TO ACCOMPANY PAPALIA AND OLDS

A CHILD'S WORLD

INFANCY THROUGH ADOLESCENCE

FIFTH EDITION

Ruth Duskin Feldman

D1473884

McGraw-Hill Publishing Company

New York St. Louis San Francisco Auckland Bogotá
Caracas Hamburg Lisbon London Madrid Mexico Milan Montreal
New Delhi Oklahoma City Paris San Juan São Paulo Singapore
Sydney Tokyo Toronto

STUDY GUIDE WITH READINGS
TO ACCOMPANY PAPALIA AND OLDS,
A CHILD'S WORLD:
INFANCY THROUGH ADOLESCENCE
FIFTH EDITION

234567890 SEM SEM 9543210

ISBN 0-07-048547-X

This book was designed and set in Palatino with Helvetica by Tim Nenno and Susan Gamer. The editors were James D. Anker and Susan Gamer; the permissions editor was Melissa Mashburn; the production supervisor was Friederich W. Schulte.
The cover was designed by Joan E. O'Connor. Semline, Inc., was printer and binder.

Credits for cover photographs (left to right):
Top row, Susanne Szasz/Photo Researchers; Nancy Durrell McKenna/Photo Researchers; Jim Pozarik/Gamma-Liaison; Richard Hutchings/Photo Researchers.
Second row, Stephen Becker; Fern Logan; Stephen Becker; Fern Logan.
Third row, Fern Logan; Sally Olds; Fern Logan; Larry Nicholson/Photo Researchers.
Bottom row, John Anerino/Gamma-Liaison; Valerie Campbell; John Anerino/Gamma-Liaison; Fern Logan.

ACKNOWLEDGMENTS FOR READINGS

Angelou, Maya: Excerpt from *I Know Why the Caged Bird Sings.* Copyright © 1969 by Maya Angelou. Reprinted by permission of Random House, Inc.

Braden, William: "Births Drawn in Black and White; Mortality Risk Haunts Middle-Class Mothers." © With permission of the Chicago Sun-Times, Inc., 1989.

Franklin, Deborah: "What a Child Is Given." Excerpted from *The New York Times Magazine.* Copyright © by The New York Times Company. Reprinted by permission.

Freud, Sophie: "Paradoxes of Parenthood: On the Impossibility of Raising Children Perfectly." From *No Way: The Nature of the Impossible,* by Philip J. Davis and David Park. Copyright © by W.H. Freeman and Company. Reprinted by permission.

Fritz, Katherine: "The Yum-Yuck Syndrome: Why Jenny Won't Eat." Reprinted by permission of *Human Development Research at Penn State.*

Garbarino, James: "Child Needs Roots—And Wings." © With permission of the Chicago Sun-Times, Inc., 1989.

Goleman, Daniel: "New Research Overturns a Milestone of Infancy; 'Stranger Anxiety' May Be a Matter of Temperament," June 6, 1989. Copyright © by The New York Times Company. Reprinted by permission.

Guthrie, Patricia: "Alcohol's Child: A Father Tells His Tale," July 30, 1989. Copyright © by The New York Times Company. Reprinted by permission.

Hand, Douglas: "Morality Lessons? Hear! Hear!" April 9, 1989. Copyright © 1989 by The New York Times Company. Reprinted by permission.

Holt, John: "Talk," from *How Children Learn,* Revised Edition. Copyright © 1967, 1983 by John Holt. Reprinted by permission of Delacorte Press/Seymour Lawrence, a division of Bantam, Doubleday, Dell Publishing Group, Inc.

Jackson, Shirley: "Charles," from *The Lottery.* Copyright © 1948, 1949 by Shirley Jackson. Copyright renewed 1976, 1977 by Laurence Hyman, Barry Hyman, Mrs. Sarah Webster, and Mrs. Joanne Schnurer. Reprinted by permission of Farrar, Straus and Giroux, Inc.

Pruett, Kyle D., M.D.: "Solving the Father Problem." Reprinted by permission of Warner Books/New York from *The Nurturing Father.* Copyright © 1987 by Kyle D. Pruett.

Roberts, Marjory: "Schoolyard Menace." Reprinted with permission from *Psychology Today* Magazine. Copyright © 1988 (PT Partners, L.P.).

Rose, Sylvia: "Out of the Garden of Eden." Reprinted from *Humanistic Judaism* by permission of Sylvia Rose.

Scott, John: "Don't Make Me Walk When I Want to Fly: An Open Letter from a Gifted Child." From *Instructor* Magazine, January 1977. Reprinted with permission of Scholastic, Inc.

Squires, Sally: "Baby Fat: A Weigh to Poor Health." © The Washington Post. Reprinted by permission.

Weston, Carol: "The Worries Teens Won't Share with Their Parents." Reprinted from *Woman's Day* by permission of Carol Weston.

CONTENTS

LIST OF READINGS

PREFACE:
TO THE STUDENT

This *Study Guide with Readings* has been designed to help you get the most out of your textbook, *A Child's World*, Fifth Edition, by Diane E. Papalia and Sally Wendkos Olds. It is not intended as a substitute for *A Child's World*; rather, it is just what its title implies—a guide to help you absorb and interpret the material in the text. Although some of the material in your textbook will be familiar to you (since you once inhabited the world of childhood), much of it will be new; and you must now see all of it from a new perspective, as an adult and a student of child development. Using this Study Guide will increase your understanding of the material and improve your ability to remember it, to apply it, and to build on it throughout this course, in related courses, and in your own life.

The Study Guide will help you to:

■ Organize and focus your learning

■ Check your mastery of the material in the text

■ Practice dealing with typical examination formats

■ Think analytically about the subject matter

■ Broaden your perspective on child development

How the Study Guide Is Organized

The Study Guide's sixteen chapters correspond to Chapters 1 to 16 of *A Child's World.* Each chapter of the Study Guide begins with a brief "Overview" of the text chapter and has the followingh five major parts:

Chapter Review
Chapter Quiz
Topics for Thought and Discussion
Chapter Reading
Answer Key

Let's look at each of these, to give you an understanding of how the Study Guide works and how you'll be using it.

CHAPTER REVIEW

The Chapter Review is a way to organize and focus your learning. It will help you identify and reexamine important material in the text chapter and also help you decide which material will need further study.

The Review is divided into sections that correspond to the major headings in the text chapter. This format lets you break your study into manageable "chunks" and makes it easier for you to locate information in the text, check answers, and concentrate on areas where you need to do more work.

Typically, each section of the Review has three elements: Framework, Important Terms, and Learning Objectives.

Framework: The Framework is an outline of all the subheadings in the text section. (When there are no subheadings within a section, this element is omitted.) The Framework shows you the section at a glance and indicates the relationship among different topics taken up in the section. You might think of it as a road map. You can use it to preview the section; you should refer to it frequently as you read, to get your bearings; and later, you can use it to remind yourself where you have been.

You can also use the Framework to guide your reading by using the "questioning" approach. You'll notice that some of the text headings are in the form of questions; others can be rephrased as questions, which you can keep in mind as you read. For example, in Chapter 1 you'll find the heading "Critical Periods in Development." You might ask yourself, "What are critical periods?" "*When* are critical periods?" If you can give a tentative answer, jot it down. Then, when you find the answer in the text, check to see if you were on the right track.

Important Terms: Important Terms is a fill-in-the-blanks exercise which covers all the "key terms" in the text section. It checks your knowledge of terms and meanings; it gives you practice with completion-type test items; and, when you have filled it in, it will serve as a glossary for the section, to be used for reference and review. (For text sections without key terms, the Important Terms exercise is omitted.)

Can you fill in the blanks in Important Terms without referring to the text? If you do need to consult the text, can you go directly to the passage you need? If you must turn to the text often, or if you have trouble finding the information you want, you'll know that you need additional study.

Check your work against the Answer Key. Your wrong answers will let you know where more work is needed.

Learning Objectives: The Learning Objectives are a list of tasks you should be able to accomplish when you have studied the section. To check your understanding of the text material, see if you can accomplish each objective without recourse to the text. If you need to look at the text, note how readily you can locate the necessary information.

You can use the space provided below each objective to make brief notes. But the Learning Objectives can also serve another purpose, since they resemble essay-type test items. Writing out complete, formal answers to some or all of them—on separate paper—will give you needed practice in the essay format.

The Answer Key provides text page references for the Learning Objectives, but it's up to you to write the actual answers.

CHAPTER QUIZ

The Chapter Quiz will check your mastery of the text material. It also gives you practice with three types of questions often found on tests:

Matching
Multiple-choice
True-or-false

Take the quiz when you are reasonably confident about your mastery of the entire chapter. This is a closed-book test. Put the textbook away—far away, if you are easily tempted—and allow about as much time to take the quiz as you would have for a classroom examination.

As you take the quiz, pay attention to your "comfort level." Are you uncertain or uneasy about many items? Do you find that you must skip many items? Do you find that you are often just guessing? If so, stop and review the text again.

If your comfort level is high—that is, if you're confident about most of the questions—complete the quiz and then check the Answer Key. You should not be satisfied unless you've gotten almost all the answers right. Remember that this quiz is easier than an actual classroom examination because you take it when you decide you're ready, you are not under so much tension, and you can pace yourself. If you miss more than a few (very few) questions, restudy the material.

TOPICS FOR THOUGHT AND DISCUSSION

The Topics for Thought and Discussion are designed to help you think analytically about the subject matter. They call not only on your grasp of the material in the text but also on your ability to interpret it and apply it. Therefore, you should work on them only after you are satisfied with your performance on the Review and the Quiz.

These questions are like essay items on examinations, topics for writing assignments, and topics presented for group or class discussions. They are open-ended and thus do not have definite "right" or "wrong" answers. But this does not mean that all answers are equally good. The value of your answers depends on how clearly and logically you make and support your points.

The material in your textbook should give you *ideas*. If you are without ideas when you consider any of the Topics for Thought and Discussion, then you are not getting all you should from the text. But, equally important, your ideas must be supported by *facts*. If you have ideas but cannot state facts to back them up, you have not really mastered the material.

To help yourself think through these questions, sketch out your answers in written form. Your sketch need not be a full, formal answer, but it *should* always include your main point or points and specific supporting details. Do not be discouraged if you have to refer back to the text. Many of these questions are quite challenging and require careful consideration, not quick recall.

For practice in dealing with essay examinations—and to improve your writing in general—develop as many of your sketches as possible into full, formal, polished answers. Examine your answers carefully. Have you stated your point clearly and organized your supporting material logically? Have you expressed yourself grammatically?

You'll also find the Topics for Thought and Discussion useful for group study, and as ideas for writing assignments when you can choose your own topic.

CHAPTER READING

The Chapter Readings have been chosen to help you broaden your perspective on child development. Each reading selection supplements an important subject treated in the text chapter. Some of the selections are classics; some are current. They have been taken from newspapers, journals, magazines, and books—autobiography, fiction, and nonfiction. They may provide additional information, present different viewpoints, demonstrate practical applications of principles or theories, report on new research, or humanize an issue. They represent a sampling of the rich material you can encounter by reading widely, and they should challenge you to read carefully and critically.

A brief Introduction sets the scene for each selection by providing background information about the author, the subject, or both.

Each selection is followed by Questions about the Reading. Like the Topics for Thought and Discussion, these questions resemble essay items on examinations, issues for group discussions, and subjects for written assignments. You should sketch out written answers—always being sure to state your point and back it up with specific evidence drawn from the selection, from your textbook, and from your own experience. Then, write complete, formal answers for some or all of the questions, to sharpen your writing skills.

ANSWER KEY

The Answer Key for each chapter gives answers, with text page references, for the Important Terms exercise and for the entire Chapter Quiz. It also gives text page references for the Learning Objectives.

Use the Answer Key wisely, to check your work. Don't use it as a crutch; don't "peek" when you should be testing your recall. If you misuse the answers, you'll be cheating no one but yourself.

Before You Begin: Learning Aids in Your Textbook

The Fifth Edition of *A Child's World* itself contains several important study aids. You should take advantage of these features as you read each chapter of the text.

Chapter Contents: On the opening page of each chapter you'll see a listing of major headings. This is your first view of the chapter; take a few minutes to examine it, asking yourself, "What topics does this chapter cover, and how are they organized?"

Preview Questions: Next you will find some questions designed to direct your attention to significant material covered in the chapter. A good way to make use of this learning aid is to check off each Preview Question as you find the answer in the text, making a brief note of the answer and the page where it appears. When you've finished the chapter, turn back to the Preview Questions. Can you answer each one fully without referring to the text?

Key Terms: In each chapter, the authors identify certain "key terms." These are printed in *bold italic* in the running text, defined in the margins, and then listed at the end of the chapter (in order of their appearance in the text, with page references). Whenever you encounter a key term, stop and read its definition. Is the definition clear to you? (If not, reread the explanation in the text.) Can you think of

a specific example? When you've finished a chapter, use the list at the end to review the vocabulary and check your mastery of it.

Boxes: The boxes (which are listed in the chapter contents) illuminate many topics covered in the text. Read them as carefully as the text itself and ask yourself questions about them: "How does this box relate to the subject matter in the text?" "Why was this topic chosen for highlighting?" If a box takes up a controversial issue, what is your opinion?

Tables and Illustrations: Pay close attention to tables, figures, and photographs. They illustrate, summarize, or crystallize material in the text, making it easier to understand and remember.

Summary: The summary at the end of each chapter, in the form of a numbered list, gives a quick review of the main points and is a good way for you to check your learning when you've completed the chapter. Is each of the numbered items familiar to you? Can you expand on each?

Suggested Readings: Also at the end of each chapter is a list of recommended readings. These interesting, informative books can be used for research or writing assignments, or simply to learn more about topics introduced in the chapter.

Glossary: The glossary at the end of the book brings together all the key terms from every chapter, in alphabetical order, with their definitions and with page references to the text. It is useful for reference and review.

Bibliography: You may not have thought of the bibliography as a study aid, but it can be: it is an excellent guide to books and articles for further research.

People who teach and write about study skills will tell you that a crucial part of learning effectively is being an "active reader"—being alert, perceptive, and involved as you read. You'll find that using these special features in *A Child's World* will help you become an active reader and thus a more efficient learner.

Acknowledgments

The author would like to thank her daughters, Heidi Feldman and Laurie Feldman, who contributed their considerable skills as teachers and writers and their insights and experience as adult learners in drafting many chapters of this Study Guide. Special appreciation goes to the editors: Susan Gamer, who helped develop the format, suggested several of the readings, and supervised all aspects of production; Jim Anker, who provided wise guidance and support; and Melissa Mashburn, who tracked down sources and obtained permission for use of the readings. Finally, very special thanks are due to Tim Nenno of McGraw-Hill's Publishing Operations group. Tim's technical expertise, step-by-step guidance, and unfailing patience made possible the computerized production of the Study Guide.

Ruth Duskin Feldman

About the Author of This Study Guide . . .

Ruth Duskin Feldman received her bachelor's degree from Northwestern University, where she graduated with highest distinction and was elected to Phi Beta Kappa. A former teacher, she has developed educational materials for all levels from elementary school through college. She is the award-winning author of two books and a coauthor of several others—including the Fourth Edition of Diane E. Papalia and Sally Wendkos Olds's widely used textbook Human Development.

A CHILD'S WORLD: THEORIES, ISSUES, AND METHODS FOR STUDYING IT

OVERVIEW

Chapter 1 introduces you to the study of child development. In this chapter, the authors:

■ Define child development and explain why its study is important

■ Outline the periods into which the text divides childhood and the aspects of development to be studied for each period

■ Point out several types of influences on how children develop

■ Discuss several important theoretical perspectives from which child development has been viewed

■ Describe the major types of methods for studying child development and discuss advantages and disadvantages of each

---

CHAPTER 1 REVIEW

Section I A Child's World: Concepts and Issues

FRAMEWORK FOR SECTION I

A. What Is Development, and Why Should We Study It?
B. The Whole Child: Aspects of Development
  1. Physical Development
  2. Intellectual (Cognitive) Development
  3. Personality-Social-Emotional Development
C. Periods of Childhood
  1. Prenatal Stage
  2. Infancy and Toddlerhood
  3. Early Childhood
  4. Middle Childhood
  5. Adolescence
D. Influences on Children's Development
  1. Normative Age-Graded Influences
  2. Normative History-Graded Influences
  3. Nonnormative Life Events
E. Critical Periods in Development

IMPORTANT TERMS FOR SECTION I

Completion: Fill in the blanks to complete the definitions of key terms for this section of Chapter 1.

1. **child development:** Scientific study of _NORMAL_ changes in children over time.
2. _QUANTITATIVE_ **change:** Change in amount, such as in height, weight, or size of vocabulary.
3. _QUALITATIVE_ **change:** Change in kind, as in the nature of intelligence.
4. **physical development:** Changes in body, brain, sensory capacity, and _MOTOR_ skills over time.
5. **intellectual development:** Changes in mental abilities, activities, or organization over time; also called _COGNITIVE_ development.
6. _PERSONALITY-SOCIAL-EMOTIONAL_ **development:** Changes in a person's unique style of responding, feeling, and reacting.

7. **normative age-graded influence:** Influence on development that is highly similar for all people in a given _AGE-GROUP_
8. **normative history-graded influence:** Biological or environmental influence on development that is common to people of a particular _GENERATION_
9. _NONNORMATIVE_ **life event:** Unusual event that may have a major influence on a person's life.
10. _CRITICAL_ **period:** Specific time during development when an event has its greatest impact.

LEARNING OBJECTIVES FOR SECTION I

After reading and reviewing this section of Chapter 1, you should be able to do the following. (Note: Here and throughout this study guide, when you are asked to give examples, try to think of examples other than those given in the text.)

1. Explain the difference between quantitative and qualitative change and give at least one example of each.

QUANTITATIVE CHANGE IS IN THE AMOUNT. SUCH AS HEIGHT, WEIGHT, SIZE ITC.

QUALATATIVE CHANGE IS IN KIND SUCH AS I.Q. OR NATURE OF INTELLIGENCE

2. Identify four goals of child development as a scientific discipline.

PAGE 10

3. List the five periods into which your text divides childhood and identify the approximate age range and distinguishing features of each.

RENATAL - CONCEPTION - BIRTH
IFANCY & TODDLERHOOD - BIRTH - 3
ARLY CHILDHOOD 3-6
IDDLE CHILDHOOD 6-12
DOLESCENCE - 12-18

GES 13-14

4. Identify three categories of noninherited influences on children's development, and give at least one example of each.

5. Explain the implications of the concept of critical periods for physical and nonphysical development. A SPECIFIC TIME WHEN A GIVEN EVENT WILL HAVE ITS GREATEST IMPACT ORE APPLICABLE TO PHYSICAL EVELOPMENT, ESPECIALLY RENATAL DEVELOPMENT HAN TO PSYCHOLOGICAL DEVEL.

Section II A Child's World: Perspectives on Child Development

FRAMEWORK FOR SECTION II

A. Early Approaches
B. Today's Approaches
  1. Psychoanalytic Perspective
    a. Sigmund Freud: Psychosexual Theory
      (1) Id, Ego, and Superego
      (2) Stages of Psychosexual Development
      (3) Defense Mechanisms
    b. Erik H. Erikson: Psychosocial Theory—The Eight Crises
    c. Evaluation of Psychoanalytic Theory
  2. Mechanistic Perspective: Learning Theories
    a. Behaviorism
      (1) Classical Conditioning
      (2) Operant Conditioning
    b. Social-Learning Theory
    c. Evaluation of Learning Theories
  3. Organismic Perspective
    a. Jean Piaget: Cognitive-Stage Theory
      (1) Cognitive Structures
      (2) Principles of Cognitive Development
    b. Evaluation of Piaget's Organismic Theory
  4. Humanistic Perspective
    a. Abraham Maslow: Hierarchy of Needs
    b. Evaluation of Humanistic Theories

IMPORTANT TERMS FOR SECTION II

Completion: Fill in the blanks to complete the definitions of key terms for this section of Chapter 1.

1. **theory:** Set of related statements about data; the goal of a theory is to integrate data, EXPLAIN behavior, and predict behavior.
2. **data:** Information obtained through RESEARCH
3. **hypothesis:** Possible EXPLANATION for an observation; a hypothesis is used to predict the outcome of an experiment.
4. PSYCHOANALYTIC **perspective:** View of humanity concerned with the unconscious forces motivating behavior.
5. **id:** In Freud's theory, the unconscious source of motives and desires; it operates on the "PLEASURE principle."
6. **ego:** In Freud's theory, the representation of reason or common sense; it operates on the "REALITY principle."
7. SUPEREGO In Freud's theory, the representation of social values, communicated by parents and other adults.
8. **psychosexual development:** In Freudian theory, the different stages of development in which GRATIFICATION shifts from one body zone to another.
9. **defense mechanism:** Unconscious distortion of reality to protect the ego against ANXIETY

10. **psychosocial development:** _ERIKSON_'s theory of personality development through the life span, stressing societal and cultural influences on the ego at eight stages.

11. _MECHANISTIC_ **perspective:** View of humanity which assumes that all change is a reaction to external events; purpose, will, and intelligence are ignored or given little weight.

12. _BEHAVIORISM_: School of psychology that emphasizes the study of observable behaviors and events and the role of the environment in causing behavior.

13. **classical conditioning:** _LEARNING_ in which a previously neutral stimulus (conditioned stimulus) acquires the power to elicit a response (conditioned response) by association with an unconditioned stimulus that ordinarily elicits a particular response (unconditioned response).

14. **unconditioned stimulus (UCS):** In classical conditioning, a stimulus that automatically elicits a(n) _UNLEARNED_ response.

15. **unconditioned response (UCR):** In classical conditioning, an automatic, _UNLEARNED_ response to an unconditioned stimulus; also called an *unconditioned* _REFLEX_.

16. _NEUTRAL_ **stimulus:** Stimulus that does not ordinarily evoke a reflex response.

17. **conditioned stimulus (CS):** In classical conditioning, an originally neutral stimulus that, after repeated pairing with an unconditioned stimulus, provokes a(n) _CONDITIONED RESPONSE_

18. **conditioned response (CR):** In classical conditioning, a response to a conditioned stimulus; also known as a *conditioned* _REFLEX_.

19. **operant conditioning:** Learning in which a response continues to be made because it has been reinforced; also called _INSTRUMENTAL_ *conditioning*.

20. **reinforcement:** Stimulus that follows a response and _INCREASES_ the likelihood that the response will be repeated.

21. **punishment:** Stimulus that follows a behavior and _DECREASES_ the likelihood that the response will be repeated.

22. _EXTINCTION_: Process whereby a response that is no longer reinforced stops or returns to its original (baseline) level.

23. _SHAPING_: Bringing about a new response by reinforcing responses that are progressively like the desired one.

24. **social-learning theory:** Theory proposed by Bandura that behaviors are learned by observing and imitating _MODELS_

25. **organismic perspective:** View of humanity that sees people as active agents in their own development, focuses on _QUANTITATIVE_ changes, and sees development as discontinuous, or occurring in _STAGES_

26. **schema:** In _PIAGETS_ terminology, the basic cognitive unit; a schema is generally named after the _BEHAVIOR_ involved.

27. **adaptation:** In _PIAGETS_'s theory terminology, the _COMPLEMENT_ processes of assimilation and accommodation.

28. **assimilation:** In _PIAGETS_'s terminology, the incorporation of a new object, experience, or concept into existing _COGNITIVE_ structures.

29. **accommodation:** In _PIAGETS_'s terminology, changes in existing _COGNITIVE_ structures to include new _EXPERIENCES_

30. **equilibration:** Striving for _COGNITIVE_ balance.

31. _HUMANISTIC_ **perspective:** View of humanity that sees people as able to foster their own development in healthy, positive ways.

LEARNING OBJECTIVES FOR SECTION II

After reading and reviewing this section of Chapter 1, you should be able to do the following. (Remember: When you are asked to give examples, try to think of examples other than those given in the text.)

1. Briefly describe five trends that led to the scientific study of child development.

PAGE 17
☐ BLUE BOXES

2. Identify the four major perspectives on human development and their main distinguishing features.

PSYCHOANALYTIC
MECHANISTIC
ORGANISMIC
HUMANISTIC

3. Name the three major components of personality according to Freud's theory, and explain each term in your own words.

ID - PLEASURE PRINCIPLE
EGO - REALITY PRICIPLE
SUPER EGO - SOCIAL
            VALUES

4. Name the first three stages of psychosexual development, according to Freud's theory, and identify the approximate age range and the chief source of pleasure at each stage.

ORAL - BIRTH to 12-18 mo.
        MOUTH
ANAL - 12-18 mon to 3 yrs
        ANAL
PHALIC 3-6 yrs / GENITAL REGION

5. Define and give an example of five common defense mechanisms, according to Freud's theory.

REGRESSION
REPRESSION
SUBLIMATION
PROJECTION
REACTION FORMATION

6. Explain how Erikson's theory of psychosocial development modifies and expands upon Freud's psychosexual theory, particularly with regard to the development of the ego.

IT FOLLOWS PERSONALITY devel THROUGH the LIFE SPAN OF PERSON STRESSING SOCIETAL + CULTURAL INFLUENCES ON the EGO at EACH OF 8 AGE STAGES.

7. Explain what Erikson means by a crisis in personality, and discuss the implications of the way in which the crisis at each stage of development is resolved.

EACH CRISIS IS a TURNING POINT FOR DEALING w/an ISSUE that IS PARTICULARLY IMPORTANT at the TIME. CRISIS EMERGE + then adjusts to the demands OF EACH CRISIS

8. Briefly discuss some criticisms of Freud's and Erikson's theories.

FREUD PATRONIZED & demeans WOMEN
ERIKSON - ANTIFEMALE bias

9. State at least two basic assumptions of the mechanistic perspective.

ALL CHANGE IS a REACTION to EXTERNAL EVENTS, PURPOSE, WILL, and INTELLIGENCE ARE IGNORED OR GIVEN little WEIGHT

10. Name the two major theories that take the mechanistic perspective, and explain the similarities and differences between them.

PAGES 23-27

BEHAVIORISM
SOCIAL-LEARNING

11. Explain why behaviorists do not describe stages of development.

BECAUSE THEY BELIEVE THAT PEOPLE OF ALL AGES LEARN the same way THEY ARE INTERESTED IN QUANTITATIVE change

12. Name and describe the two types of conditioning and give at least one example of each.

[handwritten: CLASSICAL - NEUTRAL STIMULUS ACQUIRES THE POWER TO ELICIT A RESPONSE   OPERANT - RESPONSE THROUGH REINFORCEMENT CONTINUES TO BE MADE]

13. Explain the difference between negative reinforcement and punishment.

[handwritten: 25]

14. Briefly discuss some criticisms of behaviorism and social learning theory.

[handwritten: 27]

15. State two major features of the organismic perspective.

[handwritten: 27]

16. Explain the processes by which cognitive growth occurs, according to Piaget's theory.

[handwritten: 29]

17. Briefly discuss some criticisms of Piaget's cognitive-stage theory.

[handwritten: 29-30]

18. State two basic assumptions that distinguish the humanistic perspective.

[handwritten: 30]

19. List at least three characteristics of a "self-actualized person" according to Maslow.

[handwritten: 31]

20. Briefly discuss some criticisms of humanistic theories.

[handwritten: 31]

Section III   A Child's World: How We Discover It

FRAMEWORK FOR SECTION III

A. Methods for Studying Child Development
   1. Nonexperimental Methods
      a. Case Studies
      b. Naturalistic Observation
      c. Clinical Method
      d. Interview Method
      e. Correlational Studies
   2. Experimental Methods
      a. Variables and Groups
      b. Sampling and Assignment
         (1) Selecting a Sample
         (2) Assigning Subjects
      c. Types of Experiments
         (1) Laboratory Experiments
         (2) Field Experiments
         (3) Natural Experiments
         (4) Comparing Types of Experiments

3. Methods of Data Collection
   a. Longitudinal Studies
   b. Cross-Sectional Studies
   c. Comparing Longitudinal and Cross-Sectional Studies
   d. Sequential Strategies
B. Ethical Considerations in Studying Children
   1. Rights of Participants
      a. Right to Privacy
      b. Right to the Truth
      c. Right to Informed Consent
      d. Right to Self-Esteem
   2. Social Decisions

IMPORTANT TERMS FOR SECTION III

Completion: Fill in the blanks to complete the definitions of key terms for this section of Chapter 1.

1. **scientific method:** Means of inquiry that depends on observation to establish findings, uses further observations to test alternative explanations for the findings, and then uses new observers to demonstrate the continuing _VALIDITY_ of the observations.

2. **case studies:** Studies of a single case, or individual _LIFE_.

3. **naturalistic observation:** Study of people in a(n) _REAL LIFE_ setting, with no attempt to manipulate behavior.

4. _CLINICAL_ **method:** Technique of observation in which questioning is flexible and the interviewer asks additional questions in response to particular answers.

5. _INTERVIEW_ **method:** Research technique in which people are asked to state their attitudes, opinions, or histories.

6. **correlational study:** Study that assesses the _DIRECTION_ and _EXTENT_ of a relationship between variables.

7. **experiment:** Highly controlled, _REPLICABLE_ (repeatable) procedure in which a researcher assesses the effect of manipulating variables; an experiment provides information about cause and effect.

8. _INDEPENDENT_ **variable:** In an experiment, the variable that is directly controlled and manipulated by the experimenter.

9. _dependent_ **variable:** In an experiment, the variable that may or may not change as a result of changes in the _INDEPENDENT_ variable.

10. **experimental group:** In an experiment, people who receive the treatment under study; changes in these people are compared with changes in a(n) _CONTROL_ group.

11. **treatment:** In an experiment, a(n) _CONTROLLED_ form of manipulation; a treatment is the cause of any effects observed during the experiment.

12. _CONTROL_ **group:** In an experiment, people who are similar to people in the experimental group but do not receive the treatment whose effects are to be measured; the results obtained with this group are compared with the results obtained with the experimental group to assess _CAUSE & EFFECT_

13. **sample:** In an experiment, a group of people who are used to _REPRESENT_ the total population.

14. _POPULATION_ All the members of a group to be studied.

15. **random sample:** Sampling technique in which the members of the _CONTROL_ group and the _EXPERIMENTAL_ group are randomly selected from the larger population.

16. **matching:** Sampling technique in which the members of the _CONTROL_ group and the _EXPERIMENTAL_ group are selected by comparing and matching certain _CHARACTERISTICS_

17. **laboratory experiment:** Experiment performed in a psychological laboratory setting that is subject to the experimenter's _CONTROL_

18. _FIELD_ **experiment:** Experiment performed in a setting familiar to the subject, such as a day care center.

19. _NATURAL EXPERIMENT_ Comparison of a person or a group of people who were exposed to some _NATURALLY_ occurring event (such as hospitalization or malnutrition) with a person or a group of people who were not exposed to the event.

20. _longitudinal_ **study:** Research that follows the same people over a period of time.

21. _cross-sectional_ **study:** Research that assesses different people of different ages at the same time.

22. **cross-sequential study:** Research that assesses the people in a(n) _cross-sectional_ study two or more times.

LEARNING OBJECTIVES FOR SECTION III

After reading and reviewing this section of Chapter 1, you should be able to do the following. (Remember: When you are asked to give examples, try to think of examples other than those given in the text.)

1. Name five nonexperimental methods of studying child development, give at least one example for the use of each method, and state at least one advantage and disadvantage of each.

2. Explain how and why experimenters select a random sample.

3. Explain and compare two ways of assigning subjects of an experiment to experimental and control groups.

4. Name three types of experiments, give at least one example of each, and state the two major ways they differ from each other.

5. Explain the chief differences between experimental and nonexperimental methods.

6. Name and describe three methods of data collection and give at least one example of the use of each method.

7. Explain four important ethical concerns about the rights of participants in research on child development.

CHAPTER 1 QUIZ

Matching—Who's Who: Match each person at the left with the appropriate description on the right.

1. Albert Bandura _D_
2. Sigmund Freud _I_
3. Erik H. Erikson _B_
4. Bärbel Inhelder _E_
5. Ivan Pavlov _C_
6. John B. Watson _J_
7. G. Stanley Hall _F_
8. Jean Piaget _H_
9. Abraham Maslow _A_
10. Emma Willard _G_

a. humanistic psychologist who identified a "hierarchy" of needs that motivate human behavior
b. psychologist who expanded on Freud's theory to emphasize the role of culture in personality development
c. Russian physiologist who studied classical conditioning
d. leading advocate of social-learning theory
e. experimental child psychologist who collaborated with Piaget
f. first psychologist to formulate a theory of adolescence
g. American educator and author of the first child biography published in English
h. Swiss scholar, famous for his observations of children and his theory of cognitive stages of development
i. originator of psychoanalytic theory
j. behavioral psychologist who first applied stimulus-response theories of learning to child development

Multiple-Choice: Circle the choice that best completes or answers each item.

1. Qualitative change involves change in
   a. amount
   b. kind
   c. both amount and kind
   d. either amount or kind, depending on the specific situation

2. With regard to behavior, the original focus of child development as a discipline was
   a. description
   b. explanation
   c. prediction
   d. modification

3. Which of the following best describes the goal of developmentalists today?
   a. explanation, leading to prediction of behavior
   b. behavior modification
   c. psychotherapy
   d. compensatory education

4. The distinction among physical, intellectual, and personality-social-emotional development is
   a. rarely useful
   b. convenient but somewhat arbitrary
   c. important in discussing infancy and early childhood, but less important later in the life span
   d. more important later in the life span than in infancy and early childhood

5. The prenatal stage is defined as lasting until
   a. the pregnant woman "feels life"
   b. the fetus's basic body structures and organs are formed
   c. the fetus's brain develops
   d. birth

6. Which of the following is *not* an example of a normative age-graded influence?
   a. puberty
   b. entry into school
   c. a disabling accident
   d. retirement

7. Which of the following statements about nonnormative life events is (are) true?
   a. By definition, they are unhappy in nature.
   b. People often create their own nonnormative life events.
   c. Nonnormative life events can be considered essentially the same as critical periods.
   d. all of the above

8. Apparently, professional involvement in children's lives began
   a. in the sixteenth century with books of advice on child rearing
   b. in the nineteenth century with the passage of child labor laws
   c. in 1904, when G. Stanley Hall published *Adolescence*
   d. as a result of Freud's development of the psychoanalytic perspective

9. In Freud's theory, the id is
   a. present at birth
   b. not developed until infants recognize that they are separate beings
   c. replaced by the ego when infants recognize that they are separate beings
   d. a source of gratification

10. According to Freud, which of the following incorporate(s) society's "shoulds" and "should nots"?
    a. ego
    b. superego
    c. both a and b
    d. neither a nor b

11. Which of the following is *not* a Freudian defense mechanism?
    a. regression
    b. repression
    c. reinforcement
    d. reaction formation

12. How many crises of development does Erikson envision?
    a. 8
    b. 10
    c. 8 for females and 10 for males
    d. 10 for females and 8 for males

13. Which of the following statements about Freud's and Erikson's theories is true?
    a. Neither theory goes beyond adolescence.
    b. Both theories cover the entire life span.
    c. Freud's theory covers the life span, but Erikson's "crises" end with adolescence.
    d. Erikson's theory covers the life span, but Freud's stages end with adolescence.

14. The mechanistic perspective includes
    a. cognitive-stage theory
    b. Maslow's hierarchy of needs
    c. behaviorism
    d. all of the above

15. Which of the following is an example of classical conditioning?
    a. Vicky is so used to having her picture taken with a flashbulb that she no longer blinks at the flash.
    b. Pavlov's dogs salivate when an attendant comes into the laboratory with their food.
    c. Jason will suck on a nipple more if it activates a recording of his mother's voice than if it activates a recording of a strange voice.
    d. none of the above

16. Which of the following would be considered the distinguishing feature of operant conditioning?
    a. It involves punishment.
    b. It does not involve punishment.
    c. The learner changes the environment in some way.
    d. It depends on cognitive development.

17. Reinforcement is
    a. positive
    b. negative
    c. either positive or negative
    d. another term for *shaping*

18. Social-learning theory is an outgrowth of
    a. behaviorism
    b. Maslow's hierarchy of needs
    c. Freudian theory
    d. the concept of critical periods

19. Learning theories stress
    a. cognitive factors
    b. developmental changes
    c. hereditary influences
    d. environmental influences

20. The term *schema* is associated with
    a. Freud
    b. Erikson
    c. Piaget ⟵ (circled)
    d. none of the above

21. According to Maslow, people
    a. will take risks to meet their basic physiological needs ⟵ (circled)
    b. must feel loved and accepted before they can feel secure
    c. must realize their potential in order to gain self-esteem
    d. all of the above

22. Time sampling is a type of
    a. clinical study
    b. correlational study
    c. experiment
    d. naturalistic observation ⟵ (circled)

23. A correlation describes
    a. cause and effect
    b. direction and magnitude of a relationship between variables ⟵ (circled)
    c. practical implications of a relationship between variables
    d. which variable in an experiment is dependent and which is independent

24. Which kind of experiment is used to study environmental effects on identical twins?
    a. laboratory experiment
    b. field experiment
    c. natural experiment ⟵ (circled)
    d. none of the above; experimentation on human beings is unethical

25. The longitudinal, cross-sectional, and cross-sequential methods are ways of
    a. selecting a sample
    b. collecting data ⟵ (circled)
    c. calculating correlations
    d. establishing ethical criteria for research

True or False? In the blank following each item, write T (for *true*) or F (for *false).* In the space below each item, if the statement is false, rewrite it to make it true.

1. The study of child development focuses mainly on abnormal changes in children.
   F

2. Early childhood is the years from 6 to 12.
   F   3-6

3. A critical period is a time during which it is easiest to reverse the effects of earlier events or experiences on an individual. F
   when the event will have greatest impact

4. The concept of critical periods is important in the psychoanalytic perspective. T

5. G. Stanley Hall's pioneering work *Adolescence* was not scientifically rigorous. T

6. A theory is information obtained through research. F
   a theory is an attempt to organize info. through research

7. Data are information obtained through research. T

8. A hypothesis is information obtained through research. _F_

A POSSIBLE explanation FOR something observed

9. Most of Freud's patients in Vienna were children and adolescents. _F_

UPPER-CLASS ~~teenagers~~ adults

10. In Freud's theory, the superego represents common sense. _F_

SOCIAL VALUES

11. In Freud's theory, psychosexual development is a series of stages in which gratification shifts from one part of the body to another. _T_

12. Erikson's theory is essentially based on Piaget's. _F_

on FREUDS

13. According to Erikson, successful resolution of each crisis requires discarding a negative trait entirely in order to acquire the corresponding positive trait. _F_

SUCCESFUL RESOLUTION REQUIRES a BALANCE between positive & negative traits

14. The mechanistic perspective sees change as qualitative. ~~T~~ _F_

quantative

15. Mechanistic theorists see development as occurring in clearly defined stages. _F_

EVERYONE LEARNS THE SAME NO STAGES

16. An unconditioned stimulus automatically elicits an unlearned response. _T_

17. Reinforcement is a crucial element in classical conditioning. _F_

OF OPERANT conditioning

18. *Instrumental conditioning* is another term for classical conditioning. _F_

OPERANT Conditioning

19. According to Piaget, cognitive growth results from adaptation and assimilation. _T_

20. Piaget's theory says little about emotional and personality development. ___T___

21. The "self-actualized person" is a concept associated with organismic theory. __F__

    ~HUMINISTIC theory

22. A common difficulty with case studies and naturalistic observation is observer bias. __T__

23. The clinical method was developed by Freud. __F__

    ~PIAGET

24. The experiments that are most generalizable are those that are the most rigidly controlled. __F__

    ~LEAST GENERALIZED

25. The principle of the *self-fulfilling prophecy* explains why some research may be harmful to children. __T__

TOPICS FOR THOUGHT AND DISCUSSION

---

1. The authors of your text treat infancy and toddlerhood as one period of development. What reasons, if any, might there be to view them as separate periods?

2. According to the authors, the concept of a critical period "generally seems too limiting" to be applied to nonphysical areas of development. Do you agree with this view, or do you think that the concept could be applied more broadly?

3. Freud's theory has been criticized for containing aspects that seem to demean women. If Freud's theory does contain ideas that demean women, does that make the theory useless?

4. According to the authors, both Freud and Erikson, in developing their psychoanalytic theories, were influenced by their personal experiences as well as their clinical observations. If so, does this limit the scientific value of their theories?

5. Imagine that you are a psychoanalytic theorist, striving to test and build upon Freud's and Erikson's theories. What methods would you use to assess Freud's psychosexual stages and Erikson's eight crises?

6. According to behaviorists, people of all ages learn in the same way—basically, by classical or operant conditioning. Is the idea that children and adults learn in the same way consistent with your experience, or can you think of aspects or types of learning that are different at different ages?

7. Social-learning theory contains two aspects of the organismic perspective: it sees people as playing an active role in their own learning, and it recognizes cognitive influences on

behavior. Why, then, is social-learning theory considered part of the mechanistic perspective?

8. According to the authors, many of Piaget's ideas about children's cognitive development were based on observations of his own children rather than on scientific research. Are such personal observations less scientific than clinical observations, a method which the text says Piaget also used extensively? Why or why not?

9. Of the three types of experiments, the one that is most controlled—laboratory experiments—has the least generalizability to real life. Why is this so? Does this fact limit the value of experimental findings about child development?

10. The section on ethical considerations of research with children lists four rights of subjects: privacy, truth, informed consent, and self-esteem. Is research that cannot be designed without interfering with these rights ever justified?

CHAPTER 1 READING

INTRODUCTION

The article reprinted here was the first of a series on child development published by the *Chicago Sun-Times* in 1987. James Garbarino is president of the Erikson Institute for Advanced Study in Child Development. You might expect, then, that his views would reflect the psychoanalytic perspective on child development described in your text. As you read the article, notice whether and to what extent this is true. Also, notice which of the other theoretical perspectives, if any, are reflected in points Garbarino makes about how children develop, and which theoretical perspectives are deemphasized or missing.

Child Needs Roots—And Wings

by James Garbarino

> *"There are two lasting bequests we can give our children—one is roots, the other wings."—Anonymous*

What is child development? It is the process of becoming fully human.

A child's experiences combine with a child's biological givens, and from this mixture emerges a complete person, ready for the challenges of day-to-day life—as students, as workers, as friends, as family members and as citizens.

To succeed in these roles, children need to become socially competent. They must know who they are. They must have a secure sense of their own identity. They must become proficient in thinking and speaking clearly. They must learn to understand the many ways people communicate with one another. In short, they need to learn the ropes of our culture.

But they also need to appreciate the wonder of being alive. We want them to do more than just learn to read. We want them to experience the joy of great literature and the pleasure of reading just for fun. We want them to do more than just cope with human relationships. We want them to know love and friendship. They need to be able to do more than just exist. We want them to know and appreciate the miracles of existence around us. We want our children to spread their wings and fly, just as we want them to take root and live socially responsible lives.

It's Not Automatic

How is all this to happen? First and foremost, we must recognize that it is not going to happen automatically. If it is going to happen, it is going to be because the adults who care for children approach children "developmentally." What does it mean to approach children developmentally?

It means that we recognize the child's changing capacity. As children develop, their intellectual, physical and emotional potentials change. The range of what is possible increases and alters. These changes in the child's capacity are what child development is all about.

Many experts believe these changes take place in a regular sequence, in which the child faces first one, then another issue. Erik Erikson, for example, described eight "stages," beginning in infancy and extending through old age.

The stages mean we recognize the capacity for change. The child's life is not fixed in some unalterable genetic code that predetermines what and who the child will be. Each child contains the potential to be many different children, and caring adults can do much to shape which of those children will come to life.

It means that we recognize that development is the process by which the child forms a picture or draws a map of the world and his or her place in it. As children draw these maps they move forward on the paths they believe exist.

What does it take for a child to form a realistic and positive map of the world, a map that will lead outward into the world with confidence and sympathy for love, trust, responsibility and beauty? It takes a world that offers a child roots and wings. The roots come from a family that has the means to meet a child's basic needs. Such a family has access to health care so that children can grow strong and healthy. It has access to adequate employment and income. And, it provides day-to-day stability in important care-giving relationships for the child.

Whether or not children experience these essential ingredients is critical to their development. Threats to the physical health of a child can jeopardize mental and emotional development. Poverty can stunt intellectual development and impose stress that undermines social development. Instability of child-care arrangements can threaten the child's sense of security and continuity.

Beyond these roots, what does the child need to sprout wings and fly?

It takes adults—parents, teachers, care-givers—who recognize the processes of development at work in the life of the child and who seize upon occasions to interact with the child and thus create an environment in which learning can go forward.

Much of our thinking about how children develop intellectually relies upon the pioneering work of the Swiss psychologist Jean Piaget. Mr. Piaget's view of development is based upon the idea that children form concepts that represent reality.

As their brains mature and they experience the world, they either fit these experiences into existing concepts (a process that Mr. Piaget called "assimilation") or they adjust or change the schemes to make sense of new or incongruous ideas (a process that Mr. Piaget labeled "accommodation").

But Mr. Piaget's views are not the whole story. The child does not—will not, cannot—develop in a social vacuum. There is more to development than maturation.

Development is a social process, for it is through relationships with people that the child learns about the world and how it works. Who points out that this four-legged furry creature is not a dog but rather a cat? Who reassures the child when he or she is frightened? Who affirms the child's need to play and daydream? Who guides and helps the child in learning society's rules and beliefs?

Child development proceeds through and because of social relationships. The earliest and most important of these are the early social relationships between infant and parents (and others who care for the child). These "attachment" relationships are the training ground and the foundation for subsequent social relationships.

Problems in early attachments tend to translate into social problems and emotional difficulties. Deprive the child of crucial social relationships, and the child will not move forward developmentally, but will fall back, regress, stop.

What the child needs for development to go forward are responses that are emotionally validating, that challenge the child. This is what moves development forward.

The child needs people to teach him or her how to be patient, how to follow through, how to behave responsibly, as well as how to tell dogs from cats, A's from B's and 1s from 2s. A child needs people who care for that child, know that child, and who validate that child emotionally.

The psychologist Lev Vygotsky went beyond Mr. Piaget's concept of development to emphasize the role of the adult as teacher in the child's development. The good teacher understands the distance between what the child can accomplish alone and what the child can do when helped by an adult or a more competent peer.

Indeed, it is not so much our capacity for learning that distinguishes human beings from other species but rather our capacity to teach. All animals can learn. But only the human one consciously can set out to teach as a way of facilitating development.

Children learn from adults in many ways, some of which are inadvertent on the adult's part. Deliberate teaching plays a special role in this learning process, however.

What does all this mean for understanding child development?

Children aren't computers. Their development will not move forward most efficiently if we simply turn them loose with the message "go forth and learn!" nor if we totally plan every detail in their experience.

Like Honored Dignitaries

Children need to be treated like honored dignitaries from a foreign land who do not yet understand the language and know the customs. They need to be respected but also to be taught the ropes.

What else do we need to know to begin a study of child development?

We need to know that the development of children reflects a mixture of forces and influences, some conscious, some not. Unconscious forces play an important role in the child's life. Early evidence of unconscious processes comes from the toddler's sudden resistance to going to sleep, acquiring imaginary playmates, having nightmares and the invention of monsters, ghosts, witches and boogeymen.

Fantasy and play (and particularly pretend play) are vital to a child's development. Through them, children have a chance to explore the meaning of the world around and inside them. In this sense, play is the child's vocation. It serves both the need to work through unconscious forces and the need to practice basic life skills.

This is what we mean by child development.

QUESTIONS ABOUT THE READING

1. At the beginning of the article, Garbarino gives a definition of child development which is different from the one given in your text. Are the two definitions compatible? Do you agree with the implication in Garbarino's definition that a child is not yet fully human?

2. What attitudes or beliefs does Garbarino exhibit which reveal his allegiance to Erikson's psychosocial theory of child development?

3. Garbarino specifically discusses Piaget's view of development. He does not specifically mention two other perspectives you studied in this chapter—the mechanistic and humanistic perspectives. Can you find any indication of whether he would agree or disagree with aspects of these perspectives?

4. How does Garbarino's emphasis on the importance of a child's receiving challenging, emotionally validating responses square with the various theoretical perspectives you have studied in this chapter?

5. Does Garbarino appear to place more emphasis on either qualitative or quantitative change?

6. Garbarino reminds us that children are not computers. Would a behaviorist agree?

7. Garbarino mentions a number of ways in which children need and learn from adults. Can you think of some examples of parenting practices that would seem to be consistent or inconsistent with his "recipe" for positive child development?

ANSWER KEY FOR CHAPTER 1

Note: Numbers in parentheses refer to pages in the textbook where answers can be found.

CHAPTER 1 REVIEW

Important Terms for Section I

1. normal (page 10)
2. quantitative (10)
3. qualitative (10)
4. motor (11)
5. cognitive (11)
6. personality-social-emotional (11)
7. age group (13)
8. generation (13)
9. nonnormative (14)
10. critical (15)

Learning Objectives for Section I

1. (page 10)
2. (10)
3. (12-13)
4. (13-14)
5. (14-15)

Important Terms for Section II

1. explain (page 18)
2. research (18)
3. explanation (18)
4. psychoanalytic (18)
5. pleasure (19)
6. reality (19)
7. superego (19)
8. gratification (19)
9. anxiety (21)
10. Erikson (21)
11. mechanistic (23)
12. behaviorism (23)
13. learning (23)
14. unlearned (24)
15. unlearned, reflex (24)
16. neutral (24)
17. conditioned response (24)
18. reflex (24)
19. instrumental (25)
20. increases (25)
21. decreases (25)
22. extinction (25)
23. shaping (26)
24. models (26-27)
25. qualitative, stages (27)
26. Piaget's, behavior (29)
27. Piaget's, complementary (29)
28. Piaget's, cognitive (29)
29. Piaget's, cognitive, experiences (29)
30. cognitive (29)
31. humanistic (30)

Learning Objectives for Section II

1. (page 17)
2. (18)
3. (19)
4. (19-20)
5. (21)
6. (21)
7. (21)
8. (22)
9. (23)
10. (23-27)
11. (23)
12. (23-26)
13. (25)
14. (27)
15. (27)
16. (29)
17. (29-30)

18. (30)
19. (31)
20. (31)

Important Terms for Section III

1. validity (page 32)
2. life (33)
3. real-life (34)
4. clinical (35)
5. interview (36)
6. direction, extent (36)
7. replicable (36)
8. independent (37)
9. dependent, independent (37)
10. control (37)
11. controlled (37)
12. control, cause and effect (37)
13. represent (38)
14. population (38)
15. control, experimental (38)
16. control, experimental, characteristics (38)
17. control (38)
18. field (39)
19. natural experiment, naturally (39)
20. longitudinal (40)
21. cross-sectional (40)
22. cross-sectional (41)

Learning Objectives for Section III

1. (pages 33-36)
2. (38)
3. (38)
4. (38-40)
5. (39)
6. (40-41)
7. (42-43)

CHAPTER 1 QUIZ

Matching—Who's Who

1. d (page 26)
2. i (18)
3. b (21)
4. e (29)
5. c (23)
6. j (24)
7. f (17)
8. h (28)
9. a (30)
10. g (34)

Multiple-Choice

1. b (page 10)
2. a (11)
3. a (11)
4. b (11)
5. d (12)
6. c (13)
7. b (14)
8. a (16)
9. a (19)
10. b (19)
11. c (21)
12. a (21)
13. d (22)
14. c (23)
15. d (23-25)
16. c (25)
17. c (25)
18. a (26)
19. d (27)
20. c (29)
21. a (30-31)
22. d (34)
23. b (36)
24. c (39)
25. b (40)

True or False?

1. F—The study of child development focuses on normal changes in children over time. (page 10)
2. F—Early childhood is the years from 3 to 6. (12)
3. F—A critical period is the time in development when an event will have the greatest impact. (15)
4. T (15)
5. T (17)
6. F—A theory is an attempt to organize information obtained through research. (18)
7. T (18)
8. F—A hypothesis is a possible explanation for something observed. (18)
9. F—Most of Freud's patients were adults. (22)
10. F—The superego represents social values. (19)
11. T (19)
12. F—Erikson's theory is a modification of Freud's. (21)
13. F—Successful resolution requires a balance between a positive trait and a negative one. (21)
14. F—The mechanistic perspective sees change as quantitative. (23)
15. F—Mechanistic theorists do not describe stages of development. (23, 27)
16. T (24)
17. F—Reinforcement is an element of operant conditioning. (25)
18. F—*Instrumental conditioning* is another name for operant conditioning. (25)
19. T (29)
20. T (30)
21. F—The "self-actualized person" is a concept associated with humanistic theory. (31)
22. T (33, 34, 35)
23. F—The clinical method was developed by Piaget. (35)
24. F—Laboratory experiments, which are the most rigidly controlled, are the least generalizable. (33, 39)
25. T (42)

HEREDITY AND ENVIRONMENT

OVERVIEW

Chapter 2 traces the earliest development of a child, beginning with the parents' decision to conceive. In this chapter, the authors:

■ Discuss why and when people choose to have children

■ Describe human reproduction

■ Explain the genetic mechanisms through which offspring inherit characteristics from parents

■ Explain genetic transmission of various types of birth defects and discuss how genetic counseling and prenatal diagnosis can help parents who are worried about bearing a child with such a defect

■ Discuss the relative influence of heredity and environment and how these factors interact

CHAPTER 2 REVIEW

Introduction and Section I Choosing Parenthood

FRAMEWORK FOR SECTION I

A. Why People Have Children
B. When to Have Children
C. The Nature of the Choice

IMPORTANT TERMS FOR INTRODUCTION AND SECTION I

Completion: Fill in the blanks to complete the definitions of key terms for this section of Chapter 2.

1. _____: Inborn factors inherited from parents that affect development.

2. **environment:** Combination of _____ influences such as family, community, and personal experience that affect development.

3. _____-versus-_____ **controversy:** Dispute over the the relative importance of hereditary and environmental factors in influencing human development; since both factors interact continuously, debate is widely seen as futile.

LEARNING OBJECTIVES FOR SECTION I

After reading and reviewing this section of Chapter 2, you should be able to do the following.

1. Explain why deciding whether or not to have children is more complicated today than it was in preindustrial times.

2. Identify important issues to consider in deciding whether or not to have children.

3. List at least three advantages of having children early in life and at least three advantages of having children later in life, and explain why the recent trend has been in the latter direction.

Section II The Beginning of Pregnancy

FRAMEWORK FOR SECTION II

A. Fertilization
B. The Mechanisms of Heredity
C. Determination of Sex
D. Multiple Births

IMPORTANT TERMS FOR SECTION II

Completion: Fill in the blanks to complete the definitions of key terms for this section of Chapter 2.

1. **zygote:** Single _____ formed through fertilization.

2. **gamete:** _____ cell.

3. **follicle:** Small sac containing a(n) _____ , or female gamete.

4. _____: Organ of gestation where the fertilized ovum develops until ready for birth; the womb.

5. **fallopian tube:** Either of two slender ducts connecting the _____ to the _____ ; a fallopian tube is normally the site of fertilization

6. **chromosome:** Rod-shaped particle found in every living cell; it carries the _____ .

7. **meiosis:** Type of cell division in which the gametes receive one of each pair of _____ .

8. _____ : Process by which a cell divides in half, over and over again.

9. _____ : Functional unit of heredity; determines the traits that are passed from one generation to the next.

10. **DNA (deoxyribonucleic acid):** Chemical carrying the instructions that tell all the cells in the body how to make the _____ which enable them to carry out their various functions.

11. **dizygotic twins:** Two people who are conceived by the mother and born at approximately the same time as a result of the fertilization of two _____ ; fraternal twins.

12. **monozygotic twins:** Two people with identical genes, arising from the formation of one _____ that divided; identical twins.

LEARNING OBJECTIVES FOR SECTION II

After reading and reviewing this section of Chapter 2, you should be able to do the following.

1. Contrast the beliefs of two seventeenth- and eighteenth-century schools of thought concerning the human reproductive system, the "Ovists" and the "Homunculists," and tell how both were proved incorrect.

2. Explain what happens during ovulation and fertilization.

3. Explain the process by which a zygote develops into an embryo.

4. Briefly explain the role of genes and chromosomes in inheritance of characteristics.

5. Explain how the sex of a child is determined.

6. Identify two important physical differences between the sexes, other than genital or chromosomal structure, that show up during the prenatal period and persist into adulthood.

7. Explain the difference between fraternal and identical twins and cite factors affecting the incidence of each.

Section III Genetics

FRAMEWORK FOR SECTION III

A. Patterns of Genetic Transmission
 1. Mendelian Laws
  a. Appearance of Traits
  b. Law of Independent Segregation
  c. Law of Dominant Inheritance
  d. Law of Recessive Inheritance
 2. Types of Inheritance
  a. Dominant and Recessive Inheritance
   (1) Homozygous and Heterozygous Alleles
   (2) Phenotypes and Genotypes
  b. Other Forms of Inheritance
   (1) Incomplete Dominance
   (2) Sex-Linked Inheritance
   (3) Polygenic Inheritance
   (4) Multifactorial Inheritance
 3. Transmission of Genetic Abnormalities
  a. Defects Transmitted by Dominant Inheritance
  b. Defects Transmitted by Recessive Inheritance
  c. Defects Transmitted by Sex-Linked Inheritance
 4. Chromosomal Abnormalities
  a. What Are Chromosomal Abnormalities?
  b. Down Syndrome
B. Genetic Counseling

IMPORTANT TERMS FOR SECTION III

Completion: Fill in the blanks to complete the definitions of key terms for this section of Chapter 2.

1. _____: Hereditary characteristic, such as shortness and tallness.

2. _____: One of a pair of genes affecting a trait; the genes may be identical or different.

3. **independent** _____: Mendel's law that individual traits are transmitted separately.

4. **dominant inheritance:** Mendel's law that when an offspring receives genes for _____ traits, only one of the traits—the dominant trait—will be expressed.

5. **homozygous:** Possessing _____ alleles for a trait.

6. **heterozygous:** Possessing _____ alleles for a trait.

7. **recessive inheritance:** Expression of a recessive trait, which occurs only if a person (or an animal or a plant) is _____ for the trait (has two alleles carrying it).

8. **phenotype:** _____ characteristics of a person.

9. **genotype:** Pattern of _____ carried by a person.

10. **multiple alleles:** _____ that exist in three or more allelic states.

11. **sex-linked inheritance:** Process by which certain _____ genes are transmitted differently to male and female children.

12. _____ **inheritance:** Interaction of a number of different genes to produce certain traits.

13. _____ **inheritance:** Interaction of both genetic and environmental factors to produce certain traits.

14. **carrier:** In genetics, a person with an allele which is not _____ but can be passed on to future generations.

15. **Down syndrome:** Disorder caused by a(n) _____ twenty-first chromosome; it is characterized by mental retardation and often heart defects and other physical abnormalities.

16. _____ **counseling:** Clinical service that advises couples of their probable risk of having a child with a particular hereditary disorder.

17. _____: Photograph made through a microscope showing the chromosomes when they are separated and aligned for cell division; the chromosomes are displayed according to a standard array.

18. **amniocentesis:** Prenatal diagnostic procedure for examining the chromosomes of a fetus; sample cells are withdrawn from the _____ , in which the fetus floats, and are examined for signs of birth defects.

19. **chorionic villus sampling (CVS):** Prenatal diagnostic procedure for obtaining sample villi from the _____ surrounding the embryo and then examining the embryo's chromosomes for birth defects.

20. _____ **(AFP):** Blood test used to indicate the possibility of a defect in the formation of the brain or spinal cord of a fetus.

21. _____: Medical procedure using high-frequency _____ waves to detect the outlines of a fetus and determine whether the pregnancy is progressing normally.

22. _____: Medical procedure permitting direct viewing of the fetus in the uterus.

LEARNING OBJECTIVES FOR SECTION III

After reading and reviewing this section of Chapter 2, you should be able to do the following.

1. Briefly explain the genetic basis for the appearance of traits.

2. State three important "laws," discovered through study of the reproduction of peas, which laid the foundation for our knowledge of human heredity.

3. Contrast dominant and recessive inheritance and explain how each occurs.

4. Explain how a person can be either homozygous or heterozygous for the same expressed trait.

5. Explain the difference between a person's phenotype and that person's genotype.

6. List and describe four types of inheritance other than dominant and recessive inheritance.

7. List and describe three methods of transmission of defects, and give at least one example of each.

8. Name two ways in which chromosomal abnormalities occur.

9. Identify the cause of Down syndrome and discuss the outlook for a child born with this disorder.

10. Explain how a genetic counselor assesses the probability that a child will be born with an inherited defect.

11. List and describe six techniques for prenatal diagnosis of birth defects.

Section IV
Nature versus Nurture

FRAMEWORK FOR SECTION IV

A. How Heredity and Environment Interact
B. Effects of Heredity and Environment
   1. Ways to Study the Relative Effects of Heredity and Environment
   2. Characteristics Influenced by Heredity and Environment
     a. Physical and Physiological Traits
     b. Intelligence
     c. Personality
     d. Mental Disorders with Probable Hereditary Factors
       (1) Autism
       (2) Depression
       (3) Schizophrenia
       (4) Alcoholism

IMPORTANT TERMS FOR SECTION IV

Completion: Fill in the blanks to complete the definitions of key terms for this section of Chapter 2.

1. **tabula rasa:** Philosophical metaphor implying that at birth a baby is a blank slate with no inborn predispositions, a position espoused by _____.

2. **reaction range:** In genetics, a potential _____ in the expression of a hereditary trait, depending on _____ conditions.

3. _____: Triggering of expression of a trait as a function of biology rather than of the environment.

4. **developmental behavioral genetics:** Study of interactions of _____ and _____ which create differences between people.

5. _____: Probability of agreement; used to measure the relative importance of hereditary and environmental factors in development.

6. **infantile** _____: Rare developmental disorder involving the inability to communicate with and respond to other people.

7. _____: Emotional disturbance characterized by feeble responses to stimuli, low initiative, and sullen or despondent attitude.

8. **neurotransmitter:** Chemical that transmits signals between _____ (nerve cells).

9. **schizophrenia:** Psychological disorder marked by a loss of contact with _____ ; symptoms include hallucinations and delusions.

LEARNING OBJECTIVES FOR SECTION IV

After reading and reviewing this section of Chapter 2, you should be able to do the following.

1. Summarize the two sides of the nature-versus-nurture dispute and explain why most modern theorists do not fully accept either of these positions.

2. Explain the concepts of reaction range and maturation and give at least one example of each.

3. List and describe four types of studies of hereditary factors and three types of studies of environmental factors in development.

4. Name several normal characteristics that seem to be strongly influenced by heredity.

5. Explain the significance of concordance in establishing a genetic basis for mental disorders.

6. Identify the characteristics and probable causes of autism, depression, schizophrenia, and alcoholism.

CHAPTER 2 QUIZ

Matching—Who's Who: Match each person at the left with the appropriate description on the right.

1. Daniel Freedman _____
2. Anton van Leeuwenhoek _____
3. Gregor Mendel _____
4. Wilhelm von Leibnitz _____
5. Regnier de Graaf _____
6. Sandra Scarr _____
7. B. F. Skinner _____
8. Caspar Friedrich Wolff _____
9. John Locke _____
10. Jerome Kagan _____

a. mathematician (1646-1716) who argued that children are born with complete genetic instructions which determine all their responses to situations
b. psychologist at University of Virginia, known for research on the effects of heredity and environment on intelligence and personality
c. German anatomist who demonstrated in the mid-eighteenth century that men and women contribute equally to reproduction
d. psychology professor at Harvard University who has done longitudinal studies suggesting that shyness and boldness are inborn
e. behaviorist who argued in the mid-1950s that language development depends entirely on environmental factors
f. British philosopher (1632-1704) who argued that development depends entirely on experience
g. researcher who has studied differences in reflexive behavior among newborns in western and nonwestern cultures
h. Dutch scientist, the first to view embryonic cells taken from female rabbits
i. Austrian monk whose breeding and cross-breeding of peas and other plants during the 1860s led to important discoveries about the workings of heredity
j. Dutch scientist, the first to view live sperm under a microscope, in 1677

Multiple-Choice: Circle the choice that best completes or answers each item.

1. The most important predictor of the age at which a woman will bear her first child is her
   a. age at the time of marriage
   b. educational level at the time of marriage
   c. income level
   d. own mother's age at first pregnancy

2. Approximately how many days after the beginning of a woman's menstrual period can fertilization occur?
   a. 7
   b. 10
   c. 14
   d. 21

3. Fertilization normally occurs in the
   a. uterus
   b. vagina
   c. cervix
   d. fallopian tubes

4. A newborn girl has approximately how many immature ova in her ovaries?
   a. none
   b. 40
   c. 4000
   d. 400,000

5. A normal mature male's ejaculation contains approximately how many sperm?
   a. 50
   b. 500
   c. 500 million
   d. 500 billion

6. A male zygote can result from which combination of sex chromosomes?
   a. YY
   b. XY
   c. XX
   d. any of the above

7. The gene called TDF
   a. tells the cells to manufacture essential proteins
   b. tells the cells to produce testosterone
   c. causes a fetus to develop female body parts
   d. causes a fetus to develop a sex-linked disorder

8. Which of the following hypotheses has (have) been advanced to explain why male babies are more vulnerable to miscarriage and disorder than female babies?
   a. The X chromosome contains genes which protect females against stress.
   b. The Y chromosome contains harmful genes.
   c. The mechanisms for immunity in males are inferior.
   d. all of the above

9. The incidence of fraternal twins has been increasing because of
   a. increased use of fertility drugs
   b. increased rate of sexual activity
   c. aftereffects of birth control pills
   d. none of the above

10. Which of the following statements about genes is true?
    a. Each gene acts independently of other genes in determining a trait.
    b. Most inherited defects are transmitted by dominant genes.
    c. Each gene has a fixed position on a particular chromosome.
    d. Some genes are "floaters," which may be located on more than one chromosome.

11. Which of the following statements about traits is true?
    a. Traits preserve their nature as they are passed on.
    b. Traits are transmitted in pairs.
    c. Traits blend into each other over time.
    d. none of the above

12. The pattern of alleles underlying a person's observable traits is called his or her
    a. allelic type
    b. prototype
    c. phenotype
    d. genotype

13. The blood type AB is an example of
    a. incomplete dominance
    b. sex-linked inheritance
    c. polygenic inheritance
    d. multifactorial inheritance

14. Approximately what proportion of newborns in the United States each year have physical or mental handicaps?
    a. 1 percent
    b. 5 percent
    c. 10 percent
    d. 15 percent

15. Sickle-cell anemia and Tay-Sachs disease are examples of defects transmitted by which kind of inheritance?
    a. dominant
    b. recessive
    c. sex-linked
    d. polygenic

16. A man and woman each carry the same harmful recessive allele. What is the probability that their child will have the disorder associated with it?
    a. 25 percent
    b. 50 percent
    c. 75 percent
    d. It is impossible to calculate the probability.

17. Chromosomal abnormalities are the result of
    a. inheritance
    b. accidents
    c. both a and b
    d. neither a nor b

18. A new technique that allows a doctor to draw a blood sample from a fetus to diagnose the presence of certain disorders is called
    a. chorionic villus sampling
    b. fetoscopy
    c. alpha fetoprotein (AFP) test
    d. ultrasound

19. Which of the following is a method of studying the possibility that traits may be inherited?
    a. prenatal study
    b. consanguinity study
    c. case history
    d. none of the above

20. Which of the following characteristics appear(s) to be strongly influenced by heredity?
    a. sensitivity to stimuli
    b. longevity
    c. shyness
    d. all of the above

21. Today, autism is
    a. known to be caused by cold, unresponsive parents
    b. recognized as a biological disorder of the nervous system, which is probably inherited
    c. recognized as being caused by deafness
    d. alarmingly common (about 3 cases per 100 people)

True or False? In the blank following each item, write T (for *true*) or F (for *false*). In the space below each item, if the statement is false, rewrite it to make it true.

1. In preindustrial societies, large families were frowned upon. _____

2. The ovum is the largest cell in the adult human body. _____

3. Only one sperm can penetrate an ovum. _____

4. After ejaculation, a sperm must immediately fertilize an ovum, or it will be devoured by the woman's white blood cells. _____

5. Every cell in the human body has 46 chromosomes (23 pairs). _____

6. Mitosis is a process of cell division resulting in exact duplicates of the original cell. _____

7. DNA gives each cell the biochemical instructions to make the proteins it needs to perform its functions. _____

8. Twenty-two of the twenty-three pairs of chromosomes are known as autosomes. _____

9. If a fetus is destined to be male, the male sex hormone testosterone begins to act at conception. _____

10. Male babies are stronger than female babies, and their physical development is quicker. _____

11. Identical twins are always of the same sex. _____

12. Most normal human traits can be explained by Mendel's law of dominant inheritance. _____

13. A trait of yours that does not show up in your own child may show up in your grandchild. _____

14. Red-green color blindness is a sex-linked trait. _____

15. The son of a man with hemophilia has a 50 percent chance of being a carrier of the disorder. _____

16. Down syndrome results from an extra sex chromosome. _____

17. The locations of more than 1250 genes have been identified. _____

18. Maturation is programmed by the genes and cannot be affected by environmental factors. _____

19. A woman who is a fraternal twin has a good chance of having twins herself. _____

20. Recent research suggests that environment may play a less important role in the development of intelligence than was previously thought. _____

21. Schizophrenia is typically a disorder of childhood. _____

22. Research has found some genetic basis for alcoholism. _____

TOPICS FOR THOUGHT AND DISCUSSION

1. According to the text, a 1983 study found that some women have children for the "wrong" reasons. What criteria, other than their own opinion, might the researchers have used to evaluate the soundness of the reasons women gave for having children?

2. The more educated a woman is, the older she is likely to be when she has her first child. Looking ahead to later chapters, what developmental effects do you suppose the age and educational level of a mother might have on her children?

3. Why might Henry VIII, who divorced a wife because she had a daughter instead of a son, have believed that the woman determines the sex of the child?

4. In view of the facts that females have a better chance of survival and a faster rate of physical development than males, why do you think women have been considered the "weaker sex" in most cultures throughout history?

5. Remembering what you learned about research methods in Chapter 1, imagine that you are a researcher in developmental behavioral genetics. How would you design an adoption study? A prenatal study?

6. A genetic counselor has advised you and your spouse that there is a 50-50 chance that a child conceived by the two of you would be born with sickle-cell anemia. What factors and alternatives might you consider, given this advice?

7. How would an advocate of the "nature" side of the nature-versus-nurture debate explain the growth of a generation of children who are a foot taller than their parents? Would such a

phenomenon give an advocate of the "nurture" position valid grounds to argue that height is environmentally determined? Why or why not?

8. Why do studies of the causes of physical traits seem to be more conclusive than studies of the influences on intellectual traits?

9. Applied research has found that an improved environment can lead to gains in intelligence test scores. Does this finding suggest that there may be a reaction range for intelligence? What environmental factors might be detrimental to the development of intelligence?

10. The New York Longitudinal Study concluded that many personality traits appear to be inborn. Does this finding challenge Freud's theory of psychosexual development?

CHAPTER 2 READING

INTRODUCTION

According to your text, researchers doing studies of twins and adopted children are increasingly finding evidence of the influence of heredity on personality traits. This article, condensed from the September 3, 1989, issue of *The New York Times Magazine*, summarizes recent findings and explores some implications. The author, Deborah Franklin, is a staff writer at *Hippocrates* magazine.

What a Child Is Given

by Deborah Franklin

On the August morning in 1971 when Marietta Spencer first met the birth family of her adopted son, Paul, she was prepared to be nervous. In the four years that she had worked as a social worker for the Children's Home Society of Minnesota, in St. Paul, Spencer had arranged and guided many such meetings. She had seen firsthand the fears and confusion stirred up when strangers, joined at the heart by adoption, examine the potent ties among them. But what Spencer wasn't prepared for, as she and Paul and the rest of the family spent a day swapping stories with a score of her son's birth relatives in their home in northern Germany, was how familiar all these strangers would seem.

It was more than physical appearance, she decided, though Paul's tall, slight build, blue eyes and narrow smile were echoed throughout the birth family, who had not seen the boy since they had arranged for his adoption 17 years earlier. It had more to do with the way one of the birth mother's brothers tossed a pillow up atop a bookcase to punctuate a joke, and with the jokes themselves—no slapstick here, only very dry, occasional one-liners. The conversational tone was familiar, too—mostly quiet and spare of excess emotion.

Like Paul, a gifted pianist, they reserved their passion for music; three of the birth mother's brothers had played for years in the local orchestra. In this German family of the woman who had died soon after giving birth to Paul, Spencer saw striking reflections of her son's personality.

"I felt such a tremendous sense of relief, as I realized, of course, this is Paul, here are the roots of who he is," she recalls.

For Paul, the encounter sparked a friendship that he pursued, returning again to visit the family on his own. For Spencer, it hammered home a lesson that scientific studies of the last 20 years have validated: A newborn child is not a formless bit of clay waiting to be shaped by parents or anybody else.

Rather, the core of many behaviors and most personality traits—the determinants of whether we're shy or extroverted, even the kinds of jokes we find funny and the kinds of people we like—seem largely embedded in the coils of chromosomes that our parents pass to us at conception. The question today is no longer whether genetics influence personality, but rather how much, and in what ways?

The answers, emerging in the last few years primarily from long-term studies of twins and adopted children, bring increasing clarity to the nature/nurture debate: While environmental forces *can* help shape temperament, it is apparently equally true that genes can dictate an individual's response to those environmental forces.

The cumulative evidence also suggests that it's not full-blown personality traits that are inherited, but rather predilections. And, in an interesting turnabout, that information has already begun to change the process of adoption itself. At many adoption agencies, a child is no longer passed from one family to another like a closely held secret. Instead, birth parents fill out lengthy questionnaires that probe not only their medical histories, but also their interests, talents and goals; that information is presented to the adoptive parents as a part of the child's birthright.

Spencer is unsentimental about the value of this information.

"A genetic history—psychological as well as medical—is something like a child's washing instructions," she says. "When you buy a sweater, you want to know all about its fabric content. How much more important is it to know everything you can about the care and feeding of the child you are about to nurture?"

Not long ago, such views were scandalous. James Watson, Francis Crick and Maurice Wilkins were awarded a 1962 Nobel Prize for puzzling out the structure of the human genetic code, and the medical discoveries that their work has spawned—genetic clues to Tay-Sachs disease, sickle-cell anemia and hemophilia, for example—have been universally heralded. But the notion that psychological traits and behavioral disorders may also be genetically rooted has had more difficulty escaping the pall of Nazi experiments in eugenics during World War II.

Many political activists of the 1960's and 70's, wary that genetic theories might ultimately be used to justify social inequality, attacked anyone who suggested that it wasn't within the DNA of each person to be a mathematical genius, a concert pianist or a gifted statesman. "Potential" was the buzzword; any mention of limits was deemed reactionary. It was all right to talk to your veterinarian about a sweet-tempered pup, but heaven forbid you should suggest that your child had an inherent nature. Still, even then, in a few psychology departments scattered around the world, researchers were stubbornly chipping away at the idea that every aspect of personality is learned.

It is within the family that the alchemy of nurture and nature works its strongest magic, and it is by studying families—of twins and adopted children—that behavioral geneticists have best succeeded in untangling those forces. Thomas J. Bouchard at the University of Minnesota heads one of the most dramatic of such studies.

Since 1979, Bouchard has specialized in the examination of adult identical and fraternal twins who were separated soon after their birth and reared in separate families, separate worlds. To date, he has found about 100 twin pairs—60 of them identical—and has brought each to his laboratory for a week of tests.

He finds that identical twins reared in completely different families and communities answer the 15,000 questions he asks in remarkably similar ways. In fact, in questions that reveal traits as diverse as leadership ability, traditionalism or irritability, for example, they respond just as identical twins would who grew up in the same family. When measuring traditionalism—a composite trait that includes showing respect for authority, endorsing strict child-rearing practices and valuing the esteem of the community—the similarities between twins reared in different families were striking.

By focusing on identical twins reared apart, Bouchard has found individuals who have all of their genes—and perhaps only their genes—in common. The clincher is that he and his colleagues run the same battery of tests on three other types of twins: identical pairs raised in the same families, fraternal twins reared together and fraternal twins reared apart.

Remember that identical twins arise from the fertilization of a single egg that splits in half shortly after conception, while fraternal twins are the product of two fertilized eggs. Identical twins have in common all their genes; fraternal twins, on average, half. By comparing the degree of similarity among twins in each of these four categories, Bouchard is able to look trait by trait and see how much each is influenced by genetics. In measuring I.Q., for example, Bouchard found that identical twins reared apart were more similar than fraternal twins reared together.

Internationally, there are two other major, ongoing studies of identical twins reared apart—one in Sweden, the other in Finland—encompassing more than 7,000 pairs of twins all told. Together with earlier, smaller studies, this research has allowed behavioral geneticists to begin to speak confidently about the influence of genes on a number of human characteristics.

Though the debate over the value of intelligence quotient tests continues, for example, there is ample evidence that whatever it is they measure is in large part inherited. Studies of some 100,000 children and adults internationally suggest that genes are 50 percent to 70 percent responsible for an individual's I.Q. "That's not to say that you can't reduce anybody's I.Q. to zero if you hit them over the head hard enough," says John C. Loehlin, a behavioral geneticist at the University of Texas at Austin. Physical or psychological abuse, malnutrition or even a lack of intellectual stimulation can act as environmental bludgeons to native intelligence. However, Loehlin adds, "The idea that, if raised in the same environment, we would all have the same I.Q. has pretty well been laid to rest."

The findings are trickiest to understand where what we call personality is concerned. Research of the last decade shows that genetics are as influential as environment on characteristics as varied as extraversion, motivation for achievement, leadership, conscientiousness and conservatism. But whether some traits are more genetically controlled than others is much harder to tease apart. Like Bouchard and others, Robert Plomin, a developmental psychologist at Pennsylvania State University, is trying to do just that in a study of nearly 700 pairs of Swedish twins.

"The interesting question today," says Plomin, "is, 'Are there any traits that *aren't* significantly affected by genetics?' " He thinks he has found one: agreeableness, or as he calls it, "niceness"—whether a person is more trusting, sympathetic and cooperative, or cynical, callous and antagonistic. "We found that where a person tends to fall on that scale is much more influenced by environment—mostly early environment—than by genes," Plomin says, "and as a parent, I find that very reassuring."

The same studies continue to shed light on behavioral disorders such as alcoholism—a particularly complicated area of inquiry, since research shows that "situational" alcoholism caused by environmental factors such as war and unemployment skews the findings.

Men appear to be much more susceptible to the disorder than women; an alcoholic father is a strong indicator of a possible problem in a son. Perhaps the best evidence for a genetic link comes from a 1987 adoption study in Sweden, which found that the adopted sons of alcoholic birth fathers were four times more likely to grow up to be alcoholic than were members of a control group. A smaller study of adopted daughters of alcoholic birth mothers found they were three times more likely to have the disorder.

Recent adoption and twin studies also suggest that there's a genetic link to most—but not all—forms of schizophrenia. The likelihood that a child or sibling of someone with schizophrenia will develop the disorder is about 12 percent—12 times higher than the risk for everyone else—and if one identical twin has schizophrenia, the other has a 50 percent chance of developing the illness. Researchers suspect that a constellation of genes, working in combination with environmental forces, triggers the disease.

Both adoptive and twin studies confirm that clinical depression, particularly the bipolar manic-depressive variety, has a strong genetic component. According to one of the largest studies, in Denmark in 1977, if one identical twin suffers from bipolar manic depression, the other has a 79 percent likelihood of having the same disorder. Among fraternal twins, that correlation is only 19 percent.

Mary Anne Maiser, who supervises social workers at the Children's Home Society, works in an office dotted with photographs of her three daughters, the oldest of whom, Laura, is adopted. "At the time my husband and I adopted Laura, social workers were taught—and taught clients—that each baby is a tabula rasa," Maiser says. "But by the time Laura was a year old, I knew something was wrong." She was an extremely difficult child, even alienated.

Over the years, the family sought help from a therapist. It wasn't until age 17 that Laura was diagnosed with bipolar disorder, or manic-depressive illness. Around that time, after two years of trying, Maiser was able to get more information about Laura's birth family; she had been adopted through a different agency in another state. The agency revealed that within months of Laura's adoption, her biological father had been hospitalized. "You can guess the diagnosis," Maiser says. "Bipolar disorder and schizophrenia."

If she had been given the information earlier, would it have made a difference? Maiser's voice gets tight and her mouth forms a resolute line. "Laura had so much pain and went undiagnosed for so long," she says. "She didn't just need family therapy, she needed lithium."

Despite such testimonials, some people still argue that wrapping an adopted child in genetic history does more damage than good. Laura had only about a 15 percent chance of inheriting her biological father's illness. If the disorder had never appeared, might not the label itself have twisted her life?

Marietta Spencer dismisses such objections: "Everyone I have ever worked with has said it is always better to know the history than not to know. Because, believe me, it's the parents who *don't* know who imagine the worst if they have a child who seems to be troubled."

For his part, Plomin thinks it's at least as important to tell adoptive parents that the birth father was an alcoholic as to alert them to their child's tiny risk of inheriting a rare disease. "Even if you have a genetic vulnerability," he points out, "you don't become an alcoholic unless you drink a lot over a long period. If you have the genetic history ahead of time, and you see the symptoms developing, you may be more likely to get help early."

If adoption agencies are going to do everything they can to maximize the chances of harmony in a family, should they perhaps go one step further and take temperamental factors into account when "matching" a child to new parents?

Spencer, while stressing that genetic history isn't the *only* factor to consider in an adoption, thinks it shouldn't be ignored. "Adoption, like marriage, is a process of family building, and empathy is very important," she says.

While Spencer might have a point, Plomin says, accurately predicting whether family members will be sympathetic or antagonistic to each other—in essence, predicting the chemistry of relationships—is much more difficult than she imagines. And even if adoption workers could give long, detailed personality tests to both sets of parents, they would still be a long way from predicting the baby's temperament.

Moreover, Plomin cautions, the current infatuation with genetic influences has obscured the very real importance of environment in human development.

In fact, Plomin's most recent research suggests that the influences of genes and the environment may be intractably intertwined. He asked participants in the Swedish twin study, who were an average of 59 years old, to fill out questionnaires about their parents, siblings and childhood experiences. The questions were phrased so as to get at the respondents' perceptions of their families—how cohesive or emotionally demonstrative the families were, for example, or how much stress parents had placed on achievement, organization, discipline or culture.

The results were striking: identical twins reared in different families described their early childhood environments as remarkably similar—almost as similar as if they had been raised in the same family. Fraternal twins, on the other hand, even when raised in the same family, described that family very differently.

"You can interpret the findings in one of two ways," Plomin says. "Maybe, because of their identical genes, identical twins perceive their environment in a quite similar way—sort of like looking at the world through the same shade of gray- or rose-colored glasses. But it is also possible—and we think quite likely—that their parents and others respond to them similarly because of genetically influenced quirks of personality that they share."

Bouchard is finding much the same thing in his study. He cites the example of one pair of identical twins from Britain, now middle-aged, who were separated soon after birth. One was adopted by a working-class family with little time or money for books. The other grew up exposed to a rich library as the daughter of a university professor. "From early childhood, both women loved to read," Bouchard says. "One had only to walk out into the living room and pull books off the shelf. The other went every week to the library and came home with a huge stack. Though one had to work a little harder at it than the other, they both ended up creating functionally similar environments."

However, "if one of those women had been raised in a family with *no* access to libraries, she would have been dramatically different from her sister," he explains. "The trait develops via the environment."

If the behavioral geneticists are right, then those who fear the tyranny of biological determinism can rest a little easier. Genes aren't the sole ingredient of the personality soup, they are merely the well-seasoned stock. That message should be liberating for all parents—and children.

QUESTIONS ABOUT THE READING

1. Are the findings and interpretations given in this article generally consistent with those in your text regarding the relative influence of heredity and environment on intelligence? On various personality traits? On alcoholism, depression, and schizophrenia? If not, in what ways do the two sources differ, and what might explain such differences?

2. To many people today, the idea that heredity and environment have intertwining effects on development seems quite reasonable. Why do you suppose that the "nature-nurture debate" raged so fiercely in the past? According to Franklin, what may have motivated pressures to deny the influence of heredity? Considering that scientific methods are supposed to be as free as possible of subjective bias, what conclusions might you draw from the fact that only within the past 10 to 20 years has research produced general agreement on the significant role apparently played by the genes? Why, now, does the pendulum seem to be swinging in the other direction, with genetic influences

obscuring "the very real importance of environment"?

3. In the past, adoptive parents were given little or no information about their child's natural parents. Today such policies are changing, largely in response to requests from adoptive children and their families. On the basis of this article, would you favor or oppose disclosing medical and other information about a child's background to the adoptive parents at the time of adoption? Can you think of reasons, pro or con, other than those given in the article?

4. Do you think adoption agencies should attempt to match children and families according to personality characteristics?

5. Franklin concludes that the "message" of behavioral genetics should be "liberating for all parents—and children." Do you agree? Why or why not? What conclusions about child rearing can you draw from the information about behavioral genetics presented in this article and in your text?

ANSWER KEY FOR CHAPTER 2

Note: Numbers in parentheses refer to pages in the textbook where answers can be found.

CHAPTER 2 REVIEW

Important Terms for Introduction and Section I

1. heredity (page 52)
2. outside (52)
3. nature, nurture (52)

Learning Objectives for Section I

1. (page 53)
2. (54)
3. (54, 55)

Important Terms for Section II

1. cell (page 56)
2. sex (56)
3. ovum (56)
4. uterus (57)
5. ovaries, uterus (57)
6. genes (57)
7. chromosomes (58)
8. mitosis (58)
9. gene (58)
10. proteins (58)
11. ova (60)
12. zygote (60)

Learning Objectives for Section II

1. (pages 55-56)
2. (56-57)
3. (58)
4. (58)
5. (59)
6. (59)
7. (60)

Important Terms for Section III

1. trait (page 61)
2. allele (61)
3. segregation (61)
4. contradictory (62)
5. identical (62)
6. different (62)
7. homozygous (63)
8. observable (63)
9. alleles (63)
10. genes (63)
11. recessive (64)
12. polygenic (64)
13. multifactorial (64)
14. expressed (66)
15. extra (69)
16. genetic (71)
17. karyotype (71)
18. amniotic fluid (72)
19. membrane (72)
20. alpha fetoprotein (72)
21. ultrasound, sound (72)
22. fetoscopy (72)

Learning Objectives for Section III

1. (page 61)
2. (61)
3. (62-63)
4. (62)
5. (63)
6. (63-64)
7. (65-69)
8. (69)
9. (69-71)
10. (71-73)
11. (74-75)

Important Terms for Section IV

1. John Locke (page 73)
2. variability, environmental (75)
3. maturation (75)
4. heredity, environment (77)
5. concordance (82)
6. autism (83)
7. depression (85)
8. neurons (85)
9. reality (85)

Learning Objectives for Section IV

1. (pages 73-74)
2. (75-76)
3. (77-78)
4. (78-82)
5. (82-83)
6. (83-87)

CHAPTER 2 QUIZ

Matching—Who's Who

1. g (page 84)
2. j (56)
3. i (61)
4. a (73)
5. h (56)
6. b (76)
7. e (76)
8. c (56)
9. f (73)
10. d (83)

Multiple-Choice

1. b (page 54)
2. c (56)
3. d (57)
4. d (56)
5. c (57)
6. b (59)
7. b (59)
8. d (59)
9. a (60)
10. c (61, 63, 64, 65)
11. a (61)
12. d (63)
13. a (63)
14. b (64)
15. b (65)
16. a (67)
17. c (69)
18. b (75)
19. b (77-78)
20. d (79, 82, 83)
21. b (83-85)

True or False?

1. F—In preindustrial societies, families needed to be large. (page 53)
2. T (56)
3. F—More than one sperm may penetrate an ovum, but only one sperm can fertilize it. (57)
4. F—Sperm can fertilize an ovum for up to 48 hours after ejaculation. (57)
5. F—Every cell in the human body except the sex cells has 46 chromosomes; the sex cells have 23 chromosomes. (58)
6. T (58)
7. T (58)
8. T (59)
9. F—Testosterone begins to act at about the sixth week of gestation. (59)
10. F—Male babies are more vulnerable to death and disorders, and their physical development is slower than that of female babies. (59)
11. T (60)
12. F—Simple dominant and recessive inheritance in humans can be seen mainly in inherited defects and diseases. (63)
13. T (63)
14. T (64)
15. F—The man cannot pass on the gene for hemophilia to his son, because it is carried on the X chromosome. (69)

16. F—Down syndrome results from an extra auto-some. (69)
17. T (73)
18. F—Extreme environmental deprivation can interfere with maturation. (75-76)
19. T (79)
20. T (80)
21. F—Although schizophrenia can begin in childhood, it typically occurs in young adults. (85)
22. T (86)

PRENATAL DEVELOPMENT

OVERVIEW

Chapter 3 explores the development of the child from conception to birth. In this chapter, the authors:

- Describe the experience of pregnancy and the psychological changes men and women go through as they approach parenthood
- Explain how a new human life is created
- Outline three stages of prenatal development
- Describe the developing capabilities of the fetus
- Discuss factors in a mother's lifestyle that can affect the developing fetus
- Identify some birth defects that can be transmitted by mothers and fathers
- Point out how infertility can be treated or overcome
- Discuss alternative ways for infertile couples to become parents

CHAPTER 3 REVIEW

Section I The Experience of Pregnancy

LEARNING OBJECTIVES FOR SECTION I

After reading and reviewing this section of Chapter 3, you should be able to do the following.

1. List four tasks facing expectant parents and describe how prospective parents typically accomplish each of them.

2. Name at least two possible, at least two probable, and at least two positive signs of pregnancy. For each, tell when the sign generally appears and name other possible causes, if any.

Section II Prenatal Development

FRAMEWORK FOR SECTION II

A. The Three Stages of Prenatal Development
  1. Germinal Stage (Fertilization to 2 Weeks)
  2. Embryonic Stage (2 to 8-12 Weeks)
    a. The Embryonic Stage as a Critical Period
    b. Spontaneous Abortion in the Embryonic Stage
  3. Fetal Stage (8-12 Weeks to Birth)
B. Prenatal Abilities and Activities
  1. Fetal Hearing
  2. Fetal Learning

IMPORTANT TERMS FOR SECTION II

Completion: Fill in the blanks to complete the definitions of key terms for this section of Chapter 3.

1. **gestation:** Period of time from conception to birth; normal full-term gestation is _____ days.

2. _____ **stage:** First 2 weeks of development of a conceptus, beginning at fertilization, characterized by rapid cell division and increasing complexity, and ending when the conceptus attaches to the wall of the uterus.

3. **embryonic stage:** Second stage of pregnancy (2 to 8-12 weeks), characterized by differentiation of body parts and systems and ending when the _____ begin to appear.

4. **critical period:** Specific time during development when an event has its greatest _____.

5. _____: First, second, or third 3-month period of pregnancy.

6. **spontaneous abortion:** Natural expulsion from the uterus of a conceptus that cannot survive outside the womb; also called _____.

7. **fetus:** Conceptus between _____ to _____ weeks and birth.

8. _____ **stage:** Final stage of pregnancy (_____ to _____ weeks to birth), characterized by increased detail of body parts and greatly enlarged body size.

LEARNING OBJECTIVES FOR SECTION II

After reading and reviewing this section of Chapter 3, you should be able to do the following.

1. Identify the main activity that takes place during all three stages of prenatal development.

2. Summarize the development of the conceptus during the germinal stage.

3. Define the following terms: *blastocyst, embryonic disk, ectoderm, endoderm, mesoderm, placenta, umbilical cord, amniotic sac, trophoblast, embryo.*

4. Identify three functions of the placenta.

5. Explain why the embryonic stage is considered a critical period.

6. Summarize the development that occurs during the embryonic stage.

7. Explain why some pregnancies terminate in spontaneous abortion.

8. Summarize the development that takes place during the fetal stage.

9. Discuss findings about fetal sensory and cognitive abilities.

Section III The Prenatal Environment

FRAMEWORK FOR SECTION III

A. Maternal Factors
  1. Nutrition
     a. Importance of Good Nutrition in Pregnancy
     b. Malnutrition
        (1) Malnutrition and Fetal Development
        (2) Overcoming the Effects of Malnutrition
  2. Drug Intake
     a. Birth Control Pills
     b. Diethylstilbestrol (DES)
     c. Caffeine
     d. Nicotine
     e. Alcohol
     f. Marijuana
     g. Opiates
     h. Cocaine
  3. Other Maternal Factors
     a. Illness
     b. Incompatibility of Blood Type
     c. Emotional States
     d. Environmental Hazards
        (1) Industrial Chemicals
        (2) Lead Contamination
        (3) Radiation
        (4) Video Display Terminals
     e. Exercise
B. Birth Defects Transmitted by the Father
C. Medical Therapy within the Womb
D. A Note on Prenatal Hazards

IMPORTANT TERMS FOR SECTION III

Completion: Fill in the blanks to complete the definitions of key terms for this section of Chapter 3.

1. **teratogenic:** Capable of causing
   _____.

2. _____ (abbreviated _____):
   Combination of mental, motor, and
   developmental abnormalities affecting the
   offspring of some women who drink heavily
   during pregnancy.

3. **Rh factor:** Protein substance found in the
   blood of most people; when it is present in the
   blood of a(n) _____ but not in the
   blood of the _____ , death of the
   fetus can result.

4. **mutation:** Change in a(n) _____
   that leads to the production of a new, often
   harmful trait.

LEARNING OBJECTIVES FOR SECTION III

After reading and reviewing this section of Chapter
3, you should be able to do the following.

1. List the elements of good nutrition during
   pregnancy.

2. Describe the effects of malnutrition on fetal
   development and cite two ways to prevent or
   overcome its effects.

3. Explain how drug intake during pregnancy
   can harm an embryo or fetus and list effects of
   birth control pills, diethylstilbestrol (DES),
   caffeine, nicotine, alcohol, marijuana, opiates,
   and cocaine.

4. Name four illnesses that can be passed from
   mother to fetus and describe their
   consequences.

5. Explain how incompatibility of blood type can
   arise between a mother and child and briefly
   discuss consequences, prevention, and
   treatment.

6. Compare the effects of a mother's emotional
   state on a fetus and on an infant.

7. Outline the prenatal risks involved in exposure
   to industrial chemicals, lead contamination,
   radiation, and video display terminals.

8. Summarize the relationship between exercise during pregnancy and the health of the fetus.

9. Identify several ways in which a man can contribute to the risk of birth defects in his child.

10. Describe two techniques for correcting disorders in the womb and name two conditions that can be treated prenatally.

11. Discuss factors to be weighed in considering the issue of "fetal abuse."

12. List nine ways of reducing risks during pregnancy.

Section IV   Other Ways to Parenthood

FRAMEWORK FOR SECTION IV

A. Infertility
B. Alternative Ways to Conceive
    1. Artificial Insemination
    2. In Vitro Fertilization
    3. Donor Eggs
    4. Surrogate Motherhood
C. Adoption

IMPORTANT TERMS FOR SECTION IV

Completion: Fill in the blanks to complete the definitions of key terms for this section of Chapter 3.

1. _____: Inability to conceive after 1 year of trying to have a baby.

2. **artificial** _____: Nonsexual introduction of sperm into a woman's body with the intent to cause pregnancy.

3. **in vitro fertilization:** _____ outside the body.

4. _____: Taking a child into one's family through legal means and accepting the child as one's own.

LEARNING OBJECTIVES FOR SECTION IV

After reading and reviewing this section of Chapter 3, you should be able to do the following.

1. List possible reasons for the increase in infertility during the past 25 years, and briefly discuss its effects on a marriage.

2. List four alternative ways for infertile people to conceive, and explain how each works.

3. Summarize trends in adoption in the United States since 1970 and briefly discuss attitudes toward it.

CHAPTER 3 QUIZ

Matching—Month by Month: Match each month of gestation in the left-hand column with the appropriate description (a typical development during that month) in the right-hand column.

1. First month _____
2. Second month _____
3. Third month _____
4. Fourth month _____
5. Fifth month _____
6. Sixth month _____
7. Seventh month _____
8. Eighth month _____
9. Ninth month _____

a. Sex can first be easily determined.
b. First signs of individual personality appear.
c. Body begins to catch up to head, growing to same proportions as at birth.
d. Fetus stops growing.
e. Growth is more rapid than at any other time during prenatal or postnatal life.
f. Reflex patterns are fully developed.
g. Layer of fat begins developing over entire body.
h. Skin becomes sensitive enough to react to tactile stimulation.
i. Fetus is first able to hear.

Multiple-Choice: Circle the choice that best completes or answers each item.

1. Through cell division, the single-celled zygote develops into a person with at least how many cells?
   a. 800
   b. 8000
   c. 800 million
   d. 800 billion

2. The conceptus implants itself in the wall of the uterus during which stage of prenatal development?
   a. germinal
   b. embryonic
   c. fetal
   d. uterine

3. During the germinal stage, the fertilized ovum moves from the
   a. uterus to the fallopian tube
   b. fallopian tube to the uterus
   c. ovary to the fallopian tube
   d. fallopian tube to the ovary

4. Which of the following protects the unborn child?
   a. embryonic disk
   b. endoderm
   c. amniotic sac
   d. none of the above

5. The placenta
   a. provides immunity
   b. produces hormones
   c. nourishes the fetus
   d. all of the above

6. Which of the following is (are) likely to cause a spontaneous abortion?
   a. chromosomal abnormalities
   b. defective sperm
   c. herpes virus in the uterus
   d. all of the above

7. The fetal stage is characterized by
   a. high risk of miscarriage
   b. rapid growth and increased complexity
   c. occurrence of developmental birth defects
   d. all of the above

8. Which statement about fetal learning is true, according to research?
   a. Newborns prefer male voices to female voices.
   b. Newborns cannot yet distinguish between the mother's voice and that of another woman.
   c. Newborns recognize stories that were read to them before birth.
   d. Newborns show no preferences that suggest fetal learning has taken place.

9. Which of the following is a procedure for detection of fetal disorders?
   a. amniocentesis
   b. transferrin
   c. teratogenesis
   d. radiation

10. Babies tend to develop best when their mothers gain approximately how many pounds during pregnancy?
    a. 10 to 15
    b. 16 to 25
    c. 26 to 35
    d. 36 to 45

11. Pregnant women need how many extra calories daily?
    a. about 200
    b. 300 to 500
    c. 800 or more
    d. none—extra calories may make the baby obese

12. Malnutrition in a mother affects the infant's
    a. weight
    b. chance of survival
    c. brain
    d. all of the above

13. The effects of which of the following, when ingested during pregnancy, are still in question?
    a. caffeine
    b. birth control pills
    c. DES
    d. all of the above

14. Which of the following has *not* been found to be an effect of a mother's heavy smoking during pregnancy?
    a. childhood cancer
    b. stillbirth
    c. facial abnormalities
    d. retarded growth and cognitive development

15. Of the three leading causes of mental retardation, the only completely preventable one is
    a. fetal alcohol syndrome
    b. fetal tobacco syndrome
    c. Down syndrome
    d. neural tube defects

16. The use of which of the following drugs by a mother during pregnancy has been linked to sudden infant death syndrome?
    a. heroin
    b. cocaine
    c. marijuana
    d. all of the above

17. AIDS can be passed to children through the mother's
    a. milk
    b. genetic structure
    c. blood
    d. none of the above—AIDS can be passed only through sexual contact

18. An environmental hazard that can cause gene mutations is
    a. PCBs
    b. lead
    c. radiation
    d. none of the above

19. If a father is in his late thirties or older when his baby is conceived, the child may have an increased risk of
    a. Down syndrome
    b. dwarfism
    c. bone malformations
    d. all of the above

20. Doctors can give fetuses blood transfusions or injections through
    a. the placenta
    b. amniocentesis
    c. hydrocephalus
    d. the umbilical cord

21. In vitro fertilization is
    a. a form of artificial insemination
    b. conception outside the body
    c. most likely to be used when the cause of a couple's infertility is the man's low sperm count
    d. none of the above

True or False? In the blank following each item, write T (for *true*) or F (for *false*). In the space below the item, if the statement is false, rewrite it to make it true.

1. Absence of menstruation is a positive sign of pregnancy. _____

2. A mother's emotional attachment to her unborn baby normally occurs immediately upon her discovery that she is pregnant. _____

3. It usually takes 1 week for the fertilized ovum to reach the uterus. _____

4. The embryonic disk differentiates into three layers from which the various parts of the body will develop. _____

5. Most developmental birth defects occur during the first trimester of pregnancy. _____

6. Differences in fetal activity seem to indicate temperamental patterns that may continue into adulthood. _____

7. Research suggests that the first sense to develop is smell. _____

8. Skipping breakfast during pregnancy can result in changes in the composition of the bloodstream. _____

9. The effects of fetal malnourishment cannot be overcome after birth. _____

10. It is unsafe for a pregnant woman to take aspirin. _____

11. Any ill effects on a fetus of drugs taken during pregnancy will show up at or soon after birth. _____

12. It can take 6 years for a child to recover from the consequences of drug addiction acquired in the womb. _____

13. If a mother contracts German measles at any time during her pregnancy, her baby is almost certain to be born deaf or with heart defects. _____

14. If the Rh factor is present in a mother's blood but not in the fetus's blood, death of the fetus can result. _____

15. Stress and anxiety during pregnancy have no apparent effect on the health of a baby. _____

16. Pregnant women should be sure to include fatty fish in their diet, to aid the development of fat cells in the fetus. _____

17. Women whose jobs require them to work full time at video display terminals during the first 3 months of pregnancy have an increased risk of miscarriage. _____

18. Jogging, swimming, bicycling, or playing tennis can overstrain a pregnant woman and endanger the fetus. _____

19. Infertility is by definition a permanent condition. _____

20. "Donor eggs" are the female equivalent of artificial insemination by a donor. _____

21. Surrogate motherhood is another name for adoption. _____

TOPICS FOR THOUGHT AND DISCUSSION

1. Some expectant fathers experience physical symptoms of pregnancy. What are some possible reasons for this phenomenon?

2. In ancient times, people believed that a clap of thunder or a jolt could cause a woman to miscarry. How do you imagine this belief might have affected the treatment and behavior of women during pregnancy?

3. Why would correspondence between levels of fetal activity and levels of activity in infancy or adulthood support the hypothesis that temperament is inborn? Can you think of any other explanations for this finding?

4. In India, many abortions have resulted after amniocentesis was performed solely to determine whether a baby would be a boy or a girl. In the United States, too, many parents have definite preferences regarding the sex of an expected child. If it was established that amniocentesis which is motivated by such preferences has prompted an increase in abortions, would you favor a law (as was recently passed in India) banning amniocentesis except when a risk of birth defects can be shown? Would you favor a ban on disclosure of the sex of the fetus to the parents? Why or why not?

5. The authors of your text state that ethical considerations prevent controlled experiments to study prenatal hazards. Why? Does the fact that findings regarding these hazards must be based largely on animal research and mothers' self-reports affect your confidence in these findings?

6. The first Rh-positive baby of an Rh-negative mother is usually not in danger, but the risk is greater for each succeeding child. What hypothesis can you suggest to explain this increasing risk? How might you test your hypothesis?

7. If a fetus exhibits a prenatal condition that can be cured by intrauterine transfusion, would a mother's refusal to submit to this procedure constitute "fetal abuse"? How would you weigh the fetus's right to health against the mother's right to control her own body and to avoid medical risks?

8. Surrogacy contracts, such as the one ultimately invalidated by the New Jersey Supreme Court in the "Baby M" case, have raised much controversy over such issues as "child buying" and whether a surrogate has a right to change her mind and keep the baby. The discussions of prenatal hazards and "fetal abuse" in this chapter suggest another concern: to what extent can or should a surrogate mother be held responsible for avoiding these hazards and contributing positively to fetal development? (Note: The "Baby M" contract provided that the surrogate, Mary Beth Whitehead, would not smoke, drink, or take drugs while pregnant, would assume all medical risks, and would undergo amniocentesis or abortion upon demand of the father, William Stern.)

9. The other three alternative methods of conception described in your text (artificial insemination, in vitro fertilization, and donor eggs) also raise ethical issues. For example, if eggs or sperm from a donor are used, how can or should donors be screened for physical or genetic defects or psychological problems? Does the donor have any rights and responsibilities regarding the child? Should the child be told about his or her parentage, since children fathered or mothered by the same donor (genetic half siblings) could someday meet and marry, increasing the risk that they would bear children with birth defects?

CHAPTER 3 READING

INTRODUCTION

According to your text, about 1 newborn in 750 is afflicted with fetal alcohol syndrome, a leading cause of mental retardation. One of those "FAS babies" is the subject of *The Broken Cord* (Harper and Row, 1989), a highly moving book by Michael Dorris, adoptive father of the boy he calls Adam—now grown to adulthood.

This review by Patricia Guthrie, a reporter for *The Albuquerque Tribune*, appeared in *The New York Times Book Review* of July 30, 1989. Guthrie was a winner of the 1988 George Polk Award for a series of articles on alcoholism among Native Americans.

The review quotes briefly from the last chapter of *The Broken Cord*, in which Adam's typed account of his life story is reproduced just as he wrote it, with grammar and punctuation intact.

Alcohol's Child: A Father Tells His Tale

by Patricia Guthrie

In 1971, Michael Dorris, 26 years old and unmarried, was living in an isolated Indian community in Alaska, doing fieldwork for his doctorate in anthropology. Realizing that "in a world of 'we,' I was an 'I' " he decided that he wanted to be a father. Lacking a partner, Mr. Dorris decided to try to adopt a child alone. Part American Indian himself, he asked for an Indian child, and his application was forwarded to a national adoption service. A few months later, as he was settling into a new teaching job in New Hampshire, a social worker called to tell him that a 3-year-old boy from a Sioux reservation in South Dakota was up for adoption.

Mr. Dorris was warned that the boy had been born almost seven weeks premature; his mother was a heavy drinker who neglected him; he "had not been toilet-trained or taught to speak more than a few words. He was diagnosed as mentally retarded." In the perfect abstraction of longing to be a parent, Mr. Dorris believed in the "positive impact of environment." He assured himself: "With me he'll catch up."

At their first meeting in the social worker's office the boy Mr. Dorris calls Adam looked up from his toy truck and said "Hi, Daddy." It was the beginning of a bittersweet relationship that has gone on for 18 years, lovingly and painfully described in "The Broken Cord," the story of a child afflicted by fetal alcohol syndrome and of Mr. Dorris's personal investigation of the condition that has blighted his son's life.

Despite the attention of the best teachers, countless examinations by medical doctors and psychologists and the constant, doting care of his father and family, Adam Dorris never shook his bad start. He struggled through the Cornish, N.H., public elementary school; at graduation in 1983, "he could not add, subtract, count money, or consistently identify the town, state, country or planet." He went on to high school in Claremont, a half-hour bus ride away. He was sent each day, but could not reliably get on the right bus going in the right direction to get home. He was transferred to a vocational education program at a school farther away. At the age of 20, he still could not count money or tell time. His I.Q. remained a steady 65.

In 1982, after Mr. Dorris had adopted a second son and a daughter and was on his way to having three more children with his wife, the writer Louise Erdrich, he learned at last what was really wrong with Adam. As head of Native American studies at Dartmouth College, Mr. Dorris was visiting a treatment center for chemically dependent teen-agers on South Dakota's Pine Ridge Sioux reservation when he saw three "uncannily familiar" boys who not only behaved like Adam but looked like him. He reached for a wallet photo of Adam to show the program director, who "nodded, and handed it back. 'FAS too' " he replied. It was the first time Mr. Dorris had heard the initials that stand for fetal alcohol syndrome.

"They come from alcoholic families, mothers who drank," the director told him. "Your wife too?" he asked.

"He's adopted," Mr. Dorris replied, "And, yes, his mother did drink." Alcohol, Mr. Dorris soon learned, had damaged Adam's brain while he was still in the womb. And the damage could not be undone.

In the next few years Mr. Dorris learned a lot about fetal alcohol syndrome, a condition that was being identified and explored by the international medical community in the 1970's, just when Adam's medical and learning disabilities were baffling his father.

Medical news doesn't always travel fast. While Adam was struggling to comprehend the simplest of tasks in elementary school, some doctors were still prescribing an occasional glass of wine to pregnant women for relaxation. But by 1981, the Food and Drug Administration was warning health professionals that pregnant women should drink no alcohol at all, that even small, casual doses had been linked to increased risk of low birth weight and spontaneous abortion.

The definition of fetal alcohol syndrome, Mr. Dorris writes, embraces individuals who share several recognizable characteristics: "(1) significant growth retardation both before and after birth; (2) measurable mental deficit; (3) altered facial characteristics; (4) other physical abnormalities; and (5) documentation of maternal alcoholism." By 1988 the "mental deficit" category had been refined to include "attention deficits," or the inability to concentrate on a single task; memory problems; hyperactivity; low I.Q.; and an inability, apparently connected to a defective grasp of cause-and-effect relations, to handle money, regardless of "sex, age, educational level or background."

For three years after he learned the name of Adam's condition, Mr. Dorris traveled the country, collecting the bleak stories of Indians dying from whatever alcohol product they could find: death by hair spray, death by antifreeze (the fate of Adam's natural mother). He also heard of the grim beginnings: babies born reeking of cheap wine, babies born with delirium tremens.

At the numerous medical conferences he attended, Mr. Dorris learned that thousands of children are born each year with full fetal alcohol syndrome—about 7,500 by one estimate. Thousands more suffer the lesser disabilities of fetal alcohol effect—feeding difficulties in infants, in older children marginal mental retardation, short memory span, emotional instability. These are afflictions that know no ethnic or class bounds, Mr. Dorris realized, although, as he writes, "historically and presently" it is a "major problem for American Indians." Drinking alcohol has long been "a venerable part of social culture" in many societies—for men. However, according to recent studies, the condition seems to be emerging around the world when "'modern' women, regardless of their class or ethnic background" begin drinking. As Adam had struggled, so many other children around the world struggled: to tie their shoes, to write their names, to remember to wear a coat when it is snowing outside. All because their mothers drank.

The alarming statistics and consequences of fetal alcohol syndrome are skillfully interwoven with the human story of one of its victims in "The Broken Cord." Mr. Dorris's prose is clear and affecting: "Adam's birthdays are reminders for me. For each celebration commemorating that he was born, there is the pang, the rage, that he was not born whole."

The last chapter of the book is "The Adam Dorris Story by Adam Dorris." At his father's suggestion, the young man typed out his life memories, and to everyone's surprise he finished the project. With incurably misspelled words and hopeless punctuation, Adam lists stacking wood and pulling up burdock bushes as his biggest triumphs. "I might of not told you this before but stacking wood is one of my favorite hobbies . I don,t really mind stacking wood at all . And my other hobby is mowing lawns . I don,t have any other hobby besides those two right there ."

Adam does not write about the first time he danced with a girl or about playing in his first baseball game, nor does he seem aware that he missed them. But his father knows what Adam is missing. And it is he, not Adam, who lives with this knowledge.

Mr. Dorris also raises and struggles with, but cannot answer, some Solomonic questions: what should communities do with pregnant women who insist on drinking? How can society possibly protect an unborn child against maternal behavior that is not only legal almost everywhere, but almost impossible to prevent anywhere? Should such women be incarcerated? Should mothers of fetal alcohol children be sterilized if they intend to keep drinking and reproducing? Can civil rights be abrogated for the protection of the unborn? Should liquor companies be held liable for these damaged children if adequate warnings are not on their products?

Those are abstractions, and worth consideration. Throughout his book, Mr. Dorris returns time and again to one real, haunting question: what if someone had stopped Adam's biological mother from drinking?

"The Broken Cord" should be required reading for all medical professionals and social workers, and especially for pregnant women, and women who contemplate pregnancy, who may be tempted to drink. At the very least, Michael Dorris's last comment should be prescribed:

"My son will forever travel through a moonless night with only the roar of wind for company. Don't talk to him of mountains, of tropical beaches. Don't ask him to swoon at sunrises or marvel at the filter of light through leaves. He's never had time for such things, and he does not believe in them. . . . A drowning man is not separated from the lust for air by a bridge of thought—he is one with it—and my son, conceived and grown in an ethanol bath, lives each day in the act of drowning. For him there is no shore."

QUESTIONS ABOUT THE READING

1. The basic facts about fetal alcohol syndrome, as related in *The Broken Cord* and in the review, are generally consistent with those in your text. But while the review cites a warning by the U.S. Food and Drug Administration that pregnant women should drink *no* alcohol, your text, citing other authoritative sources, does not rule out "an occasional drink." How do you think Michael Dorris would react to occasional social drinking by an expectant mother? Do you think that pregnant women should abstain from alcohol completely?

2. According to the review, Dorris raises but does not answer some difficult questions about what society can do to prevent fetal alcohol syndrome. How would you answer these questions? Does a woman have the right to knowingly ingest a substance that can permanently damage her unborn child? Should pregnant women who refuse to stop drinking be incarcerated until they give birth? (Dorris's wife, the writer Louise Erdrich, in her foreword to *The Broken Cord,* suggests that they should.) If not, how else might the problem be handled? Would your answers be the same regarding pregnant women who use cocaine or ingest other substances potentially harmful to the fetus?

3. Dorris says that alcohol use has been a social tradition for men in many cultures, including that of Native Americans; and your text points out that large amounts of alcohol can produce genetic abnormalities in a man's sperm. In view of that possibility, should men of childbearing age be forced to abstain from alcohol? If so, how could such a prohibition be enforced?

ANSWER KEY FOR CHAPTER 3

Note: Numbers in parentheses refer to pages in the textbook where answers can be found.

CHAPTER 3 REVIEW

Learning Objectives for Section I

1. (pages 93-94)
2. (93)

Important Terms for Section II

1. 266 (page 95)
2. germinal (95)
3. bone cells (98)
4. impact (98)
5. trimester (98)
6. miscarriage (98)
7. 8, 12 (99)
8. fetal, 8, 12 (99)

Learning Objectives for Section II

1. (page 95)
2. (95-98)

3. (95-98)
4. (97-98)
5. (98)
6. (98)
7. (98)
8. (99-101)
9. (100-101)

Important Terms for Section III

1. birth defects (page 102)
2. fetal alcohol syndrome (FAS) (105)
3. fetus, mother (110)
4. gene (111)

Learning Objectives for Section III

1. (page 102)
2. (103)
3. (103-108)
4. (108-109)
5. (110)
6. (110)
7. (110-112)
8. (112)

9. (112-113)
10. (113)
11. (114)
12. (115)

Important Terms for Section IV

1. infertility (page 116)
2. insemination (116)
3. conception (117)
4. adoption (117)

Learning Objectives for Section IV

1. (page 116)
2. (116-117)
3. (117-118)

CHAPTER 3 QUIZ

Matching—Month by Month

(All answers can be found on pages 96-97.)

1. e
2. h
3. a
4. c
5. b
6. i
7. f
8. g
9. d

Multiple-Choice

1. d (page 95)
2. a (95)
3. b (95)
4. c (97)
5. d (97-98)
6. d (98)
7. b (99)
8. c (100-101)
9. a (101)
10. c (102)
11. b (102)
12. d (103)
13. a (104)
14. c (105)
15. a (105)
16. b (108)
17. c (109)

18. c (111)
19. d (113)
20. d (113)
21. b (117)

True or False?

1. F—Absence of menstruation is only a possible sign of pregnancy and has many other possible causes. (page 93)
2. F—It takes time for emotional attachment to an unborn baby to develop. (94)
3. F—It normally takes 3 or 4 days for the fertilized ovum to reach the uterus. (95)
4. T (97)
5. T (98)
6. T (99)
7. F—Although babies a few hours old have shown the ability to smell, research shows that fetuses can hear and can respond to touch. (100)
8. T (102)
9. F—A malnourished fetus may benefit from intellectual enrichment after birth. (103)
10. T (104)
11. F—The effects of some drugs, such as the synthetic hormone DES, may not show up for many years. (104)
12. T (107)
13. F—If a mother contracts German measles during the first 11 weeks of pregnancy, her baby is almost certain to be born deaf and to have heart defects. (108)
14. F—When the Rh factor is present in the fetus's blood but not in the mother's blood, death of the fetus can result. (110)
15. T (110)
16. F—Fatty fish from areas such as Lake Michigan may contain PCBs, which can harm fetal development. (110)
17. T (111-112)
18. F—Regular, moderate exercise can contribute to a more comfortable pregnancy and an easier, safer delivery and seems to have no ill effects on the fetus. (112, 115)
19. F—Infertility is defined simply as inability to conceive after 1 year of trying. Many couples, after experiencing infertility, eventually are able to conceive normally. (116)
20. T (117)
21. F—Surrogate motherhood is impregnation of a woman who for a fee carries a baby to term and gives it to the biological father and his wife. (117)

BIRTH AND THE NEWBORN BABY

OVERVIEW

Chapter 4 begins with the drama of birth: the climax of fetal development and the curtain raiser on child development in the world outside the womb. In this chapter, the authors:

- Describe what happens during the three stages, or phases, of childbirth

- Discuss the pros and cons of various methods of, and alternative settings for, childbirth

- Describe how parents react to childbirth and how the transition to parenthood affects their daily lives

- Identify the effects of some potential complications of childbirth and discuss what can be done to prevent and treat low birthweight

- Describe the physical characteristics of a newborn baby and the changes in functioning of basic body systems that occur with the cutting of the umbilical cord

- Explain how the Apgar scale, the Brazelton scale, and other neonatal screening instruments are used to check the health and functioning of the newborn

- Describe the typical alternation of newborns' states of wakefulness, sleep, and activity

---

CHAPTER 4 REVIEW

Section I   The Birth Process

FRAMEWORK FOR SECTION I

A. Birth and Biology: The Phases of Childbirth
B. Birth and Society: Helping the Mother and Baby
  1. Childbearing Positions
  2. Medical Monitoring
  3. Methods of Childbirth
    a. Medicated Delivery
    b. Natural and Prepared Childbirth
    c. Gentle Birth
    d. Cesarean Delivery
    e. Alternative Settings for Childbirth
C. Parents' Reactions to Childbirth
D. Complications of Childbirth
  1. Low Birthweight
    a. Consequences of Low Birthweight
    b. Women at Risk of Having Low-Birthweight Babies
    c. Preventing Low Birthweight
    d. Treating Low-Birthweight Babies
      (1) Isolettes
      (2) Stimulation
      (3) Improving the Parent-Child Relationship
  2. Postmaturity
  3. Birth Trauma
  4. Stillbirth

IMPORTANT TERMS FOR SECTION I

Completion: Fill in the blanks to complete the definitions of key terms for this section of Chapter 4.

1. **neonate:** Newborn in the first _____ weeks of life.

2. **gestation:** Period of time from _____ to _____ ; normal full-term gestation is 266 days.

3. **electronic fetal monitoring:** Use of machines to monitor the fetal _____ during labor and delivery.

4. **medicated delivery:** Childbirth in which the mother receives _____ .

5. **natural childbirth:** Method of childbirth developed by Dr. _____ that seeks to prevent pain by eliminating the mother's fear of childbirth.

6. **prepared childbirth:** Method of childbirth developed by Dr. _____ that uses instruction, breathing exercises, and social support to eliminate fear and pain.

7. **gentle birth:** Delivering babies in dimly lit, quiet rooms, without forceps and with only local anesthesia or none; sometimes called the _____ *method.*

8. _____ **delivery:** Surgical removal of the baby from the uterus.

9. **breech position:** Misalignment of a fetus in the uterus causing the _____ or _____ to emerge before the _____ .

10. _____ **position:** Misalignment of a fetus that causes it to lie crosswise in the uterus.

11. _____ **:** Physician who specializes in delivering babies.

12. **nurse-**_____ **:** Certified nurse who has been specially trained to assist at births.

13. **low-birthweight baby:** General term used for both _____ and _____ babies; formerly called *premature babies.*

14. **preterm (premature) baby:** Baby born less than _____ after the mother's last menstrual period.

15. **small-for-date baby:** Baby whose birthweight is less than that of 90 percent of all babies born at the same _____ age.

16. _____ **:** Crib which permits full temperature regulation under antiseptic conditions; formerly called an *incubator.*

17. _____ **prophecy:** Prediction of behavior that biases people to act as though the prophecy were already true.

18. **birth** _____: Injury sustained by an infant at birth.

19. _____: Oxygen deprivation.

20. **stillbirth:** Delivery of a(n) _____ infant.

21. **fetal death in utero:** Death of a fetus while in the _____.

LEARNING OBJECTIVES FOR SECTION I

After reading and reviewing this section of Chapter 4, you should be able to do the following.

1. Describe what occurs during each of the three stages, or phases, of labor.

2. Explain why the old-fashioned birth stool is returning to favor in many hospitals.

3. Discuss advantages and disadvantages of electronic fetal monitoring during childbirth.

4. Discuss considerations that should enter into a woman's decision whether or not to have a medicated delivery.

5. Explain the theory of the Lamaze method of childbirth and describe some elements of the method.

6. Contrast the Leboyer method ("gentle birth") with conventional childbirth practices and summarize arguments made by advocates of each.

7. Discuss some common reasons for and risks of cesarean delivery.

8. Discuss significant considerations in choosing to give birth in a hospital, at home, or in a freestanding birth center.

9. Cite factors that affect parents' reactions to childbirth and the ease of their transition to parenthood.

10. Explain the difference between preterm (premature) and small-for-date babies, and explain why low birthweight is a serious problem for both types of babies.

11. Name four types of factors that put some women at risk of bearing low-birthweight babies, and give an example of each type, distinguishing between factors the woman can control and those she cannot.

12. Cite three ways in which the treatment of low-birthweight babies immediately after birth has changed in recent years, improving their chances of survival.

13. Identify some considerations involved, when a baby is postmature, in deciding whether to induce labor or deliver by the cesarean method.

14. Discuss factors affecting the long-term outlook for children who have suffered birth trauma.

15. List the typical phases in grieving for a stillborn baby.

Section II The Newborn

FRAMEWORK FOR SECTION II

A. Who Is the Newborn?
B. How Does the Newborn Function?
   1. The Newborn's Body Systems
      a. Circulatory System
      b. Respiratory System
      c. Gastrointestinal System
      d. Temperature Regulation
   2. Medical and Behavioral Screening: Is the Baby Healthy?
      a. Immediate Medical Assessment: Apgar Scale
      b. Screening Newborns for Medical Conditions
      c. Assessing Responses: Brazelton Scale
   3. The States of Infants

IMPORTANT TERMS FOR SECTION II

Completion: Fill in the blanks to complete the definitions of key terms for this section of Chapter 4.

1. _____ **period:** First 4 weeks after birth.

2. **lanugo:** Fine, soft prenatal _____ ; present on some neonates at birth, but soon lost.

3. _____: Oily substance on a neonate's body that dries within a few days after birth.

4. **meconium:** Fetal _____.

5. **neonatal** _____: Yellowing of the skin and eyeballs that is common among newborns and seldom serious.

6. **Apgar scale:** Standard measurement of a newborn's condition that assesses _____ , _____ , _____ , activity, and _____ .

7. _____ **(PKU):** Hereditary abnormality which, if not discovered and treated with a special diet, leads to mental retardation; with special diet, development is normal.

8. **Brazelton Neonatal Behavioral Assessment Scale:** Measure of a newborn's behavioral ability that assesses _____ behaviors, _____ skills, self-control, and response to _____ .

9. _____ : Periodic variation in an infant's cycle of wakefulness, sleep, and activity.

LEARNING OBJECTIVES FOR SECTION II

After reading and reviewing this section of Chapter 4, you should be able to do the following.

1. Describe the typical appearance of a neonate.

2. Contrast the circulatory, respiratory, gastrointestinal, and temperature-regulation systems in a fetus with those in a newborn.

3. Identify three tests given to newborns to assess normality of their responses or to identify babies with specific correctable defects.

4. Explain why individual babies have different patterns of eating, sleeping, and waking and the effect these early patterns have on personality development.

5. Suggest several methods of comforting a crying baby and explain why providing such comfort assists the baby's healthy development.

CHAPTER 4 QUIZ

Matching—Numbers: For each of the items in the column at the left, fill in the correct number from the column at the right.

1. Number of weeks of normal full-term gestation _____   1
2. Number of weeks in the neonatal period _____   2
3. Number of stages of labor _____   3
4. Number of gestational weeks before which a birth is considered premature _____   4
5. Age below which a woman is at risk of bearing an underweight infant _____   7
6. Age above which a woman is at risk of bearing an underweight infant _____   16
7. Number of weeks of gestation at which a birth is considered postmature _____   17
8. Approximate length in inches of the average newborn _____   20
9. Number of minutes after delivery when Apgar scale is first administered _____   34
10. Number of minutes after birth when a baby who has not yet begun to breathe may be in trouble _____   37
11. Minimum score attained by 90 percent of normal infants on Apgar scale _____   40
12. Average number of hours per day a newborn sleeps _____   42

Multiple-Choice: Circle the choice that best completes or answers each item.

1. Gestation is the period from
   a. conception to quickening
   b. conception to birth
   c. commencement of labor to delivery
   d. birth to 4 weeks

2. Which of the following events is considered a possible trigger of the birth process?
   a. decreased flow of blood to the uterus
   b. substance in fetal urine released into the amniotic fluid
   c. genetic programming of the placenta
   d. each of the above

3. During the first stage of labor
   a. the mother's cervix widens to permit passage of the baby's head out of the uterus
   b. the mother experiences "false" labor pains
   c. the mother bears down to permit passage of the baby
   d. the baby's head begins to move through the cervix and vaginal canal

4. The movement of the baby through the birth canal generally takes approximately
   a. 10 minutes
   b. 30 minutes
   c. 1½ hours
   d. 12 to 24 hours

5. The umbilical cord and placenta are expelled from the womb
   a. during the first stage of labor
   b. during the second stage of labor
   c. during the third stage of labor
   d. as soon as the cervix is fully dilated

6. Motorized birth stools are used in many hospitals because they
   a. are more comfortable for mothers
   b. take advantage of gravity to help shorten labor
   c. ease delivery for first-time mothers
   d. all of the above

7. "False positive" readings on electronic fetal monitors during childbirth suggest that fetuses
   a. are in distress when in fact they are not
   b. have normal heartbeats when in fact they do not
   c. are at risk of premature expulsion when in fact they are not
   d. are in position for delivery when in fact they are not

8. Natural childbirth involves educating and training women in order to eliminate
   a. the need for doctors
   b. severe contractions
   c. fear and pain
   d. fetal monitoring

9. Which of the following is *not* an element of the Lamaze method of childbirth?
   a. education about childbirth
   b. control of breathing
   c. dim lighting
   d. concentration on positive sensations

10. Which of the following is *not* an element of the Leboyer method of gentle birth?
    a. relaxation techniques
    b. quiet room
    c. warm bath for the baby
    d. delivery without forceps

11. Which of the following tends to be a problem with elective cesarean deliveries as opposed to vaginal deliveries?
    a. Risk of infection is higher.
    b. Stress hormones are not released in the baby.
    c. The mother's recovery takes longer.
    d. each of the above

12. A good maternity or birth center
    a. is fully staffed by physicians
    b. keeps mother and baby at least overnight
    c. provides emergency equipment for resuscitation
    d. all of the above

13. Which of the following statements about the effect of a new baby on the parents' marriage is (are) true?
    a. The initial transition is the hardest period.
    b. Boys strain a marriage more than girls do.
    c. Childless women are happier in their marriages than mothers of either girls or boys.
    d. all of the above

14. Low-birthweight babies are defined as weighing less than
    a. 3 pounds
    b. 4½ pounds
    c. 5½ pounds
    d. 7 pounds

15. Small-for-date babies are more likely to survive than
    a. full-term babies
    b. premature babies
    c. babies delivered by cesarean section
    d. none of the above; small-for-date babies rarely live

16. Which of the following is *not* a common risk for low-birthweight babies?
    a. bleeding in the brain
    b. weak lungs
    c. infection
    d. high blood sugar

17. Other things being equal, which of the following women would be *least* likely to deliver a low-birthweight baby?
    a. 23-year-old bearing her second child 2 years after the birth of the first
    b. 23-year-old smoker
    c. 35-year-old bearing twins
    d. woman who was herself low-birthweight

18. Which of the following is *not* an example of a self-fulfilling prophecy?
    a. Parents of a low-birthweight baby, fearing that the baby will not survive, rarely hold the baby, resulting in failure of the baby to thrive.
    b. The mother of a petite child, since the child does not look mature, babies the child, who responds by acting immaturely.
    c. A father who fantasizes about his son's becoming a great athlete pushes the boy so much that the boy rebels and refuses to have anything to do with sports.
    d. Parents who believe that their daughter will be a forceful speaker take her arguments seriously, and so she develops confidence and poise in expressing her views.

19. The weight of an average newborn is
    a. 6 pounds
    b. 6½ pounds
    c. 7 pounds
    d. 7½ pounds

20. The umbilical cord carries
    a. blood to and from the fetus
    b. oxygen to the fetus and carbon dioxide from the fetus
    c. food to the fetus and body wastes from the fetus
    d. all of the above

21. Which of the following is *not* assessed by the Brazelton Neonatal Behavioral Assessment Scale?
    a. alertness
    b. grimace
    c. muscle tone
    d. startle reaction

22. Which of the following sleep patterns is typical of neonates?
    a. six to eight sleep periods of 2 to 3 hours each
    b. four or five sleep periods of approximately 4 hours each
    c. shorter sleep periods in the daytime and longer sleep periods at night
    d. none of the above

True or False? In the blank following each item, write T (for *true*) or F (for *false*). In the space below each item, if the statement is false, rewrite it to make it true.

1. Twins are usually born before the normal full term of gestation. _____

2. Fasting is believed to help induce labor. _____

3. A mother's body secretes a natural chemical painkiller during childbirth. _____

4. The first stage of labor is painful because of the stretching of the vagina as the baby's head pushes against it. _____

5. The mother has no control over the baby's progress through the vaginal canal. _____

6. Electronic fetal monitoring has led to fewer cesarean births. _____

7. In the vast majority of childbirths in the United States, anesthesia is routinely administered to the mother. _____

8. Most hospitals today allow fathers to be in the delivery room during childbirth. _____

9. The rate of cesarean deliveries in the United States is lower than the rate in Sweden, France, England, or Japan. _____

10. Uterine contractions trigger release of hormones that may help babies survive the stress of birth. _____

11. It is possible for many babies with a birthweight of less than 2 pounds to survive. _____

12. A woman who gains less than 14 pounds during pregnancy risks bearing a low-birthweight baby. _____

13. The high rate of low-birthweight babies among black women is entirely attributable to poverty and teenage pregnancies. _____

14. Stroking low-birthweight babies increases the amount of weight they are likely to gain. _____

15. In the United States, the women most at risk of bearing low-birthweight babies tend to receive the least prenatal care. _____

16. The longer after its due date a baby is born, the healthier the infant is likely to be. _____

17. Research suggests that with high-quality medical care, fewer than 1 percent of babies suffer injuries at birth. _____

18. Newborns lose weight during the first few days of life. _____

19. A newborn who is quite pale, has hair covering its body, and has swollen breasts with secretions is probably unhealthy. _____

20. About half of all babies develop jaundice a few days after birth. _____

21. There is no correlation between activity levels in infancy and those later in childhood. _____

22. Parents should not pick up and hold a crying infant, or the baby will become spoiled and cry for attention. _____

TOPICS FOR THOUGHT AND DISCUSSION

1. Critics of conventional American childbirth practices charge that some of these practices meet the concerns of doctors more than the needs of mothers or babies. What practices described in this chapter seem to substantiate this charge? What defenses might doctors offer?

2. The authors state that a woman in labor is the "only person who can gauge the degree of her pain and is the one who is most personally concerned about the well-being of her child." In the light of mixed research findings about the effects on babies of anesthetics administered to the mother during childbirth, how should a woman weigh those two factors in deciding whether or not to have a medicated delivery? What voice, if any, should the father have in the decision? Considering recent attempts to prosecute mothers who used drugs such as cocaine while pregnant, does a pregnant woman owe it to her child to avoid intake of potentially harmful substances under *any* circumstances?

3. Why do you think the Lamaze method has become popular in the United States, where medicated deliveries are routine?

4. Given the risks associated with cesarean deliveries, why are they performed so frequently? Your text suggests some reasons doctors may have for performing them; what factors might motivate women to have them?

5. If attachment between father and child does not depend on the father's presence during delivery, what benefits, if any, may nonetheless be gained from the father's presence?

6. What questions should couples contemplating parenthood consider in deciding whether they are ready for this added responsibility and change in their lives?

7. The authors of your text advocate some form of government-sponsored prenatal medical care, linked with comprehensive social and financial benefits, as a means to reduce infant mortality. Do you see any disadvantages in this proposal? What additional information, if any, would you want to have in evaluating it? If it were adopted, should it apply to all mothers, or only to those in need? Are there specific elements of the health services and social support systems that exist in western European countries that you would like to see adopted in our country? Are there some elements that you would not favor or would consider unnecessary? Can you suggest any steps short of the proposal outlined here that might improve the infant mortality rate in this country?

CHAPTER 4 READINGS

INTRODUCTION

Birth is a biological process with social and cultural overtones. The roles and feelings of the mother and father concerning the experience of pregnancy, the birth itself, and the adjustment to parenthood are, to a large extent, shaped by prevailing societal attitudes. Even when these attitudes are in a state of flux, as they are today in American culture, they provide a context that gives us insight into the varying responses of individual men and women.

There are two readings for this chapter. First is a personal account by a mother of a preschooler and an infant, from the Summer 1988 issue of *Humanistic Judaism*, which was devoted to the theme "Becoming Parents." As you read this mother's story, notice the extent to which such factors as the age, education, lifestyle, and professional background of the parents appear to have affected the birth experience and the transition to parenthood.

The second reading is an excerpt from *The Nurturing Father*, by Kyle D. Pruett, M.D. (Warner, 1987). Dr. Pruett is a clinical professor of psychiatry at the Yale University Child Study Center. The book from which this selection was taken presents pioneering research on the experiences of fathers who assume the role of primary nurturers of their babies, but the research also has implications for all fathers who want to be deeply involved in their children's lives. The excerpt presents an argument for the father's involvement from the very beginning—the prenatal period and the birth process.

Out of the Garden of Eden

by Sylvia Rose

Parenthood isn't what I expected. I can't remember what I had expected. Maybe I didn't even have expectations. I just knew I wanted children. I thought my life would be incomplete without them and the longing would last till my grave. Now I have two daughters, a three-year-old and a four-month-old, and I barely remember our lives before they arrived. I do remember getting up on Saturdays and wondering how to spend the day. Now I wonder why we didn't go to more movies, eat out more often, and stay up on New Year's Eve. The change is so thorough, the responsibility so complete, I can only describe it as a shock. Whatever else I am, whatever I may or may not accomplish, the inexorable fact of my life has been the arrival of my children.

Rebekah's birth, our first, taught us a vivid cardinal lesson in parenting: Little Ever Goes As You Expect It To. My husband, Paul, and I were thrilled when labor began. The thought of finally seeing our baby kept our morale up for sixteen hours at home. We had gone to the classes and done our homework. Good at taking exams, we were going to ace this one. Paul had reread his medical school obstetrics textbook and was prepared for anything. Anything except demoralization.

The seventeenth hour was a blur of tears and desperation. Had any woman, however Spartan, gone through this and kept on ploughing? The page operator found the doctor on call in a restaurant. (Could it be dinnertime? I was amazed that time hadn't stopped for everyone.) Reluctantly, he let us come to the hospital, even though the contractions were stuck seven minutes apart. The staff there pronounced me "not really in labor," sent Paul home to sleep, gave me enough morphine to understand why people become addicted, and left me alone in a darkened room.

Bobbing somewhere near the ceiling, I felt every pain but didn't care. Five hours and eight centimeters later, I buzzed the nurse. She checked me cheerfully and asked where my husband was. I was ready to push. Paul needn't have hurried. It took two and a half hours. I remember thinking that women died in childbirth. It was a comfort to be in Beth Israel, one of the best hospitals in Boston.

Paul caught her head as it appeared, sunnyside up, molded to a point like a kewpie doll's. He cut the cord and handed her to me. Her eyes were wide open, and she made not a sound as she searched my face with rapt curiosity. I will never forget that gaze, so intelligent, so human. I said hello to her a hundred times. Paul said he had never seen me so happy, even on our wedding day.

We marveled at how complete she was: toes like tiny shrimp, eyes as blue as blueberries. (Recessive luck.) She was beautiful. She was perfect. We were awed by our own offspring. Although we were not believers in miracles, she seemed miraculous to us.

It Had All Been Worth It—our second rule of parent-hood.

The first night home from the hospital—the first night of Hanukka—we unplugged the phone and lay in bed watching a Peter Sellers movie. I laughed until my stitches made me cry. The baby slept all the way through it on Paul's chest. We took pictures of that, we were so happy. Our futon was right on the floor, and for days we lived and ate and nested there, oblivious to the outside world. At night we lit the *hanukkia* (the eight-branched Hanukka menora, or candelabrum) and thought about parents through the millennia who had gazed at their firstborn without electric lights: the radiant faces in Rembrandt's serene etchings, da Vinci's madonnas, George de la Tour's hushed nativities. If I could paint, I would have made a Chagall, our mattress floating forever in a night sky, menoras and Pampers and a Pink Panther tumbling by.

But reality set in soon enough. Paul went back to work, and my mother came to take care of us. (I had injured my back in a prenatal class and had damaged it badly again during the delivery.) When Mom left two weeks later, I felt as if my life was caving in on me. I was as sleep-deprived as any intern, with no end in sight. The baby needed me about forty-five minutes out of every hour, twenty-four hours a day. I lived in my bathrobe for weeks. It was so physical, so consuming. I moved through my life like a zombie.

Not that we weren't prepared. Paul is a child psychiatrist. I have a master's degree in child development and, at thirty-nine, have taught in day care, early intervention programs, and preschool for years. But your shift never ends when the child's your own, and you can't say no when she needs you. And when it's your first baby, the "shift" feels like an eternity because you have no idea when the pressure will ease up.

Which it does. Thus our third rule of parenting: Things Do Get Better. Eventually you habituate to your little ones' dependency. They cry for you, call for you, watch for you, creep towards you, crawl after you, toddle around you, shimmy up you, hang onto you, and, one day, run away from you. They gum on you, teethe on you, and pull your hair, your glasses, your fingers, your hands, your clothes, and, like a ball and chain, your legs. They do outgrow each phase, finally, but waiting for that day could make an atheist pray for patience.

Meanwhile, the quality of your life hinges on minute details, most of which are beyond your control. Will the baby take a bottle from this sitter? Can you even find a sitter? Will she nap? Will the diaper rash heal before vacation? Will the chicken pox wait until after vacation? And on and on. Your friends with teenagers tell you to enjoy these years while they last.

And, actually, they're right. If this is the worst of times, it's also the best. Your child will never be cuter, sweeter, or more innocent, probably never more spontaneous, and certainly never more ingenuous. It's proverbial but true: the first words, the first steps, the first anything will thrill you. The word *naches* (pride and joy from children) takes on new meaning. By and by, you forget how rugged the past couple of years have been, and you decide to try for a sibling.

Arielle's birth could not have been more different from Rebekah's. I went into labor at the same time, 5 a.m., but this was after eight hours' sleep, the first good night's sleep I had enjoyed in months of an uncomfortable pregnancy. In between contractions, I got Bekah ready for preschool, showered, blew my hair dry, and even put on makeup. This would be the last peaceful chance to pay attention to myself for weeks.

By 9 a.m., there was nothing to do but wait, so I got under the electric blanket and sipped herbal tea. My belly anchored to the sheets, my thoughts drifted loosely. Who was this little person in me? Could I ever love it as much as Bek? Was "he" a girl? Was "she" a boy? Were its eyes open right now?

The face of the alarm clock floated before me. Every ten minutes, Paul came over to push hard against my lower back. I closed my eyes and concentrated on the pain. As the contraction peaked, I would look up; the red hand had swept the seconds into eternity and I was triumphant again. And so it went for the next three hours: ten fast minutes, sixty slow seconds.

My mother came and went from the room, asking me questions about the washing machine, where the vanilla was, did I want to talk to so-and-so. It surprised me that I wasn't embarrassed to labor in front of her. She seemed pleased, in a matter-of-fact sort of way. I felt her equal.

At noon we phoned our private duty nurse to say that nothing was happening. (We had hired her against the prospect of another day-long ordeal.) As Paul hung up, I had a contraction so different from the previous forty-two that we decided to leave, stat (immediately). Some wordless thought made me grab my pillow on the way. At the bottom of the stairs I looked past the open door to the car parked beyond thirty feet of lawn. An ocean of lawn. I didn't think I could walk that far.

But I did, and as I lowered myself awkwardly onto the flattened front seat, the first scary thought of the morning hit me. I was going to have to labor alone.

It was fifty minutes to the hospital. Paul started the car; I had another contraction. Six minutes later, I had the next. I told Paul to turn on the headlights and the flashers. Six minutes later, another contraction. We didn't talk. He started beeping his horn at intersections. Four minutes later, another. We flew through every red light except one. Why hadn't we made a sign? Two minutes later, another. Then another. Things were getting blurry; I couldn't keep track of time any more. By the roof lines and treetops, I knew we were still in Jamaica Plain, a mile from the hospital. No more contractions—the pain was continuous. Was I in transition? There was nothing to hold onto, nothing to squeeze. I pulled at the air above me.

Two blocks from the hospital, the road narrowed to one lane. A construction worker looked in the window. At Children's Hospital the light turned red. It was 12:30. I felt safe. The intersection was full of physicians on their lunch break. One more block and we turned into Beth Israel's emergency entrance. I was panting uncontrollably; my arms were numb from the elbows down. They say no man is a hero to his wife. Paul had taken twenty minutes off the trip. My hero.

He ran for a wheelchair. I couldn't get out of the car. I felt hands lifting me. A stretcher appeared from nowhere. "Get on." Somehow I did, but I couldn't lie down. Someone lowered me onto my own lovely pillow. The croaky voice pushing me shouted for everyone to get out of the way. The hand I was scrunching wasn't Paul's. I called his name and felt the reassuringly familiar squeeze.

Up one floor and across the corridor connecting two buildings. My body heaved, and a tide of water broke over me. Up eleven more express floors and out past the nurses' station. I cried that I had to push, and the entire entourage shouted, "Don't push!" Into the first empty room, where another faceless voice ordered me to the bed. As they lifted me, I moaned that I had to push again. Again the Greek chorus droned, "Don't push!" Our private-duty nurse, still in her street clothes, told me to throw my arms around her neck and blow hard against closed lips to hold back the birth. I put her in a headlock, made a guttural compromise in my throat, and like magic, like another miracle, Ellie was out.

Arielle Simone. Our second blue-eyed beauty. Screaming louder than I had, she arrived covered with so much vernix that she could have swum the English channel. The only doctor in his scrubs, who had run after the stretcher, caught her head. Paul cut the cord. Without stitches and feeling no pain, I sat up and asked for my girl. Her little mouth moved rhythmically between sobs, so I lifted my sweatshirt and she went to work.

The nameless obstetrician was wishing us *"mazel tov"* (congratulations) when our doctor arrived. His elevator had stopped at every floor. "Missed you again!" Paul took pictures obsessively in hopes of getting "one good one." I cried all the way through the first roll. This was it. The day we had awaited for nine months and two days was over. And it was only 12:50.

We brought Ellie home on November 5, temperatures in the 70s and spring in every breath. She was alert and lovely. Rebekah was respectful. I took the stairs two at a time, buoyant to have my body back. Mom did the cooking and Paul took off two weeks from work. It had all been so easy that I fantasized about having a third child, the son Paul had hoped for; I made such beautiful babies. We sent out eighty copies of our "one good photo" and heard from everyone we knew.

But honeymoons don't last. The day after Thanksgiving, Ellie fussed all day. Each day got worse, and the pediatrician pronounced it three-month colic. Three months? It felt terminal, this shrieking in our ears, the arched back and tight legs, tears that ran down her little cheeks and off her chin. We tried everything: swings and strollers in the house, hot water bottles, swaddling, and car rides. Was the problem with my milk? I cut out chocolate and eggs, dairy products and peanut butter. Ellie was rarely quiet for more than twenty minutes at a time, and never slept longer than an hour until evening. I felt as if I was walking around with a knife between my shoulders.

Rebekah, pushed to her limit by Ellie's need for attention, went over the brink. She talked twice as loudly as she needed to, hopped heavily everywhere she went, and uttered well-timed screams to make the baby cry. We found blankets over the baby's head, dump trucks in her crib, and one day a graham cracker wedged in her mouth. I couldn't leave the two alone for a minute.

This acting out we had expected. What we had not anticipated was her depression. As the weeks wore on, she got quieter and sadder and began to withdraw from me. We wondered whether she would ever get over Ellie's arrival.

But, as I had learned the first time, Things Do Get Better. Ellie is calmer now, though she still startles at her own sneeze. Bekah is more civilized and happier with Ellie as an adoring audience. There's more than twice the work with two children, but at least I know the ground rules. I'm not as angered by their incessant demands—though some evenings I feel not merely dead, but scavenged by starving little creatures.

At times like that, I remind myself of all the humanist blessings in my life: a *mensch* (person of admirable character) of a husband, healthy children, parents who are well and independent and together. I'm grateful for antibiotics, Sesame Street, and disposable diapers. Yet when I try to put my life in perspective, I can't focus beyond the domestic chaos. I once believed I could change the world, and now I'm hard pressed to put dinner on the table. This can't last forever and I'm sure I'll go to work again, however mythical that perfect part-time job may prove to be. But will anything ever be more important than the responsibility and love I feel for my children?

Maybe it's enough to raise children well. Maybe this is the hardest job of all, and the most I can hope for is enough years and enough inner strength to accomplish it. Sometimes I think about human history, 130 million years of it. I think of women who wept and hid their babies in bullrushes. Women who wept and pleaded and made Solomon seem wise. They preserved life and are remembered. Dare I hope to do more?

QUESTIONS ABOUT THE READING

1. Your text mentions that men and women undergo a great deal of development as they respond to birth and the experience of parenthood. In what ways is that true of Sylvia Rose?

2. In what specific ways does Rose's experience bear out or contradict the conclusions in Box 4-3, "The Transition to Parenthood"?

3. Although the article focuses primarily on Rose's own reactions to childbirth and parenthood, are there any indications of how her husband has handled the transition?

4. Does this couple's experience seem fairly typical, or would you suppose that they have had an easy or a hard time adjusting to their roles compared with other new parents?

5. Can you find any evidence that Rose's experience as a teacher of very young children

and her husband's experience as a child psychiatrist affected their reactions to parenting?

6. Rose says near the end of the article, "There's more than twice the work with two children, but at least I know the ground rules." Do you think it would be helpful to a prospective first-time parent to be told Rose's "cardinal rules" (or lessons) of parenting? Why, with her professional preparation and her husband's, did Sylvia and Paul have to learn these rules from their own experience?

7. According to the authors of your text, the scientific literature on parenting tends to focus on its stresses and dissatisfactions rather than on its joys and satisfactions. The authors suggest that this tendency may be a reaction to "rose-colored views" of childbirth and child rearing. Is the personal account in this article skewed in either direction? On the whole, would you says that Rose's experience of parenting so far has been predominantly positive or negative?

8. Think back to the categories of research methods described in Chapter 1. Would this article fall into any of these categories? What value, if any, might a subjective account like this, based on one person's experience, have for students of child development?

Solving the Father Problem: An Excerpt from "The Nurturing Father"

by Kyle D. Pruett, M.D.

Fatherhood is the single most creative, complicated, fulfilling, frustrating, engrossing, enriching, depleting endeavor of a man's adult life. So often, as the septuagenarian reflects on life's rewards, we hear that "in the final analysis" of money, power, prestige, and marriage, fathering alone was what "mattered."

Men can and most often should be involved in nurturing their children. What's most needed is a fundamentally new scheme for a man's life and especially the use of his time—a scheme that enhances the quality of life more than it centers on work and that doesn't conflict with one's worth as a working, successful, even powerful man. When a man can truly and honestly examine fatherhood in this way, he is well on his way to solving the private dilemmas of the father problem.

Next comes the hard part: getting involved. This step is farther-reaching in its implication than is the decision to become a father. It means getting educated, taking decisive action, doing it early, and then staying there—right there in the life of his child, firmly fixed.

So where to begin?

We begin where a man needs to start thinking of himself as father: when he and his mate are making ready for the birth of progeny.

The obstetrician, clinic, or health care system chosen for the mother's prenatal care should be chosen by both mother *and* father, if they're lucky enough to have a choice. Questions will come throughout the pregnancy, and the father should have access to answers, just as the mother does, especially if trouble appears. He also must make certain early on that he can attend the birth, even if it's a cesarean section. He must be able to ask about the growth and health of "his" fetus too, not to mention what is happening to his wife's body. The father can play a critical role in support of his wife if he's allowed to and has enough of the facts.

Just as important as the physical change and growth, however, is the evolution of an image of the child in the father's own mind and heart. Fantasies, daydreams, random thoughts, preoccupations are important in this early attachment, whether positive or negative. Far too many fathers concern themselves only about the gender of their unborn child, with a heavy preference for male offspring.

The mother also contributes, often unwittingly, to limitations in the way a man thinks about himself as father. She may define his fathering in terms of her own needs and perceptions, delineating her mate as someone to "father" her, or be the security force, master repairman, or financial center. The widespread, unthinking acceptance of such "father defining" makes it critical that men get involved immediately.

It is vital that the pregnant father get himself educated in the physical care and feeding of his coming baby. This is so fundamental because men don't often think of themselves as "pregnant" and consequently don't prepare themselves for the arrival of a *body* that will need care and attention. Most need all the education they can get, and a lot of it is available. Many hospitals offer such group experiences, and the better ones are run by women and men, with real live babies. (Some fathers worry that they don't feel immediate attraction to such infants in the education process. The real attraction, however, usually occurs with one's own child.) The prepared birth movement has been a strong incentive for father involvement in the actual birth of the baby. Lamaze classes are widespread and offer fathers an active role in the birthing process.

The birthing of the baby affords the father his first direct physical experience of his child. For most men it's one of the single most moving moments of their lives. But men shouldn't assume automatically that attending the birth will be available to them as an option. It's still far from a universal practice in the United States. But there will be no other event in the life of the father that will so profoundly affect his early attachment to his child, not to mention his wife. Therefore, it's crucial that he be there at the beginning, otherwise he may have the feeling that he has been left at the starting gate.

Some hospitals permit only those fathers who have attended prebirth classes to watch. Our research shows that men should be there regardless of whether or not they have had preparation. All fathers should be allowed to be there—it's that important, period. The father's presence means laboring mothers need less medication, thereby lowering the prevalence of birth complications. It means that babies go home from the hospital sooner. It means the father develops an attachment to and understanding of his baby as a person more quickly, is more likely to be involved in the baby's care, and is far less likely to be abusive. The list of benefits goes on.

Once the baby is out, the father should be permitted, encouraged, and helped by the obstetrician, midwife, or maternity nursing staff to touch, look at, or hold his baby. This is what happens in the ideal situation, but often the father himself must insist on doing these things rather than just letting the "pros" take over. These first few moments of intimate contact will make the baby real and alive for the father, often for the first time in a truly physical, sensual sense. Since he did not, nor ever can, feel his baby inside his own body, he has had to hold another place open, perhaps in his mind or soul, for this child. Such an open space is a fertile garden indeed, in which to grow attachments and feelings for babies.

If the father has had the advantage of child-handling instruction or experience, or feels strongly committed to trying, he might even bathe his newborn baby in the delivery room (albeit with help nearby if needed). If not, diapering, bathing, and bottle-feeding must be in the father's repertoire before his baby leaves the hospital.

The importance of this early contact with the baby cannot be overemphasized. The father should plan somehow to spend a few hours directly with his baby as soon as it's born.

A young Black father had the last word on why. "I stood there a long time just staring at her in that little plastic bed. The nurse said I could pick her up. I said, 'Are you kidding? She's only two hours old.' She looked like a little puppy to me. I did pick her up with my hand under her head like they showed me, and then I held her in close—just pulled her in—kind of like a magnet. And then you know what she did—all by herself? She turned her head toward my chest like she was looking to suck on something that sure wasn't there! But you know she didn't look too disappointed when she didn't find much. She opened her eyes and we just looked at each other. She's the greatest, Doc, and I'm not kidding! I'm going back there later to get some more of that!"

"That" is the beginning of an attachment that no adult can give or teach to a father. He must be there to have it happen with his baby. Once it does happen, he will never be "a babysitter" again.

QUESTIONS ABOUT THE READING

1. Your text states that although attendance at the birth of a child is often a peak experience for fathers, research has not demonstrated that it makes them better fathers or affects the development of attachment to the baby. Dr. Pruett, on the other hand, concludes that attendance at the birth is a crucial factor in developing attachment. How good a case do you think he makes for that position?

2. Did you find Dr. Pruett's reference to "pregnant" fathers jarring? Do you think such terminology is appropriate? Does it serve a useful purpose?

3. Should a father who feels uncomfortable about being present at the birth be there anyway?

4. Can some of the benefits of participation be achieved if a man who does not attend the birth is permitted to hold his baby immediately afterward?

ANSWER KEY FOR CHAPTER 4

Note: Numbers in parentheses refer to pages in the textbook where answers can be found.

CHAPTER 4 REVIEW

Important Terms for Section I

1. 4 (page 124)
2. conception, birth (124)
3. heartbeat (128)
4. anesthesia (128)
5. Grantly Dick-Read (130)
6. Fernand Lamaze (130)
7. Leboyer (130)
8. cesarean (131)
9. feet, buttocks, head (131)
10. transverse (131)
11. obstetrician (133)
12. midwife (133)
13. preterm, small-for-date (137)
14. 37 weeks (137)
15. gestational (137)
16. isolette (140)
17. self-fulfilling (142)
18. trauma (143)
19. anoxia (143)
20. dead (143)
21. uterus (143)

Learning Objectives for Section I

1. (pages 125-126)
2. (126-127)
3. (128)
4. (128-130)
5. (130)
6. (130-131)
7. (131-133)

8. (133-135)
9. (135-137)
10. (137-138)
11. (138-140)
12. (140-142)
13. (142-143)
14. (143)
15. (144)

Important Terms for Section II

1. neonatal (page 144)
2. hair (145)
3. vernix caseosa (145)
4. waste matter (146)
5. jaundice (146)
6. appearance, pulse, grimace, respiration (147)
7. phenylketonuria (148)
8. interactive, motor, stress (148)
9. state (148)

Learning Objectives for Section II

1. (pages 144-145)
2. (145-147)
3. (147-148)
4. (148-151)
5. (150)

CHAPTER 4 QUIZ

Matching—Numbers

1. 40 (page 137)
2. 4 (124)
3. 3 (125)
4. 37 (137)
5. 17 (139)
6. 34 (139)
7. 42 (142)
8. 20 (144)
9. 1 (147)
10. 2 (146)
11. 7 (147)
12. 16 (148)

Multiple-Choice

1. b (page 124)
2. d (125)
3. a (125, 126)
4. c (125)
5. c (125)
6. d (127)
7. a (128)
8. c (130)
9. c (130)
10. a (130)
11. d (132)
12. c (134)
13. b (136)
14. c (137)
15. b (137)
16. d (138)
17. a (138-139)
18. c (142)
19. d (144)
20. d (146)
21. b (148)
22. a (149)

True or False?

1. T (page 125)
2. T (125)
3. T (125)
4. F—The first stage of labor is painful primarily because of the stretching, or dilation, of the cervix. (125)
5. F—The mother's bearing down with her abdominal muscles during each contraction helps the baby leave her body. (125)
6. F—Electronic fetal monitoring often leads doctors to deliver babies by cesarean section rather than vaginally. (128)
7. T (128-129)
8. T (130)
9. F—The rate of cesarean deliveries in the United States is the highest in any of 19 industrialized countries, including Sweden, France, England, and Japan. (131)
10. T (132)
11. T (137, 138)
12. T (138, 139)
13. F—Even when factors such as poverty and age are controlled, black women are more likely than white women to bear low-birthweight babies. (139)
14. T (140)
15. T (141)
16. F—Postmature babies tend to have received insufficient food and oxygen and are at higher risk of brain damage or death; therefore, after 42 weeks gestation, doctors sometimes induce labor or perform cesarean deliveries. (142-143)

17. T (143)
18. T (144)
19. F—Paleness, body hair, and swollen breasts with secretions are normal attributes of many newborns. (145)
20. T (146)

21. F—Studies show that activity levels in infancy correlate with those in childhood. (151)
22. F—Babies whose cries bring relief tend to become more self-confident and to communicate more without crying than babies whose cries are ignored or punished, and quiet babies maintain their weight better. (150, 151)

PHYSICAL DEVELOPMENT IN INFANCY AND TODDLERHOOD

OVERVIEW

Chapter 5 describes babies' physical growth and their rapidly developing sensory capabilities and motor skills, which are intertwined with their intellectual and personality-social-emotional development. In this chapter, the authors:

- Identify the principles that govern physical development

- Describe the growth of body and brain and explain how this growth may be affected by environmental influences

- Explain the significance of inborn reflexes

- Discuss how babies should be nourished

- Trace highlights of infants' sensory and motor development

- Discuss factors that contribute to infant mortality

CHAPTER 5 REVIEW

Section I How Physical Development Takes Place

FRAMEWORK FOR SECTION I

A. Two Principles of Physical Development
B. Physical Development of the Two Sexes

IMPORTANT TERMS FOR SECTION I

Completion: Fill in the blanks to complete the definitions of key terms for this section of Chapter 5.

1. _____ **principle:** Principle that development proceeds in a "head-to-tail" direction: the upper body parts develop before the lower parts.

2. _____ **principle:** Principle that development proceeds in a near-to-far manner: the parts of the body near its center (spinal cord) develop before the extremities.

LEARNING OBJECTIVES FOR SECTION I

After reading and reviewing this section of Chapter 5, you should be able to do the following.

1. Give two examples of the cephalocaudal principle of physical development and two examples of the proximodistal principle.

2. Compare the physical development of boys and girls during infancy and toddlerhood.

Section II Growth

FRAMEWORK FOR SECTION II

A. Growth of the Body
B. Growth of the Brain
   1. The Nervous System
   2. How the Environment Influences Brain Development
   3. Reflex Behaviors
C. Nutrition in Infancy
   1. Breastfeeding
   2. Bottle-Feeding
   3. Solid Food and Cow's Milk
   4. Is Obesity a Problem in Infancy?

IMPORTANT TERMS FOR SECTION II

Completion: Fill in the blanks to complete the definitions of key terms for this section of Chapter 5.

1. **cerebral cortex:** Upper layer of the _____.

2. _____ **period:** Specific time during development when an event has its greatest impact.

3. **reflex behavior:** _____ reaction to stimulation.

LEARNING OBJECTIVES FOR SECTION II

After reading and reviewing this section of Chapter 5, you should be able to do the following.

1. Describe typical changes in weight, height, body shape, and tooth development during the first 3 years.

2. Identify genetic, environmental, and gender influences on body growth.

3. Describe the growth and development of an infant's brain and nervous system.

4. Give one negative and one positive example of the effect of environment on brain development in humans.

5. Name at least four primitive reflexes; explain their purpose and the significance of their disappearance during infancy.

6. Explain why breast milk has been described as the "ultimate health food" for babies.

7. List at least four signs of a well-nourished baby and at least four signs of a malnourished baby.

8. List three reasons women give for bottle-feeding and cite one important risk of bottle-feeding.

9. Write an appropriate daily menu for a 3-month-old, a 7-month-old, and a 12-month-old baby.

10. Summarize research on the long-term effects of obesity in infancy.

Section III Early Sensory Capacities

FRAMEWORK FOR SECTION III

A. Sight
 1. Depth Perception
 2. Visual Preferences
B. Hearing
C. Smell
D. Taste
E. Touch—and Pain

IMPORTANT TERMS FOR SECTION III

Completion: Fill in the blanks to complete the definitions of key terms for this section of Chapter 5.

1. **visual cliff:** Apparatus for testing _____.

2. _____: Simple type of learning in which familiarity with a stimulus reduces, slows, or even stops a response.

LEARNING OBJECTIVES FOR SECTION III

After reading and reviewing this section of Chapter 5, you should be able to do the following.

1. Summarize research on the capacities of the five senses at birth and in the early weeks and months thereafter.

2. Discuss two ideas about the origin of depth perception.

3. Identify two ways in which very young babies' visual preferences change.

4. List four milestones of response to sounds and the typical age for each.

5. Explain two methods of studying babies' hearing.

6. State three practical implications of recent findings regarding newborns' ability to feel pain.

Section IV Motor Development of Infants and Toddlers

FRAMEWORK FOR SECTION IV

A. Milestones of Motor Development
   1. Head Control
   2. Hand Control
   3. Locomotion
B. Repetitive Processes in Motor Development
C. Environmental Influences on Motor Development
   1. How Environment Can Retard Development
   2. Can Motor Development Be Speeded Up?

IMPORTANT TERM FOR SECTION IV

Completion: Fill in the blank to complete the definition of the key term for this section of Chapter 5.

1. _____ **Screening Test:** Screening test given to children (1 month to 6 years old) to identify abnormal development; it assesses personal-social, fine motor-adaptive, language, and gross motor behavior.

LEARNING OBJECTIVES FOR SECTION IV

After reading and reviewing this section of Chapter 5, you should be able to do the following.

1. List at least five milestones of motor development and the average age at which each is attained.

2. Explain how crawling is significant for physical, intellectual, and emotional development.

3. Discuss research findings on the early appearance and later disappearance of certain motor abilities.

4. Give examples of differing rates of development of motor skills in different societies or cultures and suggest reasons for these differences.

5. Discuss research findings on the extent to which environment can or cannot retard or speed up motor development.

Section V Death in Infancy

FRAMEWORK FOR SECTION V

A. Infant Mortality
B. Sudden Infant Death Syndrome (SIDS)

IMPORTANT TERMS FOR SECTION V

Completion: Fill in the blanks to complete the definitions of key terms for this section of Chapter 5.

1. **infant mortality rate:** Proportion of babies who die within the first _____ of life.

2. **sudden infant death syndrome (SIDS):** Sudden and unexpected death of an apparently healthy infant; also known as _____ *death*.

3. **apnea:** Temporary cessation of _____.

LEARNING OBJECTIVES FOR SECTION V

After reading and reviewing this section of Chapter 5, you should be able to do the following.

1. Compare the infant mortality rate in the United States with rates in other industrialized nations.

2. Give reasons for the decline in infant mortality in this country and analyze differences in infant mortality rates among various population groups.

3. Discuss the relationship between low birthweight and neonatal mortality, especially among black babies.

4. Cite possible explanations and risk factors for sudden infant death syndrome.

CHAPTER 5 QUIZ

Matching—Numbers: Match each description in the left-hand column with the correct number in the right-hand column.

1. Percent of neonatal deaths caused by low birthweight _____	2
2. Age in months at which the average baby's birthweight doubles _____	3
3. Number of teeth the average child has by age 2½ years _____	4
4. Age in months at which babies can safely begin drinking cow's milk _____	5
5. Height in inches of the typical 1-year-old _____	6
6. Age in years at which the average baby can hold and drink from a cup _____	12
7. Age in months at which the average baby's birthweight triples _____	17
8. Age in years at which vision reaches adult range _____	20
9. Age in months at which the average baby can walk up steps _____	30
10. Earliest age in months at which babies should begin eating solid foods _____	70

Multiple-Choice: Circle the choice that best completes or answers each item.

1. According to the cephalocaudal and proximodistal principles, it would take longest for a baby to develop the ability to
   a. focus the eyes
   b. wiggle the toes
   c. hold a rattle
   d. kick the legs

2. Growth is fastest in which of these periods?
   a. birth to 1 year
   b. 1 year to 2 years
   c. 2 years to 3 years
   d. 13 years to 15 years

3. At birth, the cells in the brain
   a. number fewer than half the quantity present in adulthood
   b. are fully connected but not yet functioning
   c. are more developed in the subcortex than in the cerebral cortex
   d. are developed only in the cerebral cortex

4. The brain grows from about what percent of its adult weight at birth to about what percent of its adult weight at 1 year?
   a. 1 to 10
   b. 10 to 50
   c. 25 to 70
   d. 50 to 100

5. Which of the following is *not* an example of reflex behavior?
   a. coughing
   b. crawling
   c. shivering
   d. yawning

6. The group of reflexes which are present at birth but disappear during the first year are called
   a. subcortical
   b. Darwinian
   c. infantile
   d. primitive

7. Which of the following is *not* considered a benefit of breast milk over formula for newborns?
   a. straighter teeth
   b. less fat
   c. protection against disease
   d. special composition for premature babies

8. One study shows that the ability of newborns to differentiate between patterns is predictive of their
   a. intelligence
   b. artistic talent
   c. visual acuity
   d. independence

9. A baby turns toward a squeaking stroller wheel the first day he or she hears it, shows mild interest the second day, and shows no interest the third day. This is an example of
   a. discriminative hearing
   b. habituation
   c. auditory sensitivity
   d. auditory preference

10. Which of the following tastes would most newborns prefer?
   a. pure water
   b. sugar solution
   c. lemon juice
   b. none of the above; newborns cannot discriminate among these tastes

11. The first sense to develop is
   a. sight
   b. hearing
   c. touch
   d. taste

12. Which of the following is *not* present in newborns?
   a. precision grip
   b. directional smell
   c. visual preference
   d. auditory discrimination

13. A child's failure to pass an item on the Denver Developmental Screening Test is considered a sign of developmental delay if what percent of children the same age ordinarily pass it?
   a. 50
   b. 75
   c. 80
   d. 90

14. The average baby begins to roll over at about
   a. 3 weeks
   b. 2 months
   c. 3 months
   d. 5 months

15. Crawling helps to promote "social referencing," meaning that a crawling baby is more likely than one who does not yet crawl to
   a. interact with other babies
   b. perceive how near or far away a person or object is
   c. compare his or her size with that of adults
   d. look at the mother to check whether a situation is safe

16. Which of the following is *not* an example of an ability that appears, disappears, and later reappears in many babies?
   a. depth perception
   b. stepping
   c. eye-hand coordination
   d. ear-hand coordination

17. According to research, which of the following statements about the environment and motor development is true?
   a. Because many aspects of motor development are genetically programmed, the environment cannot retard it.
   b. A deficient environment can retard motor development significantly.
   c. In numerous experiments, children have been trained to walk, climb stairs, and contol bladder and bowels much earlier than usual.
   d. Although children in experiments have not learned to climb stairs or control bladder and bowels early, infant "walkers" have helped many children to walk early.

18. The infant mortality rate in the United States is lower
   a. than ever before
   b. among black babies than among white babies
   c. than in any other industrialized nation
   d. than the rate in Singapore

19. Seventy percent of infant deaths occur within how long after birth?
   a. 10 hours
   b. 4 weeks
   c. 3 months
   d. 1 year

20. The most likely explanation for sudden infant death syndrome appears to be
   a. suffocation
   b. vomiting
   c. contagious infection
   d. brain abnormality

True or False? In the blank following each item, write T (for *true*) or F (for *false*). In the space below each item, if the statement is false, rewrite it to make it true.

1. Normal physical development seems to follow a predetermined sequence. _____

2. Baby boys tend to be more active than baby girls. _____

3. By the second birthday, the average child weighs 4 times as much as at birth. _____

4. Most babies get the first tooth at about 4 months. _____

5. About 250,000 brain cells per minute form in the developing fetus. _____

6. The subcortex controls thinking and problem solving. _____

7. Undernourishment before or just after birth can result in brain damage. _____

8. If a baby does not outgrow the rooting reflex by approximately 9 months, the cerebral cortex is probably not developing properly. _____

9. Breastfeeding is more popular than bottle-feeding among poor and minority women. _____

10. A breastfeeding baby can become intoxicated if the mother uses drugs. _____

11. A baby who takes a bottle of milk to bed can develop tooth decay. _____

12. Pediatric nutritionists recommend starting solid foods by 2 months to foster healthy growth and help babies sleep through the night. _____

13. Babies should not be given skim milk or low-calorie diets. _____

14. A fat baby or toddler is more likely than a thin one to become a fat adult. _____

15. Babies cannot perceive colors in the first few months. _____

16. Babies at 2 months can perceive heights but do not fear them. _____

17. Babies at 1 month can recognize their mothers from the shape of the chin or hairline. _____

18. The inner and middle ear reach adult size and shape at approximately 6 months. _____

19. Within the first week of life, infants learn to recognize the smell of their mothers. _____

20. Circumcision is not painful for an 8-day-old baby, because nerve endings are not yet developed. _____

21. Baby boys have erections before birth. _____

22. A baby who never saw anyone walk would be unlikely to learn how to walk. _____

23. Babies in some cultures develop gross motor skills at slower or faster rates than American babies. _____

24. More than twice as many black babies as white babies are low-birthweight. _____

25. Sudden infant death syndrome is the leading cause of postneonatal death. _____

TOPICS FOR THOUGHT AND DISCUSSION

1. Environmental factors seem to exert varying influences on different aspects of physical development. While body and brain growth can be either retarded or advanced, only the former seems to be true of motor development. What might explain this difference?

2. Research shows that baby boys and girls typically are about even in physical development. However, as you will see in Chapter 7, some parents encourage baby boys to be more active than baby girls. What effect, if any, do you think such parental treatment might have? (Note: Keep this question, and your answer, in mind as you read the chapters to come.)

3. Research on animals has shown that brain growth and functioning can be enhanced by environmental stimulation. Such stimulation can also promote the physical and mental development of retarded children, aging people, and victims of brain damage. If these findings are generalizable to normal children, what are the practical implications for parents? Can you suggest some simple, inexpensive ways to enrich a baby's environment? (Note: Keep these findings, and these questions, in mind as you read about environmental influences on intellectual development in Chapter 6.)

4. Since some primitive reflexes seem to serve no purpose, why do you think babies are born with them?

5. According to a group of prominent pediatricians, "little is known about long-term consequences of infant feeding practices." Remembering the ethical limitations on research with humans, which type of experiment described in Chapter 1 would be most feasible in investigating the long-term effects of breastfeeding and bottle-feeding—a natural experiment, a field experiment, or a laboratory experiment? What would be the difficulties and drawbacks of such an experiment?

6. Given the advantages of breastfeeding, why do you think this feeding method declined in popularity for half a century, and what might explain its resurgence?

7. Were you surprised to read about the sensory capabilities of very young infants? How might you design an infant's environment with these capabilities in mind?

8. The rate of routine circumcision has declined by one-third, in part because of findings about newborns' sensitivity to pain and in part because of questions about the medical benefits of the procedure. What factors would play the greatest part in your decision whether to circumcise a baby boy? What additional information would you want to have before making the decision?

9. The authors of your text refer to the need to "baby-proof" a home when infants learn to crawl or walk. Yet the text also points out the importance of an enriched environment. How can parents reconcile these needs?

CHAPTER 5 READING

INTRODUCTION

The infant mortality rate is twice as great among blacks as among whites, and the lower average birthweight of black babies seems to be an important factor in this differential. But why are black babies smaller than white babies? Are the reasons socioeconomic, or are other factors involved?

The following article by William Braden, reprinted from the August 18, 1987, issue of the *Chicago Sun-Times,* was one of a series on infant mortality.

Births Drawn in Black and White; Mortality Risk Haunts Middle-Class Mothers

by William Braden

The riddle of the black middle class continues to puzzle researchers who study the U.S. rate of infant mortality.

The rate for both blacks and whites has been declining for years.

For both races, the rate goes down as income and education go up.

Middle-class blacks have a lower rate than poor blacks, just as middle-class whites have a lower rate than poor whites. And recent years have seen the emergence of a large black middle class.

And yet, blacks compared with whites remain at a 2-to-1 greater risk for infant mortality.

The problem was underscored by an important study in Northern California that was analyzed by a group of researchers from the National Institute of Child Health and Human Development.

The study involved some 29,000 largely middle-class women of various ethnic groups. It looked at low birth weight, which is the main predictor of infant mortality. And Wendy Baldwin of the National Institute wrote that the result was *"stunning in its simplicity. . . . The disparity between blacks and whites endures."*

These were middle-class women. Not poor women.

The study controlled for 22 factors including education, employment, marital status and length of prenatal care. But none of those factors explained the persistence of major ethnic differences. And in all of the control subgroups, the rates of low birth weight for blacks were "at least double that of the rates for whites." The researchers wrote, in 1986: "The rates were highest among blacks (7.70 percent), moderate among Asians (5.57 percent) and others (5.52 percent), and low among whites (3.55 percent) and Hispanics (4.00 percent.)"

The Hispanics were predominately Mexican-Americans. And the study said that Mexican-Americans in general "are of particular interest because their favorable low-birth-weight rate persists despite low educational attainment and a substantial number of teenage births."

Other studies cited by a federal Task Force on Black and Minority Health confirm the favorable Mexican-American rate and also have reported good pregnancy outcomes among Asian-Americans and native Americans. Puerto Ricans on the other hand have high rates of low birth weight and infant mortality.

It's important to stress that the middle-class blacks in the California study did much better than blacks as a whole. There's an obvious link between infant mortality and socioeconomic status. But the exact nature of that link is far from obvious. And Baldwin concluded that researchers should not shrink from the possibility that a genetic factor is also involved in the mortality statistics.

"There are clearly genetic questions involved in the whole issue of the size of the baby," said Dr. Heinz Berendes, one of the analysts who reported on the California study in the Journal of the American Medical Association. "And I don't think anyone at this point can say how much of the disparity between blacks and whites has to do with genetic or environmental factors. My own suspicion is that most of it is purely environmental and not genetic."

Berendes, an epidemiologist, said the "hottest" research now involves "intergenerational effects." This refers to the fact that mothers who had a low birth weight tend to have babies with a low birth weight.

This could reflect a genetic influence. But it also raises interesting possibilities, suggested by a study conducted years ago in Aberdeen, Scotland.

That study is cited by a University of Chicago neonatologist, Dr. Kwang-sun Lee. It found, said Lee, that a baby's birth weight correlates with the socio-economic status of the baby's maternal grandfather.

This in turn suggests to Lee that birth weight is related to upbringing and lifestyles, and that it could take decades before an improvement in socioeconomic status is translated into an improvement in birth weight.

"Winning the lottery overnight doesn't necessarily change a lifetime of disadvantage," said Dr. Woodie Kessel, chief of research and training for the Division of Maternal and Child Health, U.S. Public Health Service.

Eleanor Holmes Norton agrees.

Income itself is less important than time spent in the middle class, said the civil rights activist and Georgetown University law professor. Racism historically impeded black movement into the middle class, she said, and most middle-class blacks today are only first-generation middle class. To compare them with whites, she said, is to compare apples and oranges.

"If you compare blacks and whites," she said, "you're comparing blacks who are two or three generations behind whites whatever their incomes. In the same way, if you were looking at Italians and Irish in the early 20th century and comparing them to WASPs, you would find a whole set of lifestyle differences that would be based essentially on class and time in the country. They would influence everything from food and exercise to attention to health. And they would produce a healthier WASP probably."

The implication is that many middle-class blacks are still living like poor people in terms of their nutrition, exercise and health-seeking activity. Many of them eat the same food that poor blacks do, fail to exercise and steer clear of doctors, said Northwestern University sociologist William Sampson.

"Blacks come from a tradition where people go to the doctor when they get sick," said Norton. "Preventative medicine is not part of that tradition."

"I'm as middle-class as you can get," said Sampson. "But I don't go to a doctor until I can't walk any more." And he suggested the best way to reduce black infant mortality might be to get more blacks into the middle class, then wait two generations.

Norton noted that Ebony magazine in recent years has begun to publish many articles on nutrition, exercise and weight reduction.

"When it gets into that kind of mass market," she said, "you know that something is going to happen. The problem is, it's happening at a slower rate than with whites, because blacks—even when their incomes are middle class—do not put together all the elements of middle-class status because of the effects of racism."

Norton called for more refined research. The Public Health Service's Kessel said federal investigators are trying to provide it.

"We haven't really been successful in comparing comparable populations," he said. So the researchers are working in cooperation with Meharry Medical College, the nation's foremost black medical school, to identify blacks who have what Kessel calls a sustained history of high socioeconomic status.

That won't be easy.

Talk to David Satcher, president of Meharry, and he will tell you: "Black middle class in this country is a very deceiving class description." And he will refer you to the Meharry Cohort Study.

"This is a study," he said, "that follows a group of physicians from the time they were students at Meharry, following their blood pressure and their weight and so forth. It turns out there was a similar group followed by Johns Hopkins. And the results just came out. The risk of hypertension was more than 40 percent higher among the black group. The death rate from heart disease was 10 times as great.

"You might say, 'But they're all physicians!' But most of the Meharry graduates are *first-generation* college graduates. Look at their sodium intake, and the fact that habits as far as salt are concerned begin early in life, and continue throughout. I can guarantee you that because people are in the same socioeconomic group doesn't mean they have the same sodium intake.

"That's one thing. And another thing is, the black middle class is a very stress-filled group in this country, and for many reasons—in terms of what it means to be first-generation black middle class and still be worried about whether you're going to be able to stay there, and whether your children are going to be able to make it."

Stress among blacks also is singled out by Kwang-sun Lee as a possible factor contributing to low birth weight and infant mortality.

"This is just my imagination," he said. "It requires a study. But when a woman gets pregnant and has much stress in her life, what happens to her hormonal environment, or the biochemical environment of her body? And something very interesting happened in World War II. In Amsterdam, in Holland, no food could get into the city. And the population starved there. But there was no bombardment. Do you think their low-birth-weight rate increased very much because of malnutrition? No. It increased very little. But in Russia, in Leningrad, there was a lot of starvation—and bombardment. There was a lot of stress. And infant mortality was sky-high. Was this nature's experiment?"

Many researchers are interested in the stress factor. Wendy Baldwin suggests that the first generation to pull itself out of poverty may suffer stress related to "a disjunction with the past." But Eleanor Holmes Norton, for one, isn't sure she buys into the concept.

"I'm reluctant on things like that," she said. "Stress is so ubiquitous in this country. The stress from racism is clear. But I would not underestimate the kind of stress that is on Wall Street lawyers and investment brokers and journalists. I just don't know how you measure that. Everyone has his peculiar kind of stress. I really wonder at the science of saying the stress of racism is more deadly than the stress of people who are screaming those numbers at the Chicago commodity exchanges."

Another possible explanation of the 2-1 disparity between black and white populations is offered by Dr. Richard L. Naeye, chairman of pathology at the Pennsylvania State University College of Medicine.

Naeye cited the U.S. Public Health Service's collaborative perinatal study. He said data from that study suggest that when blacks and whites with the same education and income are compared, the 2-1 ratio shrinks to 5-4. He added:

"There are two big differences between blacks and whites. Number one is a disorder known as acute chorioamnionitis. This is when bacteria get into the membranes that surround the baby before birth and hold the amniotic fluid. This is more frequent in blacks than in whites, and it actually will explain about 85 percent of the difference in mortality—in the stillborn and newborn death rates between blacks and whites.

"These infections are the single biggest cause of premature delivery in the United States. The bacteria get into the membranes, and they start a reaction that so far nobody's been able to stop. It leads to premature labor, to premature rupture of the membranes. Big efforts are being made right now by a number of groups in Canada and the U.S. to deal with this disorder. If you could get rid of it, or control it, almost all of the difference in pregnancy outcome in blacks and whites would disappear. But it's a very difficult disorder to prevent. And the reason is that we don't really know for sure why the bacteria get into the membranes. I have no idea when we will ever have success in preventing these infections. It might take a decade, or more."

What about the other 15 percent in the black-white disparity?

"The other 15 percent is not so clear," said Naeye. "But I will tell you one other difference between blacks and whites that might be genetic. For reasons which we do not know, there are some differences between the interrelationship of mother's blood pressure during pregnancy and pregnancy outcome.

"In whites, for example, in general, as blood pressure rises from very low levels to high normal levels, this improves the outcome of pregnancy in whites. The death rates go down. In blacks, there's very little response. As those blood pressures rise, the unborn infant grows more rapidly in whites. But it has very little effect on blacks. Again, I can only speculate. But we do know there are some subtle differences in some of the mechanisms that regulate blood pressure in blacks and whites. And this might be a genetic difference."

But if socioeconomic status explains 85 percent of the 2-1 disparity and infection explains 85 percent, isn't this a 170 percent explanation?

"They're highly interrelated," said Naeye. "The poorer people are, the more infection there is. I'm talking about blacks. When you get into other groups, there's great complexity. Mexican-Americans have bad socioeconomics and very little low birth weight. And the same could be said of Chinese and Japanese living in California. Even the poor ones. They have very good pregnancy outcomes. Better than whites, as a matter of fact."

Baldwin said black susceptibility to infection at least theoretically could be genetic. Naeye said: "Nobody knows for sure. But if it did turn out to be genetic, I would be very much surprised."

"There have been lots of hypotheses over time on the relationship of infection and premature rupture of membranes," said Kessel. "The National Institute of Child Health and Human Development has a major study under way on vaginal infection in pregnancy, and it hopefully will identify that. When that study's completed, we should know a bit more about what Naeye is postulating."

Satcher said of Naeye's work:

"It just begs the question, doesn't it? He thinks the disparity can be accounted for by infections. Then what accounts for the infections? You're back where you started from. And I think you're going to find out when you get back there that it's going to be related to things related to poverty, nutrition, and even access to care."

QUESTIONS ABOUT THE READING

1. What possible explanations for the disparity between rates of infant deaths among blacks and whites are presented in this article? Which hypotheses are based on scientific evidence? Which appear to be primarily opinions or hunches?

2. Arguments for both genetic and environmental factors are advanced in this article. If you had a limited amount of research money at your disposal, which of these factors would you consider most worthy of immediate investigation?

3. What is the significance of the finding that the rate of low birthweight among Mexican-Americans is similar to that among whites?

ANSWER KEY FOR CHAPTER 5

Note: Numbers in parentheses refer to pages in the textbook where answers can be found.

CHAPTER 5 REVIEW

Important Terms for Section I

1. cephalocaudal (page 159)
2. proximodistal (159-60)

Learning Objectives for Section I

1. (pages 159-160)
2. (160)

Important Terms for Section II

1. brain (page 162)
2. critical (164)
3. involuntary (164)

Learning Objectives for Section II

1. (pages 160-161)
2. (162)
3. (162-163)
4. (163-164)
5. (164-166)
6. (166-168)
7. (167)
8. (168-169)
9. (169-170)
10. (170)

Important Terms for Section III

1. depth perception (page 171)
2. habituation (173)

Learning Objectives for Section III

1. (pages 171-175)
2. (171)
3. (172)
4. (173)
5. (173-174)
6. (175-176)

Important Term for Section IV

1. Denver Developmental (page 177)

Learning Objectives for Section IV

1. (pages 178-181)
2. (180)
3. (181)
4. (182)
5. (182-185)

Important Terms for Section V

1. year (page 185)
2. crib (188)
3. breathing (189)

Learning Objectives for Section V

1. (pages 185, 186)
2. (185-187)
3. (185-187)
4. (188-189)

CHAPTER 5 QUIZ

Matching—Numbers

1. 70 (page 185)
2. 5 (160)
3. 20 (161)
4. 6 (169)
5. 30 (161)
6. 2 (179)
7. 12 (160)
8. 3 (171)
9. 17 (178)
10. 4 (169, 170)

Multiple-Choice

1. b (pages 159-160)
2. a (160-161)
3. c (162)
4. c (163)
5. b (166)
6. d (164-66)
7. b (167)
8. a (173)
9. b (173-174)
10. b (175)
11. c (175)
12. a (172, 173-174, 176)
13. d (178)
14. c (178)
15. d (180)
16. a (181)
17. b (183-185)
18. a (185-186)
19. b (185)
20. d (189)

True or False?

1. T (page 159)
2. F—Baby boys and girls are equally active. (160)
3. T (161)
4. F—Most babies get the first tooth between 5 and 9 months. (161)
5. T (162)
6. F—The subcortex controls basic biological functions such as breathing and digestion; the cerebral cortex controls thinking and problem solving. (162, 163)
7. T (163-164)
8. T (164, 166)
9. F—Breastfeeding is less popular than bottle-feeding among poor and minority women. (167)
10. T (168)
11. T (169)
12. F—Pediatric nutritionists recommend withholding solid foods before 4 to 6 months so as not to interfere with intake of breast milk or formula. (169-170)
13. T (169, 170)
14. F—Recent research has found no long-term correlation between obesity in infancy and adulthood. (170)
15. F—By about 2 months, babies can distinguish between red and green, and by 4 months they can distinguish among red, green, blue, and yellow. (171)
16. T (171)
17. T (172)
18. F—The inner and middle ear reach adult size and shape before birth. (173)
19. T (174, 175)
20. F—Even on the first day of life, babies can feel pain. (175)
21. T (177)
22. F—Basic motor skills depend primarily on maturity of the central nervous system, muscles, and bones, though environmental factors may slow development. (177, 182, 183)
23. T (182)
24. T (185)
25. T (186, 188)

INTELLECTUAL DEVELOPMENT IN INFANCY AND TODDLERHOOD

OVERVIEW

Chapter 6 examines the rapid intellectual development that takes place during the first 3 years of life. In this chapter, the authors:

- Discuss the relationship between learning and maturation

- Describe three ways in which babies learn

- Compare the psychometric, Piagetian, and information-processing approaches to understanding intellectual development and discuss how each approach addresses and assesses infants' intelligence

- Outline milestones in language development during the first 3 years and compare theories about, and influences on, language development

- Present findings on the growth of competence and how parents can contribute to that growth

- Describe how society can help parents foster their children's intellectual development

CHAPTER 6 REVIEW

Section I Early Learning

FRAMEWORK FOR SECTION I

A. Learning and Maturation
B. Types of Learning
    1. Habituation
    2. Classical Conditioning
    3. Operant Conditioning
    4. Complex Learning
C. Infants' Memory

IMPORTANT TERMS FOR SECTION I

Completion: Fill in the blanks to complete the definitions of key terms for this section of Chapter 6.

1. _____: Relatively permanent change in behavior that results from experience.

2. _____: Unfolding of patterns of behavior in a biologically determined, age-related sequence.

3. _____: Simple type of learning in which familiarity with a stimulus reduces, slows, or even stops a response.

4. **classical conditioning:** Learning in which a previously neutral stimulus (_____ stimulus) acquires the power to elicit a response (_____ response) by association with a(n) _____ stimulus that ordinarily elicits a particular response (_____ response).

5. _____ stimulus (abbreviated _____): In classical conditioning, a stimulus that automatically elicits an unlearned response.

6. _____ response (abbreviated _____): In classical conditioning, an automatic, unlearned response to a(n) _____ stimulus; also called a(n) _____ *reflex.*

7. **neutral stimulus:** Stimulus that does not ordinarily evoke a(n) _____ response.

8. _____ stimulus (abbreviated _____): In classical conditioning, an originally neutral stimulus that, after repeated pairing with a(n) _____ stimulus, provokes a(n) _____ response.

9. _____ response (abbreviated _____): In classical conditioning, a response to a(n) _____ stimulus; also known as _____ *reflex.*

10. _____ (or instrumental) **conditioning:** Learning in which a response continues to be made because it has been reinforced.

LEARNING OBJECTIVES FOR SECTION I

After reading and reviewing this section of Chapter 6, you should be able to do the following.

1. Distinguish between learning and maturation and give an example of how they interact.

2. Name three simple types of learning babies do, and briefly describe how each occurs.

3. Summarize research findings about newborns' memory capabilities.

Section II Three Approaches to Studying Intellectual Development

FRAMEWORK FOR SECTION II

A. What Is Intelligence?
B. Psychometric Approach
   1. Intelligence Tests
      a. How Are Intelligence Tests Developed?
         (1) Standardization
         (2) Validity
         (3) Reliability
         (4) Calculating IQ Scores
      b. Can Infants' and Toddlers' Intelligence Be Measured?
      c. Is Intelligence Fixed?
   2. Developmental Tests
      a. What Are Developmental Tests?
      b. Bayley Scales
C. Piagetian Approach
   1. Piaget's Theory
   2. Piaget's Sensorimotor Stage (Birth to about 2 Years)
      a. Cognitive Concepts of the Sensorimotor Stage
         (1) Object Permanence
         (2) Causality
         (3) Representational Abilities
      b. Substages of the Sensorimotor Stage
         (1) Substage 1: Use of Reflexes (Birth to 1 Month)
         (2) Substage 2: Primary Circular Reactions—The First Acquired Adaptations (1 to 4 Months)
         (3) Substage 3: Secondary Circular Reactions (4 to 8 Months)
         (4) Substage 4: Coordination of Secondary Schemes and Their Application to New Situations (8 to 12 Months)
         (5) Substage 5: Tertiary Circular Reactions (12 to 18 Months)
         (6) Substage 6: Beginning of Thought—Mental Combinations (18 to 24 Months)
      c. Research Based on the Sensorimotor Stage

   3. Piaget's Timing: When Do Children Actually Attain Various Abilities?
      a. Achievement of Object Permanence
      b. Invisible Imitation
      c. Deferred Imitation
      d. Understanding of Number Concepts
      e. Achievement of Conservation
D. Information-Processing Approach
   1. Information Processing in Infancy
      a. Information Processing as a Predictor of Intelligence
      b. Influences on Information Processing and Cognitive Development
      c. Using Information-Processing Tests to Measure Disabled Children's Intelligence
   2. Play as a Measure of Intelligence

IMPORTANT TERMS FOR SECTION II

Completion: Fill in the blanks to complete the definitions of key terms for this section of Chapter 6.

1. _____ **approach:** Study of intellectual development based on attempts to measure the quantity of intelligence.

2. _____ **approach:** Study of intellectual development based on describing qualitative changes in thinking that are typical of children at particular stages; named after its founder, _____.

3. _____-**processing approach:** Study of intellectual development based on the mental capacities and processes that support thought.

4. **intelligence:** Ability to _____ , or appropriately alter behavior, in pursuit of a(n) _____.

5. **standardization sample:** Large, _____ group of people used in developing a statistical standard against which other people will be compared.

6. **norm:** _____ performance, with which a person's score on a test is compared.

7. _____: Extent to which a test measures what it is designed to measure.

8. **reliability (test-retest reliability):** _____ of scores when a person is tested more than once.

9. _____ (abbreviated _____): Assessment of a person's intellectual ability, determined by administering an intelligence test and matching the test taker's score with the average age of those who have scored similarly.

10. **intelligence quotient (IQ):** Score calculated by dividing a person's _____ age by his or her _____ age and multiplying the result by 100.

11. _____ **Scales:** Standardized test of infants' intelligence.

12. _____ **development:** Changes in mental powers and qualities that permit understanding.

13. _____ **stage:** In Piaget's theory, the first stage in human cognitive development (birth to about age 2), during which infants acquire knowledge through _____ experience and _____ activity.

14. _____: In Piaget's theory, awareness that a person or thing continues to exist when out of sight.

15. **representational ability:** Capacity to represent objects and actions in _____ , largely through the use of _____ .

16. _____: Organized pattern of behavior.

17. **circular reaction:** In Piaget's theory, a simple behavior that is _____ often.

18. **primary circular reaction:** Simple _____ act, centered on the baby's own body, to reproduce a pleasant sensation first achieved by _____ .

19. _____ **adaptation:** Change in behavior to accommodate a new situation.

20. **secondary circular reaction:** _____ of an action to see results _____ the body.

21. **tertiary circular reaction:** Deliberate_____ of actions to see what will happen.

22. **deferred imitation:** Ability to _____ an action and _____ it after a passage of time.

23. **invisible imitation:** Imitation of an action with a part of the body that cannot be seen by _____ , such as imitation of facial expressions.

24. **visible imitation:** Imitation of an action with a part of the body, such as the hands or feet, that can be seen by _____ .

25. **weight** _____: Understanding that an object weighs the same if nothing is added to it or taken away from it, even though its appearance may change.

26. _____ **memory:** Remembrance of a visual stimulus.

27. _____ **memory:** Ability to remember and recognize sounds.

LEARNING OBJECTIVES FOR SECTION II

After reading and reviewing this section of Chapter 6, you should be able to do the following.

1. Compare the concerns and methods of the psychometric, Piagetian, and information-processing approaches to understanding and assessing intelligence.

2. Describe how intelligence tests are developed and standardized so as to ensure validity and reliability.

3. Explain how mental age (MA) and intelligence quotient (IQ) are calculated.

4. Give at least two reasons why it is difficult to measure infants' intelligence reliably.

5. Explain why children's IQ scores often change as they grow older.

6. Give two good reasons to administer developmental tests to infants and describe one such test.

7. Describe the major change that occurs during the sensorimotor stage, according to Piaget, and list three important concepts that have developed or have begun to develop by the end of that stage.

8. List the substages of Piaget's sensorimotor stage, describe the development that occurs during each substage, and give an example of typical behavor at each substage.

9. Trace the development of object permanence through the six substages of Piaget's sensorimotor stage, and explain why current researchers believe that Piaget may have underestimated the age at which infants achieve this capacity.

10. List four other abilities which may be achieved earlier than Piaget thought, according to recent research.

11. Explain how visual- and auditory-recognition memory, attentiveness, novelty preference, and efficiency of information-processing are related to prediction of childhood intelligence.

12. Explain how interaction with parents can enhance babies' ability to process information.

13. Explain why information-processing tests can assess intelligence of infants (especially those with motor disabilities) more accurately than psychometric tests can.

14. Explain how children's play can be an indicator of cognitive development.

Section III   Language

FRAMEWORK FOR SECTION III

A. How Children Acquire Language
　1. Prelinguistic Speech
　2. Linguistic Speech
　　a. The First Word
　　b. The First Sentence
　　c. Stages of Linguistic Speech
　　d. Some Characteristics of Early Speech
B. Theories of Language Acquisition
　1. Learning Theory
　2. Nativism
C. Influences on Language Acquisition
　1. Genetic Influences
　2. Influence of Adults
　3. "Motherese"

IMPORTANT TERMS FOR SECTION III

Completion: Fill in the blanks to complete the definitions of key terms for this section of Chapter 6.

1. **language:** _____ system that uses words and grammar.

2. **prelinguistic speech:** Communicative use of _____ by infants without using words or grammar.

3. **linguistic speech:** Spoken use of language; besides words and grammar, it relies on pronunciation, _____ , and _____ to convey meaning.

4. **holophrase:** _____ that conveys a complete thought; the typical speech form of children aged 12 to 18 months.

5. **mean length of utterance (MLU):** Average length of a child's utterance, measured in _____.

6. **morpheme:** Smallest _____ unit of speech.

7. _____ **speech:** Children's speech with an average of three morphemes per utterance, conveying a complete idea but not including any extra ideas or using complex grammar.

8. _____**theory:** Theory that most behavior is learned from experience.

9. _____: Theory that behavior is inborn; _____ linguistics holds that speech arises from an inborn capacity.

10. **language _____ device (abbreviated _____):** In _____ linguistics, the inborn ability to learn a language.

11. _____: Simplified, slow, repetitive, high-pitched speech used by most adults and slightly older children when speaking with an infant.

LEARNING OBJECTIVES FOR SECTION III

After reading and reviewing this section of Chapter 6, you should be able to do the following.

1. List in sequence at least six milestones in language development during the first 3 years.

2. Identify at least four forms of prelinguistic speech.

3. Name five types of holophrases often spoken by 1- and 2-year-olds.

4. Explain the role of symbolic gesturing in cognitive development, identify five types of symbolic gestures, and give an example of each.

5. Outline five stages of linguistic speech, and give an example of a typical utterance at each stage.

6. Describe and give examples of three characteristics of early speech.

7. Contrast the views of learning theorists and nativists, identify the single most important factor in language acquisition according to each theory, and discuss research that supports and challenges each.

8. Discuss the evidence for hereditary and environmental influences on variations in linguistic ability.

9. Discuss the pros and cons of "motherese."

10. Give at least four suggestions for stimulating babies' language development.

Section IV   Competence

FRAMEWORK FOR SECTION IV

A. What Is Competence?
B. What Influences Competence?

LEARNING OBJECTIVES FOR SECTION IV

After reading and reviewing this section of Chapter 6, you should be able to do the following.

1. List at least two social skills and two cognitive skills of competent preschoolers.

2. Identify three major aspects of child rearing that can affect the development of competence.

3. List at least five guidelines for enhancing young children's competence.

Section V When Families Need Help

LEARNING OBJECTIVES FOR SECTION V

After reading and reviewing this section of Chapter 6, you should be able to do the following.

1. Explain why the "myth of the self-sufficient family" can deprive families and children of needed help.

2. Identify at least three key elements of a successful program to help low-income parents enhance children's intellectual development.

CHAPTER 6 QUIZ

Matching—Who's Who: Match each name in the left-hand column with the appropriate description at the right. (Note: Here, a description may be used to identify more than one name.)

1. John B. Watson _____
2. Noam Chomsky _____
3. Théodore Simon _____
4. Nancy Bayley _____
5. Jean Piaget _____
6. T. G. R. Bower _____
7. Rosalie Rayner _____
8. Roger Brown _____
9. Alfred Binet _____
10. Burton L. White _____

a. studied mothers' influence on preschoolers' competence
b. devised the first psychometric intelligence test
c. found that certain abilities show up early, then disappear, and then reappear later
d. developed a standardized psychometric test of infants' intelligence
e. described five stages of linguistic speech
f. proposed the existence of an inborn language acquisition device
g. developed a theory of cognitive development based on observation of children
h. conducted a famous conditioning study, teaching a baby to fear a white rat

Multiple-Choice: Circle the choice that best completes or answers each item.

1. An infant's fear of falling is an example of
   a. learning
   b. maturation
   c. instinct
   d. temperament

2. Which of the following can reliably predict an infant's later intelligence?
   a. Stanford-Binet Intelligence Scale
   b. Bayley Scales of Infant Development
   c. both a and b
   d. neither a nor b

3. As a baby sucks on a dry nipple, an experimenter plays a tape of a woman singing a lullaby. When the baby stops sucking, the singing stops; when the baby resumes sucking, the singing resumes. This is an example of
   a. habituation
   b. classical conditioning
   c. operant conditioning
   d. complex learning

4. Which theoretical approach to intellectual development sees intelligence as fixed at birth?
   a. psychometric
   b. Piagetian
   c. information-processing
   d. none of the above

5. According to the traditional method of calculation, an IQ of 110 means that
   a. chronological age is greater than mental age
   b. mental age is greater than chronological age
   c. mental age and chronological age are the same
   d. 110 test takers per 1000 have this IQ

6. Which of the following is *not* something babies learn to do during the sensorimotor stage, according to Piaget?
   a. organize their behavior toward goals
   b. generalize from one situation to another
   c. coordinate new and previously learned behaviors
   d. understand the concept of number

7. A 10-month-old baby who purposely drops a cup from the high chair and laughs when it falls is developing the concept of
   a. object permanence
   b. causality
   c. representation
   d. weight conservation

8. Thumb-sucking by a 2-month-old baby is a
   a. primary circular reaction
   b. secondary circular reaction
   c. tertiary circular reaction
   d. form of deferred imitation

9. A 9-month-old baby who sees a toy on the floor, crawls to it, and picks it up is showing
   a. an acquired adaptation
   b. a tertiary circular reaction
   c. coordination of secondary schemes
   d. object permanence

10. According to Piaget, the approximate age at which babies typically begin to think is
    a. 8 months
    b. 12 months
    c. 15 months
    d. 18 months

11. Research discussed in your text has challenged Piaget's estimate of the age at which children develop *all but which* of the following abilities?
    a. object permanence
    b. invisible imitation
    c. conservation
    d. trial-and-error problem solving

12. An infant's later intelligence can be predicted from his or her
    a. speed of habituation
    b. age of attaining object permanence
    c. novelty preference
    d. all of the above

13. A baby's earliest means of communication is
    a. cooing
    b. babbling
    c. crying
    d. smiling

14. A 12-month-old baby who reaches for a ball and says "da" is using
    a. a holophrase
    b. prelinguistic speech
    c. telegraphic speech
    d. none of the above

15. The word *undressed* consists of how many morphemes?
    a. 1
    b. 2
    c. 3
    d. 4

16. The sentence "Mama goed bye-bye" is an example of a young child's tendency to
    a. overregularize rules
    b. speak ungrammatically
    c. use primitive speech
    d. all of the above

17. According to the nativist view of language acquisition, children learn to speak their native language by
    a. imitating their parents and caregivers
    b. analyzing the language they hear and figuring out its rules
    c. repeating sounds that receive positive reinforcement
    d. all of the above

18. Research shows that babies tend to become more competent when given
    a. challenging educational toys
    b. as much parental attention as possible
    c. freedom to explore
    d. all of the above

19. Parents can best influence a child's competence beginning when the child is how old?
    a. 3 to 5 months
    b. 6 to 8 months
    c. 10 to 12 months
    d. 2 years

20. A key to the success of a federally sponsored program for enhancing low-income children's intellectual development was
    a. frequent psychometric testing of the children
    b. financial assistance to permit purchase of books and toys
    c. recognition of cultural differences in parenting practices
    d. each of the above

True or False? In the blank following each item, write T (for *true*) or F (for *false*). In the space below each item, if the statement is false, rewrite it to make it true.

1. The first thing infants learn is to suck. _____

2. Infants less than 1 week old can distinguish between certain sights and sounds. _____

3. Newborns can learn by classical conditioning. _____

4. Maturation is essential to the success of toilet training. _____

5. Infants younger than 2 months cannot remember past events. _____

6. Intelligence tests were originally developed to identify bright students. _____

7. The Stanford-Binet Intelligence Scale is especially good for predicting ability with numbers. _____

8. Standardized IQ tests provide a reliable measure of 3-year-olds' intelligence. _____

9. About two-thirds of the population have IQs between 85 and 115. _____

10. A 6-month-old infant's DQ can help diagnose a neurological deficit. _____

11. According to Piaget, deferred imitation depends on the ability to make mental representations. _____

12. Research has failed to confirm the sequence of Piaget's stages. _____

13. Research suggests that babies as young as 7 months may have a rudimentary understanding of counting. _____

14. According to information-processing research, a child's intellectual development is continuous from birth. _____

15. Socioeconomic status has a strong influence on individual differences in early information processing. _____

16. Information processing tests are useful only for predicting intelligence of motor-disabled infants. _____

17. Babies about 1 year old begin to generate new ideas for ways to use their toys. _____

18. A baby's first word is typically said by the age of 17 months. _____

19. A 16-month-old baby who gestures as if turning a knob to signify "I want to go out," instead of using words, shows slowed cognitive development. _____

20. The development of linguistic speech is closely tied to age. _____

21. Toddlers' speech is a simplified version of adult speech. _____

22. Children who do not hear adult speech tend to be slow in developing spoken language. _____

23. Repeating babies' babbled sounds slows their speech development by reinforcing meaningless utterances. _____

24. Late talkers tend to be less verbal than early talkers. _____

25. Parents can be taught to contribute to the development of children's competence. _____

TOPICS FOR THOUGHT AND DISCUSSION

1. Aldous Huxley, in his novel *Brave New World*, envisions a society of the future in which conditioning is used to totally control human behavior. Babies destined to work in factories are conditioned to reject "time-wasting" books and flowers by associating those objects with frightening noises and painful electric shocks. Is this an example of classical conditioning or operant conditioning, or does it have elements of both? Do you think Huxley might have been caricaturing Watson and Rayner's conditioning of "Little Albert"? In what ways are the two situations similar? In what ways are they different? Does the purpose of conditioning affect the ethics involved? Can you think of a situation in which associating a stimulus with pain or discomfort for an infant might be warranted?

2. The suggestions for toilet training in Box 6-1 draw upon a variety of learning methods: social learning (imitation of models), classical conditioning (pairing), and operant conditioning (reinforcement, shaping, and mild punishment). In your experience with young children, which (if any) of these methods seems most effective? Keeping in mind the ethical standards for experimentation with children, can you devise a way to test the relative effectiveness of various methods of toilet training?

3. Meltzoff and Moore found that newborn babies can imitate adults' facial expressions, like sticking out the tongue. Other researchers, unable to replicate this result except in the youngest infants, suggest that the tongue thrust may be a reflex, which disappears as babies get older. Meltzoff and Moore reply that these other researchers' methods mask the babies' imitative abilities. Can you suggest a method to more conclusively confirm or disprove these findings?

4. In your view, does Piaget's apparent underestimation of the age of development of certain abilities seriously undermine the value of his theory of cognitive development? Why or why not?

5. Considering the points made by advocates and opponents of "motherese," as reported in your textbook, which side do you think has made the stronger case? Why? Do the authors seem to favor one point of view or the other? Which view is more consistent with your own observations?

6. The Harvard Preschool Project resulted in the development of guidelines for successful

parenting, which then were taught to a pilot group of parents. The children's progress was similar to, but not as good as, that of children in the original study whose mothers exhibited the behaviors on which the guidelines were based. Can you suggest any possible reasons for this result, other than those given in your textbook?

7. Which of the research findings reported in this chapter would you consider most helpful in stimulating a baby's intellectual development?

CHAPTER 6 READING

INTRODUCTION

John Holt was a writer, a teacher, and a very perceptive observer of children. His observations and comments were always fascinating, often provocative, and sometimes controversial. He became well known—to educators and to laypeople—through his first book, *How Children Fail.* The following selection, "Talk," is excerpted from *How Children Learn,* his second book, which was published in 1967. This book, like the first, has the format of a journal or diary of Holt's experiences with children and his thoughts about them.

Talk: Excerpts from "How Children Learn"

by John Holt

Sitting in his stroller, in a local store the other day, was a child about a year old. His mother was busy in the store, and he was absorbed in his own affairs, playing with his stroller, looking at cans of fruit and juice. I watched him. Suddenly he said to himself, "Beng-goo." After a few seconds he said it again, then again, and so perhaps ten times. Was he trying to say, "Thank you?" More probably he had hit on this sound by accident and was saying it over and over because he liked the way it sounded, and felt in his mouth.

Why does a baby begin to make sounds in the first place? Is it instinctive, like crying? It seems not to be. A puppy raised apart from other dogs will know how to bark when he gets old enough. But the few children we know of who grew up without human contact, grew up almost wholly mute. Babies in understaffed foundling hospitals, who see very little of older people, are said, except for crying, to be almost silent. Apparently it is from hearing people speak around them that babies get the idea of "speaking." When they make their first sounds, are they imitating the sounds they hear around them? Or are they inventing, so to speak, from scratch? Perhaps at first they mostly invent, and imitate more later.

It is a remarkable business. We are so used to talking that we forget that it takes a very subtle and complicated coordination of lips, tongue, teeth, palate, jaws, cheeks, voice, and breath. Simply as a muscular skill it is by far the most complicated and difficult that most of us ever learn, at least as difficult as the skill required to master a serious musical instrument. We realize how difficult speech is only when we first try to make the sounds of a language very different from our own. Suddenly we find that our mouths and tongues won't do what we want. Yet every child learns to make the sounds of his own language. If he lives where more than one language is spoken, he makes the sounds of them all. How does he do it? His coordination is poor to start with; how does he manage to do what many adults find so difficult?

The answer seems to be by patient and persistent experiment; by trying many thousands of times to make sounds, syllables, and words; by comparing his own sounds to the sounds made by people around him; and by gradually bringing his own sounds closer to the others; above all, by being willing to do things wrong even while trying his best to do them right.

Bill Hull once said to me, "If we taught children to speak, they'd never learn." I thought at first he was joking. By now I realize that it was a very important truth. Suppose we decided that we had to "teach" children to speak. How would we go about it? First, some committee of experts would analyze speech and break it down into a number of separate "speech skills." We would probably say that, since speech is made up of sounds, a child must be taught to make all the sounds of his language before he can be taught to speak the language itself. Doubtless we would list these sounds, easiest and commonest ones first, harder and rarer ones next. Then we would begin to teach infants these sounds, working our way down the list. Perhaps, in order not to "confuse" the child—"confuse" is an evil word to many educators—we would not let the child hear much ordinary speech, but would only expose him to the sounds we were trying to teach.

Along with our sound list, we would have a syllable list and a word list.

When the child had learned to make all the sounds on the sound list, we would begin to teach him to combine the sounds into syllables. When he could say all the syllables on the syllable list, we would begin to teach him the words on our word list. At the same time, we would teach him the rules of grammar, by means of which he could combine these newly-learned words into sentences. Everything would be planned with nothing left to chance; there would be plenty of drill, review, and tests, to make sure that he had not forgotten anything.

Suppose we tried to do this; what would happen? What would happen, quite simply, is that most children, before they got very far, would become baffled, discouraged, humiliated, and fearful, and would quit trying to do what we asked them. If, outside of our classes, they lived a normal infant's life, many of them would probably ignore our "teaching" and learn to speak on their own. If not, if our control of their lives was complete (the dream of too many educators), they would take refuge in deliberate failure and silence, as so many of them do when the subject is reading.

Last summer, in a supermarket, a young mother came with her baby to the meat counter, and began to discuss with him, in the most lively and natural way, what meat they should get for supper. This piece of meat looked nice, but it was too expensive—terrible what was happening to food prices. This piece might be all right, but it would take too long to cook; they had many other errands to do and would not get home before four o'clock. These chops looked good, but they had had them just two nights ago. And so on. There was nothing forced or affected in her words or her voice; she might have been talking to someone her own age.

A year or more ago, some friends and I dropped in on some people who had a six-month-old baby. She was well-rested and happy, so they brought her in to see the visitors. We all admired her before going on with our talk. She was fascinated by this talk. As each person spoke, she would turn and look intently at him. From time to time she would busy herself with a toy in her lap; then after a few minutes she would begin watching and listening again. She seemed to be learning, not just that people talk, but that they talk to each other, and respond to each other's talk with smiles, and laughter, and more talk; in short, that talk is not just a kind of noise, but messages, communication.

Babies and young children like to hear adult conversation, and will often sit quietly for a long time, just to hear it. If we want to help little children as they learn to talk, one way to do it is by talking to them—provided we do it naturally and unaffectedly—and by letting them be around when we talk to other people.

For the first few years of her life, Lisa grew up on a cattle ranch. When she was about 18 months old, she pointed at some cattle one day and said, "See cows, see cows." We were very pleased; these were about the first real words we had heard her say. We agreed that there were indeed cows out there, and said other things about them. But a few days later, going by a field with some horses in it, she said again, "See cows." Later, passing some sheep, she said the same thing. This was puzzling. Surely she didn't think they were all the same animal. Yet, if she knew the horses and sheep were different, why did she call them cows? Or, if she thought all animals were called "cows," why didn't she call the family dog and cats "cows"? Apparently, out of all the many things she saw, heard, and felt, she had isolated a group, a class, that we would call "large animals in the fields," and to this class she had given the name "cows." We did not correct her, but just went on talking about cows, horses, and sheep in a normal way. Before long she divided her class of animals in the fields into sub-groups, and put the proper label on each one.

Long before I got into teaching, I met Jackie, about two years old, who had created in his mind a class of objects that we would call "dry, crumbly things to eat"—cookies, crackers, dry toast—to which he had given the name "Zee." Neither his father or mother knew how he had come to pick that word. They assured me that he had not picked up the name from them—they never called crackers "Zee." Clearly the baby had decided for himself that it was a good name for this class of things.

Some of Tommy's first words were not names of things, but other kinds of words. When he was still little enough to be carried around a good deal of the time, he used to show where he wanted to go to whomever was carrying him by pointing his hand in the desired direction and saying, imperiously, "Way!" When he said this to me, I used to answer, "Way," and then add, using my language, "Shall we go over this way?" Another of his early words was "Down." If he was being carried, "Down" meant "Put me down." If he wasn't being carried, "Down" meant "Pick me up." His older sister, when she was very little, had invented a word, "Tup-tup," which meant exactly the same thing.

One day, when Tommy was very little, he decided that he needed to find out the names for a lot of things. He suddenly began to look very intently at various objects in the room, pointing out to me each of them in turn. At first I had no idea what he wanted. I thought he was asking me to give him whatever he was looking at, or to do something with it. But he showed me that that was not what he wanted. For a while I was baffled. Then, on a hunch, I tried telling him the name of what he was showing me. Instantly he showed by his expression that I had guessed right. He began to point to many other objects.

I was careful, when I told him the name of something, not to tell him as if it were a lesson, something he *had* to remember. Nor did I test him by saying, "What's this? What's that?" This kind of checking up is not necessary, and it puts a child in a spot where he will feel that, if he says the wrong thing, he has done wrong and is in the wrong. I have seen kindly, well-meaning parents do this to young children, hoping to help them learn. Almost every time the child soon took on the kind of tense, tricky expression we see on so many children's faces in school, and began the same sad old business of bluffing, guessing, and playing for hints. Even in the rare case when a child does not react this defensively to questions, too much quizzing is likely to make him begin to think that learning does not mean figuring out how things work, but getting and giving answers that please grownups.

We should also remember that children (like adults), and above all young children, know and understand much more than they can put into words. If we point to a lamp and say to a young child, "What's that?" we may not always get an answer. If we get none, or the wrong one, does it mean that the child doesn't know the name for lamp, or doesn't know what the word "lamp" refers to? Not necessarily. In other contexts, he might know the word perfectly well. His reason for not answering the question "What's that?" may be only that the question itself confuses him, that he doesn't know what we want him to say or do.

One good way to help children learn the names of things is by talking about anything we do together. Many mothers, getting a child ready to go out, say something like this: "Now we'll tie up this shoe; pull the laces good and tight; now we'll get the boots; let's see, the right boot for the right foot, then the left boot for the left foot; all right, coat next, arms in the sleeves, zip it up nice and tight; now the mittens, left mitten on the left hand, right mitten on the right hand; now comes the hat, on it goes, over your ears . . . " This kind of talk is companionable and fun, and from it the child learns, not just words, but the kinds of phrases and sentences they fit into.

One winter morning, when we were eating breakfast, Tommy began to say "Toe! Toe! Toe!" Putting helpful expressions on our faces, we said, "Toe?" It was clear that we did not know what he meant. Again he said, "Toe! Toe! Toe!," looking furiously at us. We knew that he had been using the word to mean toe, coat, cold, and toilet. So we said, pointing at his toe, "Does your toe hurt?" Wrong. "Do you want your coat? Your blue coat?" Wrong again. "Do you want to go towet?" (family expression inherited from previous baby). Still wrong. "Are you cold?" Now we were on the right track. Asking more questions, we eventually found that someone had left an outside door open, letting in a draft, and that Tommy wanted us to close the door—which we did. This shows that a baby's speech may be more varied than it sounds. He may *know* the difference between a number of words, even if he cannot say the difference.

When a baby shows us, by his expression, by the insistent tone of his voice, and by repeating his words over and over, that he is trying hard to tell us something, we must try just as hard to understand what he is saying. Often it will not be easy. Some people, if they don't understand the first or second time, say, "I don't know what you're saying," and give up. But we must not give up. It sometimes helps to ask the next oldest child in the family. He may be able to interpret, perhaps because he knows the smaller child better and hears him talk more, perhaps because he himself is closer to early speech and remembers what it is like. Or, if there is no other child to interpret for us, we can say to the child who is speaking, "Can you show me?" I remember seeing one mother do this with her little boy. At first he did not understand her question, and looked puzzled. She then took a step or two in one direction, pointing, and saying, "Is it in here? Is it this way?" Then she went in another direction and asked again, while the child watched, puzzled and intent. After a while he saw what her question meant, and was soon able to lead her to what he wanted to tell her about.

Bruno Bettelheim has many times pointed out that if a child's efforts to get a response from the world and the people around him fail more than a very few times, he may well decide that there is no use in trying. This throws new light on the matter of I.Q. scores. We know that so-called intelligence tests largely measure skill at understanding and using words. We also know that both high and low I.Q. scores tend to run in families. From this it is easy to infer that the kind of verbal skill measured by these tests is inherited from parents.

It seems more likely, at least to me, that I.Q. scores tend to run high, or low, in families, because people who are skillful with words are able, most of the time, to encourage the growth of that skill in their children. Such children, when still babies, are encouraged to try to talk by hearing talk around them. When they begin real talking, they are further encouraged, because their parents (and other older people) are persistent and resourceful in trying to understand them. In a family with little verbal skill, a baby can be handicapped, not just because he hears so little talk, but also because, when he does try to talk, he is less often understood, and hence less often encouraged. If people do not try very hard to understand what he says, he may come to feel that most of the time there is not much point in saying anything.

When Patrick was just over two years old, he could not pronounce S, Z, SH, CH, or any other sibilant sounds. He just left them out. Words like "spoon" came out "poon." It did not take long to learn to understand him, and when we adults could not tell what he wanted to say, his three-and-a-half-year-old sister could always translate. Nobody fretted about the missing sounds. As a result, the little boy spoke confidently and freely, and before long was able to speak like everyone else. What would have happened if we had dealt with him as we deal with children in school? Instead of giving him time to correct his own speech, to grow competent and confident in making his sibilants, we would have been correcting him every time he spoke. "No, not 'poon,' 'spoon.' S-s-s-s-poon. Say it, spoon, spoon, spoon." We might have grown more impatient and angry, the child more discouraged and frightened. It would not have been long before he would have become anxious at the very thought of speaking. Perhaps he would have tried to avoid all words with sibilants in them. Perhaps he might have decided to stop talking altogether, since it always got him into so much trouble. Or he might have developed a stutter or stammer.

Lisa (age 2½) is usually the first awake in the morning, after me. When she wakes, she begins to talk to herself. It is an odd mixture. Nonsense syllables, funny noises, snatches of songs, remarks about what she did yesterday and may do today all tumble out in profusion. She goes on talking all day. Sometimes she talks to get something she wants. Sometimes she talks to make something happen, that might uncover the meaning of what she says. Much of the time she talks just because she likes the sound of it.

Much of her talk might be called experiments with grammar, that is, exercises in putting together words in the way that people around her put them together. She makes word patterns, sentences, that sound like the sentences she hears. What do they mean? Often they may not mean anything, and are not meant to mean anything. Not long ago she said, in the middle of a conversation about something different, "I fell out of a big blue mountain into a car." My mind reeled. What was she trying to say? Then it occurred to me that perhaps she was not trying to say anything, but was making up a nice-sounding sentence, a pattern of words, using words and phrases that she knew and liked to say.

One morning at breakfast she began to say, "Pass the sugar. Pass the pepper. Pass the toast. Pass the jam." At first, we passed them along. I noticed after a while that she did not use them. Often she had no use for them; what she asked for had nothing to do with what was on her plate. She would ask for milk when she already had some, or for sugar when there was nothing to put it on. Why was she asking for these things? Clearly, because everyone else was. When you sit down at breakfast you ask people to pass things. The grownups were all doing it, so she was going to do it, too.

This may have been one reason for playing the "please pass" game, but it was not the only reason. I soon saw that, although she did not use any of the things that were passed to her, she watched very carefully each time to *see* what was passed to her. In short, she is using talk to make something happen which will, in time, help her find out what the talk means.

I don't want to make her word-experiment seem more precise than it really was. If she could have put into words her reason for looking carefully at all that was passed to her, I don't think it would have been, for example, "I'm going to ask them to pass the sugar, and I'm going to watch and see what comes up the table, and then I'll know that's what the sugar is." It was much more probably something like: "I'm going to ask them to pass things, and I'm going to watch what they do, and from that I'll probably find out something interesting, maybe what all these things are called." No doubt she had to ask for, and get, the sugar a good many times before she began, first to suspect, then to feel sure, that the white sandy-looking stuff in the bowl *was* what everyone called "sugar." But children are good at gathering and storing this kind of vague information—too vague to be useful to most adults—and waiting patiently until, someday, they find they know what it means. By such means children learn the five thousand or so words they are said to know when they first come to school.

QUESTIONS ABOUT THE READING

1. Compare Holt's descriptions of language acquisition with the section on language in Chapter 6 of your text. What similarities and differences do you find?

2. This selection does not contain the terms *learning theory* or *nativism.* Do you think Holt would have supported either of these theories of language acquisition?

3. The selection quotes Bill Hull (Holt's friend and fellow teacher) as saying, "If we taught children to speak, they'd never learn." Do you agree?

4. Holt apparently believed that IQ is entirely—or almost entirely—a result of environmental influences. What evidence can you find in the selection to support this view? Can this view be reconciled in any way with the discussion in your textbook, which concludes that intelligence is affected by both heredity and environment?

5. What do you think would have been Holt's view of "motherese"?

6. Are Holt's ideas about how adults can help children learn language consistent with the findings of the Harvard Preschool Project about how to foster children's competence?

ANSWER KEY FOR CHAPTER 6

Note: Numbers in parentheses refer to pages in the textbook where answers can be found.

CHAPTER 6 REVIEW

Important Terms for Section I

1. learning (page 195)
2. maturation (195)
3. habituation (196)
4. conditioned, conditioned, unconditioned, unconditioned (197)
5. unconditioned, UCS (198)
6. unconditioned, UCR, unconditioned, unconditioned (198)
7. reflex (198)
8. conditioned, CS, unconditioned, conditioned (198)
9. conditioned, CR, conditioned, conditioned (198)
10. operant (198)

Learning Objectives for Section I

1. (pages 195-196)
2. (196-199)
3. (199-201)

Important Terms for Section II

1. psychometric (page 201)
2. Piagetian, Jean Piaget (202)
3. information (202)
4. adapt, goal (202)
5. representative (203)
6. average (203)
7. validity (203)
8. constancy (203)
9. mental age, MA (203)
10. mental, chronological (203)
11. Bayley (206)
12. cognitive (206)
13. sensorimotor, sensory, motor (207)
14. object permanence (207)
15. memory, symbols (208)
16. scheme (208)

17. repeated (209)
18. repetitive, chance (210)
19. acquired (210)
20. repetition, outside (210)
21. varying (211)
22. observe, repeat (212)
23. oneself (213)
24. oneself (213)
25. conservation (215)
26. visual-recognition (216)
27. auditory-recognition (216)

Learning Objectives for Section II

1. (pages 201-202, 206-207, 215-216)
2. (203)
3. (203-204)
4. (204)
5. (205)
6. (205-206)
7. (207-208)
8. (208-212)
9. (210-212, 213)
10. (213-215)
11. (216-217)
12. (217-218)
13. (205, 218-219)
14. (219-220)

Important Terms for Section III

1. communication (page 220)
2. sounds (221)
3. intonation, rhythm (222)
4. single word (222)
5. morphemes (224)
6. meaningful (224)
7. telegraphic (224)
8. learning (225)
9. nativism, nativist (225)
10. acquisition, LAD, nativist (226)
11. motherese (228)

Learning Objectives for Section III

1. (pages 221-224)
2. (221-222)
3. (222)
4. (222, 223)
5. (224)
6. (224-225)
7. (225-226)

8. (226-228)
9. (228-229)
10. (230)

Learning Objectives for Section IV

1. (pages 230-231)
2. (231)
3. (232)

Learning Objectives for Section V

1. (page 233)
2. (233)

CHAPTER 6 QUIZ

Matching—Who's Who

1. h (page 198)
2. f (225, 226)
3. b (202)
4. d (205, 206)
5. g (206-207)
6. c (215)
7. h (198)
8. e (223-224)
9. b (202)
10. a (230-231)

Multiple-Choice

1. a (page 196)
2. d (202-203, 204, 206)
3. c (198-199)
4. d (205, 206, 216)
5. b (203)
6. d (207, 215)
7. b (208)
8. a (209, 210)
9. c (209, 210)
10. d (209, 212)
11. d (213-215)
12. d (197, 213, 216-217)
13. c (221)
14. a (222)
15. c (224)
16. a (225)
17. b (226)
18. c (231)
19. b (232)
20. c (233)

True or False?

1. F—Infants are born with a sucking reflex. (pages 195, 209)
2. T (197, 216)
3. T (198)
4. T (200)
5. F—Infants younger than 2 months can remember past events, particularly pleasurable ones. (200)
6. F—Intelligence tests were originally developed to identify children least likely to benefit from schooling. (202)
7. F—The Stanford-Binet Intelligence Scale is especially good for predicting success in verbal courses like English, not for mathematics. (203)
8. F—IQ tests are unreliable for children under age 5. (203, 204)
9. T (204)
10. T (206)
11. T (212, 214)
12. F—Research has confirmed the basic sequence of Piaget's stages of cognitive development. (212-213)
13. T (215)
14. T (216)
15. F—Socioeconomic status seems unrelated to individual differences in infants' information processing. (217)
16. F—Information-processing tests are useful for predicting intelligence of normal infants as well as motor-disabled infants. (218, 219)
17. T (219)
18. T (221)
19. F—Sixteen-month-old babies typically use gestures to communicate before they know or can say words. (222, 223)
20. F—The development of prelinguistic speech is fairly closely tied to age; linguistic speech is not. (223)
21. F—Toddlers' speech is not just a simplified version of adult speech; it has its own special characteristics. (224)
22. T (228)
23. F—Repeating babies' babbled sounds helps them experience the social aspect of speech. (230)
24. F—Most children who begin talking fairly late catch up eventually. (230)
25. T (232, 233)

PERSONALITY AND SOCIAL DEVELOPMENT IN INFANCY AND TODDLERHOOD

OVERVIEW

Chapter 7 begins the exploration of personality and social development with themes that continue, with variations, at each stage of childhood. In this chapter, the authors:

- Present two theoretical perspectives on personality development in infancy and toddlerhood

- Summarize what is known about infants' emotions and how they show these emotions

- Discuss the influences of temperament, gender, and the family situation on personality development

- Trace the development of sociability in infants and toddlers

- Outline stages in the development of self-control and self-regulation

CHAPTER 7 REVIEW

Introduction and Section I
Early Personality Development:
Two Theories

FRAMEWORK FOR SECTION I

A. Sigmund Freud: Psychosexual Theory
   1. Oral Stage (Birth to 12-18 Months)
   2. Anal Stage (12-18 Months to 3 Years)
B. Erik H. Erikson: Psychosocial Theory
   1. Crisis 1: Basic Trust versus Basic Mistrust
      (Birth to 12-18 Months)
   2. Crisis 2: Autonomy versus Shame and
      Doubt (18 Months to 3 Years)
C. Evaluating the Theories

IMPORTANT TERMS FOR INTRODUCTION AND SECTION I

Completion: Fill in the blanks to complete the definitions of key terms for this section of Chapter 7.

1. **personality:** Person's unique way of behaving, feeling, and _____.

2. _____ **stage:** In Freud's theory, the psychosexual stage of infancy (birth to 12-18 months), characterized by gratification in the area around the _____ ; _____ is the most common gratifying situation.

3. _____: In Freud's theory, the unconscious source of motives and desires; it operates on the "_____ principle."

4. _____ **principle:** In Freud's theory, the attempt to gratify needs immediately; the operating principle of the _____.

5. _____: In Freud's theory, the representation of reason or common sense; it operates on the "_____ principle."

6. _____ **principle:** In Freud's theory, the search for acceptable and realistic ways to obtain gratification; the operating principle of the _____.

7. **anal stage:** In Freud's theory, the psychosexual stage of toddlerhood (_____ to _____ months), in which the child receives pleasure through anal stimulation; toilet training is the most important gratifying situation.

8. _____ **versus** _____: In Erikson's theory, the first critical alternative of psychosocial development, in which infants (birth to 18 months) develop a sense of how reliable people in their world are.

9. _____ **versus** _____: In Erikson's theory, the second critical alternative of psychosocial development (18 months to 3 years), in which the child achieves a balance between self-determination and control by others.

10. _____: Self-control.

LEARNING OBJECTIVES FOR SECTION I

After reading and reviewing this section of Chapter 7, you should be able to do the following.

1. Describe the oral and anal stages proposed by Sigmund Freud.

2. Describe the first two crises proposed by Erik Erikson and compare these theories with Freud's oral and anal stages.

3. Cite three criticisms of Freud's and Erikson's theories of personality development in infancy and toddlerhood.

4. List at least four suggestions for dealing with toddlers' negativism.

Section II Factors in Personality Development

FRAMEWORK FOR SECTION II

A. Emotions: The Basis of Personality and Social Development
  1. Studying Babies' Emotions
  2. How Babies' Emotions Develop: The Sense of Self
  3. How Do Babies Express Their Emotions?
    a. Crying
      (1) Patterns of Crying
      (2) Responding to Crying
      (3) Crying as a Diagnostic Tool
    b. Smiling
    c. Laughing
B. Differences in Personality
  1. Temperamental Differences
    a. Aspects of Temperament
    b. Three Temperamental Patterns
    c. Influences on Temperament
    d. How Temperament Affects Children's Adjustment: "Goodness of Fit"
  2. Gender Differences
C. The Family and Personality Development
  1. The Mother's Role
    a. The Mother-Infant Bond
      (1) Is There a Critical Period for Forming the Mother-Infant Bond??
      (2) What Do Babies Need from Their Mothers?
    b. Attachment: A Reciprocal Connection
      (1) Studying Attachment
      (2) Patterns of Attachment between Mother and Child
      (3) How Is Attachment Established?
        (a) What Does the Mother Do?
        (b) What Does the Baby Do?
      (4) Changes in Attachment
      (5) What Are the Long-Term Effects of Attachment?
      (6) Effects of Other Caregivers on Mother-Child Attachment
  2. The Father's Role
    a. When Do Infants Form Attachments to Their Fathers?
    b. How Do Fathers Act with Babies?
    c. What Influences Fathers' Involvement with Their Infants?
    d. What Is the Significance of the Father-Infant Relationship?
  3. Brothers and Sisters—or No Siblings
    a. Birth Order
    b. Early Sibling Relationships
  4. Stranger Anxiety and Separation Anxiety
    a. Cognitive Factors
    b. Attachment-Related Factors
    c. Other Factors
  5. Social Referencing
    a. How Babies Use Adults as Resources
    b. Whom Do Babies Reference?
    c. Social Referencing and the Visual Cliff
  6. Disturbances in Family Relationships: Separation from Parents
    a. Institutionalization
    b. Hospitalization
    c. Other Temporary Separations

IMPORTANT TERMS FOR SECTION II

Completion: Fill in the blanks to complete the definitions of key terms for this section of Chapter 7.

1. **emotion:** Psychological response to a situation; although the response can lead to altered behavior, the primary characteristic is a change in _____ feeling rather than in _____ action.

2. **self-_____:** Ability to recognize one's own actions, intentions, states, and abilities.

3. **self-recognition:** Ability to recognize one's own _____.

4. **crying:** Innate nonlinguistic form of communication that in newborns and infants expresses a need for attention or a strong emotion; basic infants' cries include the rhythmic cry of need, the angry cry, the cry of pain, and the cry of _____.

5. **smiling:** Innate form of communication that begins as a(n) _____ and soon expresses pleasure, trust, and contentment.

6. _____: Person's style of approaching other people and situations.

7. _____ child: Child with a generally happy temperament, regular biological rhythms, and a readiness to accept new experiences.

8. _____ child: Child who has an irritable temperament, irregular biological rhythms, and intense responses to situations.

9. _____ child: Child whose temperament is generally mild and who is hesitant about accepting new experiences.

10. _____: Learning of behaviors deemed appropriate by one's culture.

11. _____: Instinctive form of learning in which, after a single encounter, an animal recognizes and trusts one particular individual.

12. **mother-infant bond:** Mother's feeling of _____ to her child.

13. _____: Active, affectionate, reciprocal relationship between two people; their interaction reinforces and strengthens the bond. The term often refers to an infant's relationship with parents.

14. _____ situation: Experimental procedure used to assess the attachment between a mother and her infant.

15. _____ attachment: Attachment style in which an infant separates readily from the primary caregiver and actively seeks out the caregiver when he or she returns.

16. _____ attachment: Attachment style in which an infant rarely cries when the primary caregiver leaves and avoids contact on his or her return.

17. _____ attachment: Attachment style in which an infant becomes anxious before the primary caregiver leaves but both seeks and resists contact on the caregiver's return.

18. **gender-typing:** Process by which a person learns a gender _____.

19. _____ anxiety: Wariness of strange people and places often shown by infants in the second half of the first year.

20. _____ anxiety: Distress shown by an infant when a familiar caregiver leaves.

21. **social** _____: Understanding an ambiguous situation by seeking out another person's perception of it.

LEARNING OBJECTIVES FOR SECTION II

After reading and reviewing this section of Chapter 7, you should be able to do the following.

1. Name at least five emotions babies seem to show during the first year.

2. Explain the relationship between self-awareness and the development of emotions.

3. Identify four patterns of crying and explain the impact of mothers' responses to their babies' cries.

4. Trace changes in what makes babies smile and laugh.

5. Explain how a mother's depression can affect her baby.

6. Identify nine aspects of temperament that show up soon after birth and remain relatively stable through adulthood.

7. Identify and describe three temperamental patterns and discuss hereditary and environmental influences on temperament.

8. Explain the significance of "goodness of fit" and its implications for parenting.

9. Summarize what is known about differences in baby boys' and girls' personalities.

10. Discuss the effects of changes in family life on children's socialization and personality development.

11. Discuss the results of research on mother-infant bonding.

12. Describe four patterns of attachment between infants and mothers; discuss influences on the development of these patterns and their long-term effects.

13. Compare infants' interactions with their mothers and with their fathers, and discuss the significance of the father-infant relationship.

14. Discuss the influence of sibling relationships and birth order on infants' and toddlers' development.

15. Cite three factors that affect children's adjustment to a new baby in the family.

16. Discuss the relationship between attachment, object permanence, and the development of separation anxiety.

17. Cite at least three factors that may affect a baby's reaction to strangers.

18. Describe how babies exhibit social referencing.

19. Discuss the effects on young children of institutionalization, hospitalization, and temporary separations from parents or primary caregivers, and suggest ways of avoiding or minimizing harmful effects.

Section III Development of Sociability

FRAMEWORK FOR SECTION III

A. Changes in Sociability
B. Individual Differences in Sociability

LEARNING OBJECTIVES FOR SECTION III

After reading and reviewing this section of Chapter 7, you should be able to do the following.

1. Trace changes in typical interactions among babies during the first 2 years of life.

2. Cite hereditary and environmental influences on individual differences in sociability.

Section IV Development of Self-Control and Self-Regulation

FRAMEWORK FOR SECTION IV

A. Phases Leading to Self-Regulation
B. Helping Babies Develop Self-Control and Self-Regulation

IMPORTANT TERM FOR SECTION IV

Completion: Fill in the blank to complete the definition of the key term for this section of Chapter 7.

1. **self-regulation:** Control of behavior in order to conform with social _____.

LEARNING OBJECTIVES FOR SECTION IV

After reading and reviewing this section of Chapter 7, you should be able to do the following.

1. Name and describe the four phases in the development of self-regulation.

2. Suggest at least three ways in which caregivers can help babies develop self-control and self-regulation.

CHAPTER 7 QUIZ

Matching—Who's Who: Match each name in the left-hand column with the appropriate description at the right. (Note: Here, a description may be used for more than one name or may not be used at all.)

1. Sigmund Freud_____
2. Stella Chess_____
3. Margaret Mead_____
4. Michael Lewis_____
5. Konrad Lorenz_____
6. Harry and Margaret Harlow_____
7. Carroll Izard_____
8. René Spitz_____
9. Erik Erikson_____
10. Alexander Thomas_____

a. studied infants' emotions by observing their facial expressions
b. studied effects of institutionalization on babies
c. studied emergence of self-recognition
d. believed that a child's good or bad conduct depends entirely upon the mother
e. got newborn ducklings to "love him like a mother"
f. believed that personality is formed through conflict between biological urges and societal requirements
g. suggested that children should be raised in diversified communities with people of all ages
h. traced temperamental traits from infancy to young adulthood and identified temperamental patterns
i. emphasizes achievement of a healthy balance of opposite qualities
j. studied mothering needs of rhesus monkeys

Multiple-Choice: Circle the choice that best completes or answers each item.

1. According to Freud, babies who receive too little gratification during the oral stage may become orally fixated, with the result that as adults they may be
   a. compulsive eaters
   b. nail biters
   c. smokers
   d. gullible "swallowers"

2. Toilet training is a key factor in personality development during
   a. Freud's anal stage
   b. Erikson's crisis of trust versus mistrust
   c. both a and b
   d. neither a nor b

3. Erikson, unlike Freud,
   a. does not emphasize the lifelong effects of early experiences
   b. places more importance on the influence of biology than on that of society and culture
   c. is less interested in feeding itself as a source of gratification than in the ways mothers and babies interact during feeding
   d. has only one "crisis" of ego development, instead of two stages, oral and anal

4. According to Erikson, the proper balance of autonomy versus shame and doubt gives a child the virtue of
   a. will
   b. hope
   c. self-determination
   d. trust

5. Which of the following emotions does *not* seem to appear during the first year?
   a. anger
   b. guilt
   c. fear
   d. surprise

6. Which of the following is *not* one of the four patterns of infants' crying?
   a. hunger cry
   b. pain cry
   c. cry of frustration
   d. cry of anxiety

7. The earliest smile of newborns is produced by
   a. gas
   b. pleasure
   c. recognition of parents
   d. spontaneous reflex

8. Which of the following is *not* attributable to temperament?
   a. insomnia
   b. sensitivity to tickling
   c. creativity
   d. loud laughter

9. Differences between infant boys' and girls' personalities
   a. are evident almost from birth
   b. reflect physiological differences between the sexes
   c. reflect different treatment by adults
   d. cannot be clearly described

10. Experiments with rhesus monkeys, raised in cages with plain and cloth-covered wire-mesh surrogate "mothers," produced *all but which* of the following conclusions?
    a. Baby monkeys cling more to a surrogate "mother" that provides soft bodily contact than to one that feeds them.
    b. Baby monkeys will not take food from an inanimate "mother."
    c. Baby monkeys raised with inanimate "mothers" do not grow up normally.
    d. Baby monkeys remember a cloth surrogate "mother" better than a plain wire one.

11. Research suggests that the *least* securely attached babies are those whose attachment pattern is characterized as
    a. disorganized-disoriented
    b. ambivalent
    c. avoidant
    d. resistant

12. Which of the following has been identified as a probable contributor to insecure attachment?
    a. irregular "demand" feedings
    b. presence of siblings close in age
    c. mother's use of alcohol
    d. mother's low income level

13. If a mother is to resume outside work, it is best *not* to begin when her baby is how old?
    a. 3 months
    b. 8 months
    c. 14 months
    d. 17 months

14. Engrossment causes fathers to be
    a. preoccupied with outside work
    b. primary caregivers
    c. as active in child rearing as mothers
    d. strongly influential in their babies' development

15. Which of the following is *not* cited by researchers as an influence on the extent to which sibling rivalry is likely to develop after the birth of a new baby?
    a. mother's fatigue
    b. age of the older child
    c. sex of the older child
    d. father's attention to the older child

16. Stranger anxiety seems to be related to
    a. insecure attachment
    b. temperament
    c. both a and b
    d. neither a nor b

17. As 12-month-old Emily plays in the sandbox, her mother sits nearby on a park bench. When another woman sits down on the bench, Emily looks at her mother uncertainly. Only after Emily sees her mother give the woman a friendly greeting does Emily smile and resume playing. This is an example of
    a. stranger anxiety
    b. separation anxiety
    c. insecure attachment
    d. social referencing

18. *Hospitalism* means
    a. fear of hospitals
    b. disturbance due to hospitalization
    c. movement to make hospitals more homelike
    d. long-term effects of institutionalization

19. According to John Bowlby, hospitalized babies experience the following stages of separation anxiety:
    a. detachment, anger, regression
    b. protest, despair, detachment
    c. protest, detachment, anger
    d. despair, anger, regression

20. When 2-year-old Ross's father tells him not to cross the street alone, Ross obeys the first time. But at the next corner they approach, he runs into the street. Ross has exhibited
    a. self-control but not self-regulation
    b. self-regulation but not self-control
    c. self-awareness but not social referencing
    d. social referencing but not self-control

True or False? In the blank following each statement, write T (for *true*) or F (for *false*). In the space below each statement, if the statement is false, rewrite it to make it true.

1. The theories of both Freud and Erikson place the major responsibility for the way a child turns out on the mother. _____

2. According to Freud, rigid toilet training practices can result in a person's becoming a stickler for punctuality. _____

3. According to Erikson, it is important for mothers to avoid creating mistrust on the part of their babies. _____

4. Infants' emotional development is governed by a "biological clock" unaffected by individual experience. _____

5. By 18 months, babies typically can recognize themselves. _____

6. Babies whose parents regularly respond soothingly to their cries tend to become spoiled and cry more to get what they want. _____

7. Laughter may indicate tension in a 2-year-old. _____

8. Babies of depressed mothers tend to become sad because of inability to elicit responses from the mother. _____

9. Research has shown that temperament is largely the result of early experience. _____

10. A difficult child is one who is hard to raise. _____

11. Research has demonstrated that the mother-infant bond may not develop normally if mother and child are separated in the first hours after birth. _____

12. An essential part of human personality development appears to be an infant's attachment to the mother. _____

13. The stronger a child's attachment to the mother, the easier it is for the child to leave her. _____

14. More than 50 percent of mothers of infants under 1 year old are in the work force. _____

15. Studies have shown that mothers' employment has a negative effect on babies' security of attachment. _____

16. Fathers, more than mothers, treat infant sons and daughters differently. _____

17. The youngest child in a family tends to be the highest scholastic achiever. _____

18. Sibling rivalry is typically the predominant factor in early sibling relationships. _____

19. The most significant problem for children growing up in institutions is separation from parents. _____

20. Babies become more sociable around the age of 1 year, when they start to walk. _____

TOPICS FOR THOUGHT AND DISCUSSION

1. Infants during the first year constantly put things into their mouths. Is this observation strong evidence for Freud's theory regarding the oral stage, or could some other explanation for the infants' behavior be equally plausible?

2. In Erikson's theory, how can parents or caregivers tell when they are striking the "right" balance of trust versus mistrust, or autonomy versus shame and doubt? Can you suggest any guidelines?

3. In your experience with children, how effective are the suggestions given in this chapter for the following? (a) Tackling the "terrible twos." (b) Helping children adjust to a new baby. (c) Helping babies develop self-control and self-regulation. Do you have any additional or better suggestions for dealing with any of these situations?

4. Izard and his colleagues have identified babies' emotions on the basis of their facial expressions. How conclusive is this evidence? Does agreement by a large number of observers that a baby *looks* angry establish that the baby *is* angry? Can you suggest any other basis for identifying babies' emotions?

5. Jerome Kagan is quoted on page 248 of your text as saying, "Perhaps there is no self prior to the second year, as there is no frog in the tadpole." On the basis of the discussion in the previous paragraphs, what do you think Kagan meant? Do you think Freud would agree? Would Erikson? Do you?

6. Research suggests that basic temperament is largely inborn and remains fairly stable. In thinking about people you have known since childhood, do you consider this finding surprising or not?

7. Although research shows that differences in boys' and girls' behavior cannot be clearly seen before the age of 2, the authors of your text suggest that differences in the ways adults (particularly fathers) treat infant boys and girls may contribute to the shaping of personality differences. On what might this inference be based? Can you suggest an alternative explanation for behavioral differences between the sexes?

8. Research seems to have discredited the idea that there is a critical period immediately after birth for forming the mother-infant bond. Yet one of the readings for Chapter 4 of this Study Guide implies that there *is* such a critical period for formation of the father-infant bond. Is it possible that bonding in fathers proceeds differently? Might the sample of fathers in that reading be unrepresentative?

9. Why do you suppose the Harlows did their classic experiments on mothering with monkeys rather than with human babies? If their conclusions are applicable to humans, do they seem consistent with either Freud's or Erikson's theory?

10. The authors of your text caution that almost all the research on attachment is based on the "strange situation," which they say is artificial and therefore questionable. Yet, as you read in Chapter 1, all laboratory research is necessarily artificial, in that the experimenter interferes with the natural course of behavior by setting up situations and manipulating variables. Are there aspects of the attachment experiments that are more questionable than others described in your text?

11. Is Margaret Mead's advocacy of family-based rather than institutional child care consistent with research findings about the major source of the psychological problems caused by institutionalization? What key element do institutional child care and institutionalization tend to have in common? What significant differences are there between them?

12. The authors of your text suggest that as more fathers assume the role of primary caregiver, the nature of father-infant attachment may change. The authors also suggest that differences in the way fathers and mothers behave toward their babies may be largely due to societal expectations. How convincing do you find the evidence given for these assertions? Do you think the father-as-primary-caregiver trend is likely to grow substantially?

CHAPTER 7 READING

INTRODUCTION

You have undoubtedly seen a baby break into tears when faced with—or left with—a stranger. As your text explains, it has long been thought that stranger anxiety (along with separation anxiety, or distress when a parent or other familiar caregiver leaves) is a sign that healthy attachment has occurred. Recent research, mentioned briefly in your text, challenges this long-established interpretation.

Developmental psychologists are now coming to believe that stranger anxiety may be a matter of temperament. Some healthy babies apparently do not experience it at all, while some who do experience it to an extreme degree may have emotional problems.

A recently published study on this topic, done with sensors that measure babies' brain activity, is just one example of today's technologically sophisticated research. Such studies, which can directly assess aspects of infants' emotional development that formerly could be studied only indirectly, may very well overturn some other strongly held beliefs about infant development.

This article, which appeared in the science section of *The New York Times* on June 6, 1989, also refers to research done in Ainsworth's "strange situation," which is described in your text.

New Research Overturns a Milestone of Infancy; "Stranger Anxiety" May Be a Matter of Temperament

by Daniel Goleman

For years it was considered a mark of healthy development for infants at around nine months of age to show distress at the presence of a stranger. Indeed, the dogma that "stranger anxiety" is a major milestone in an infant's emotional growth is still espoused in most books of advice for parents, and in many textbooks on child psychology.

But now developmental psychologists have concluded from recent research that whether an infant cries or not when a parent leaves or a stranger appears is determined by its temperament, not its level of emotional security. Some babies who cry in that situation may be emotionally healthy, while others may not.

The best measure of emotional health in an infant, many experts now say, is the day-to-day rapport between baby and parents, not the degree of anxiety when meeting strangers.

"Many infants who are quite healthy emotionally don't have stranger anxiety at all," said Stanley Greenspan, a psychiatrist who specializes in treating infants, and a clinical professor at George Washington University Medical School in Washington. "Indeed, stranger anxiety, if extreme enough, can be a sign of problems, not healthy adaptation."

Jay Belsky, a developmental psychologist at Pennsylvania State University, said that only in the last five years have a majority of experts "begun to acknowledge that it's totally misguided to see such anxiety as a sign of security."

The widely held if paradoxical belief that a baby's anxiety over strangers or separation from parents is a sign of emotional security followed from the pioneering work in the 1950's of John Bowlby, a British psychoanalyst, and others who studied the bonds between infants and their parents. It was thought that at around 7 to 10 months of age stranger anxiety was a positive developmental step, a first indication that the infant could distinguish familiar from unfamiliar people. Such anxiety was also taken as an indirect sign of the depth of attachment the infant had formed with his or her parents.

Studies in orphanages had shown that infants raised there, who were presumed to be emotionally insecure because of lack of caring attention from an adult, often reached out to be held by any stranger, while children who were brought up in secure homes were more likely to show fear of strangers.

The most recent, and strongest, evidence against that view was published in the May issue of The Journal of Abnormal Psychology. The small but illuminating study was conducted by Richard Davidson, a psychologist at the University of Wisconsin, and Nathan A. Fox, a developmental psychologist at the Institute for Child Study at the University of Maryland.

They analyzed the brain-wave patterns of 13 infants, 10 months of age, and found marked differences between those who later cried when their mothers left the room and those who did not. Those who cried tended to have far more brain-wave activity on the right front side of their brain than on the left even before their mothers left the room. Those who did not cry tended to have the reverse pattern.

Negative and Positive Emotions

In other studies, Dr. Davidson has determined that activity in the right frontal area of the brain is associated with negative emotions like fear, while activity in the left frontal area is found during positive emotions like joy. They have observed these effects in infants as young as three days old.

In the new study, the brain activity was measured by a special cap, containing electric sensors, that the infants wore while they sat at a feeding table. Their mothers then left the room. All but one of the infants who cried when their mothers went out of the room had much stronger activity on the right side, the seat of negative emotions, than the left. And every one of those who did not cry had stronger activity on the left side. The results strongly suggest that whether or not a baby cries in this situation is largely a matter of the baby's temperament.

In unpublished research done with Jerome Kagan, a psychologist at Harvard University, Dr. Davidson found that 3-year-olds who are inhibited and fearful had the same pattern of higher brain activation in the right frontal region as did the younger infants who cried when their mothers left the room. The research suggested that the pattern of brain activity was a sign of temperament, which shows up in different ways at different ages.

Experts on child development now say that security in infants is not measured by whether they get upset when confronted with a stranger but rather by whether they are able to find solace and be soothed after becoming upset. The baby's capacity to be consoled has been studied in a test called the "strange situation," developed by Mary Ainsworth, a developmental psychologist at the University of Virginia.

Managing the Temperament

The test involves observations of an infant as a stranger enters the room and as the baby's mother leaves for three minutes and then returns. Of particular significance is what the infant does when the mother returns, whether or not the infant cried in her absence.

"The secure babies are able to find solace in their mother's arms when she returns if they were upset when she left, or give her a greeting that shows they're glad she's back if they weren't distressed," Dr. Belsky said. "The insecure ones, though, either stay upset and resist comforting if they were upset by her leaving, or avoid or ignore her if they didn't get upset."

He added, "It's babies' innate level of emotionality that dictates whether a child cries or not. A kid with an emotional temperament may still be secure. Security has to do with how well they manage that predisposition."

Infants who are insecure are unable to find solace, even in their mother's arms, Dr. Belsky's research has found.

The key to emotional security lies in the rapport between parents and their infants, experts say. In a study published in the April issue of Developmental Psychology, conducted with Russell A. Isabella of Utah State University, Dr. Belsky found that certain kinds of interactions between mothers and infants were more likely to make the infants insecure, while others built a sense of security.

The researchers observed infants interacting with their mothers at home when the infants were one month, three months, and nine months of age. Then, at one year, the infants and mothers were observed during the "strange situation" test.

Overstimulating and Intrusive

Mothers of infants who were secure in the strange situation test at one year were found to have been highly responsive to their infants in the earlier home observations. For instance, if the infant made some sound, the mother would make a similar sound back; if the infant cried the mother would soothe it.

But mothers of infants who ignored attempts to console them had behaved differently during the observations at home. Many of these mothers seemed to overwhelm their infants; they were overstimulating and intrusive. They would talk incessantly to their babies, no matter what the baby was doing, crying, looking around, or even sleeping. Oddly, the one thing these mothers responded to the least was the sounds the baby actually made.

Anger or resistance to a mother's attempts to console the infant was associated with interactions at home in which the mothers were relatively indifferent to their baby's needs. These mothers, for instance, tended to make minimal responses to their baby's cries, or to ignore them. Though the studies were done with mothers, experts say the results could equally apply to fathers or other care takers.

"The establishment of a sense of security begins in the first months of life, in the baby's ability to use its parents to calm down," Dr. Greenspan said. "The best sign that a baby is developing security is that the baby and its parents have well-attuned interactions no matter what the emotion, whether it's fear, anger, curiosity, or joy. The baby does something and the parent responds accordingly, and the baby closes the circle by responding to that."

QUESTIONS ABOUT THE READING

1. The article says that the pioneering studies on stranger anxiety were based on comparisons between institutionalized children and children raised in "secure homes." Can you suggest a way in which this research methodology may have been flawed?

2. The Davidson research described here found that some babies have stronger brain-wave activity on the right side of the brain, which appears to be the seat of negative emotions, than on the left. Does this suggest an explanation not only for stranger anxiety but for the three basic temperamental patterns described in your text?

3. Are Jay Belsky's findings concerning mother-child interactions in the "strange situation" consistent or inconsistent with the patterns of secure and insecure attachment described in your text?

4. Compare Dr. Stanley Greenspan's comment about "closing the circle" (at the end of the article) with the "mutual regulation model" described in Box 7-2 of your text. Would you expect that an infant with a depressed mother is more or less likely than an infant with a normal mother to show stranger anxiety?

ANSWER KEY FOR CHAPTER 7

Note: Numbers in parentheses refer to pages in the textbook where answers can be found.

CHAPTER 7 REVIEW

Important Terms for Introduction and Section I

1. reacting (page 240)
2. oral, mouth, feeding (242)
3. id, pleasure (242)
4. pleasure, id (242)
5. ego, reality (242)
6. reality, ego (242)
7. 12-18, 36 (242)
8. basic trust, basic mistrust (243)
9. autonomy, shame and doubt (243)
10. autonomy (243)

Learning Objectives for Section I

1. (pages 241-242)
2. (242-244)
3. (245)
4. (244)

Important Terms for Section II

1. subjective, objective (page 245)
2. awareness (247)
3. image (247)
4. frustration (248)
5. reflex (249)
6. temperament (252)
7. easy (253)
8. difficult (253)
9. slow-to-warm-up (253)
10. socialization (256)
11. imprinting (257)
12. attachment (257)
13. attachment (259)
14. strange (259)
15. secure (259)
16. avoidant (260)
17. ambivalent (260)
18. role (267)
19. stranger (271)
20. separation (271)
21. referencing (273)

Learning Objectives for Section II

1. (pages 246, 247)
2. (247)
3. (248-249)
4. (249-250)
5. (252)
6. (252-253)
7. (253-254)
8. (254-255)
9. (255-256)
10. (256)
11. (257-258)
12. (259-264)
13. (265-268)
14. (268-270)
15. (269, 271)
16. (271-272)
17. (271-273)
18. (273-274)
19. (274-276)

Learning Objectives for Section III

1. (pages 276-277)
2. (277)

Important Term for Section IV

1. expectations (page 278)

Learning Objectives for Section IV

1. (page 278)
2. (279)

CHAPTER 7 QUIZ

Matching—Who's Who

1. f (page 241)
2. h (253)
3. g (265)
4. c (247)
5. e (257)
6. j (258)
7. a (245-246)
8. b (274)
9. i (242)
10. h (253)

Multiple-Choice

1. b (page 242)
2. a (242)
3. c (242, 243, 245)
4. a (243)
5. b (246)
6. d (248)
7. d (249)
8. c (253)
9. d (255-256)
10. b (257-258)
11. a (260)
12. c (261)
13. b (264)
14. d (265-266)
15. c (269, 271)
16. b (272-273)
17. d (273-274)
18. d (274)
19. b (275-276)
20. a (278)

True or False?

1. T (page 245)
2. T (242)
3. F—According to Erikson, although trust predominates in a healthy personality, some degree of mistrust is necessary for children to learn to protect themselves. (243)
4. F—Experience affects emotional development; for example, some abused infants show fear several months earlier than other babies do. (247)
5. T (247)
6. F—Research suggests that babies whose cries bring relief gain confidence in their ability to communicate and eventually cry less than other babies. (249)
7. T (250)
8. T (252)
9. F—Research has shown that temperament is inborn and largely hereditary, though it can be affected to some degree by experience. (253)
10. F—A difficult child is one who exhibits a specific temperamental pattern. Although difficult children have a greater tendency than other children to develop behavior problems, many make a healthy adjustment. The key factor is "goodness of fit" between the child's temperament and the demands made on the child. (254-255)
11. F—Current research has not demonstrated that contact between mothers and their infants in the

first hours after birth has any long-term effects on bonding. (257)

12. F—An essential part of human personality development appears to be an infant's attachment to a mother figure, who may be any primary caregiver. (259)

13. T (262)

14. T (263)

15. F—Studies of the relationship between mothers' employment and babies' security of attachment are inconclusive, suggesting that other factors must be taken into account. (264)

16. T (267)

17. F—Firstborn and only children tend to be higher scholastic achievers than middle or younger children. (268)

18. F—While sibling rivalry is common, early sibling relationships are characterized by a complex variety of contradictory emotions, both positive and negative. (269-271)

19. F—Research suggests that the most significant problem for institutionalized children is frequent changes in caregivers, which prevent close attachment to a specific person. (275)

20. F—Babies become less sociable around the age of 1 year, when they start to walk; their interest at that age becomes more focused on mastering physical coordination. (277)

PHYSICAL DEVELOPMENT IN EARLY CHILDHOOD

OVERVIEW

Chapter 8 covers physical development in the 3 years following infancy and toddlerhood. In this chapter, the authors:

■ Describe children's physical growth and change between ages 3 and 6

■ Point out health issues that arise during these predominantly healthy years

■ Identify normal sleep patterns and common sleep problems

■ Trace the development of motor coordination and artistic skill

■ Discuss causes and effects of child abuse and neglect and methods of prevention and treatment

CHAPTER 8 REVIEW

Section I Physical Growth and Change

FRAMEWORK FOR SECTION I

A. Appearance, Height, and Weight
B. Structural and Systemic Changes
C. Nutrition

LEARNING OBJECTIVES FOR SECTION I

After reading and reviewing this section of Chapter 8, you should be able to do the following.

1. Describe how boys and girls change in appearance, height, and weight between ages 3 and 6.

2. Describe structural and systemic changes during this period.

3. Summarize nutritional needs in early childhood.

Section II Health

FRAMEWORK FOR SECTION II

A. Health Problems
    1. Minor Illnesses
    2. Major Illnesses
    3. Accidents
    4. The Environment and Health Problems
        a. Exposure to Other Children
        b. Stress
            (1) Stressful Life Events
            (2) Emotional Stress: Suicide
        c. Poverty and Hunger
B. Dental Health
    1. Preventive Care
    2. Thumb-Sucking

LEARNING OBJECTIVES FOR SECTION II

After reading and reviewing this section of Chapter 8, you should be able to do the following.

1. Explain the frequency of minor respiratory illnesses among young children.

2. Discuss current trends in the incidence of contagious childhood diseases in the United States and in developing countries.

3. State three ways in which experiencing minor illness may benefit young children.

4. Name the two most common sites of accidents fatal to young children, and discuss the effectiveness of laws aimed at preventing such accidents.

5. Discuss three major factors that affect young children's health.

6. Explain the importance of dental care in early childhood and list guidelines for effective preventive care, including treatment of thumb-sucking.

Section III   Sleep: Patterns and Problems

FRAMEWORK FOR SECTION III

A. Normal Sleep Behavior
B. Problems with Sleep
   1. Bedtime Struggles
   2. Night Terrors and Nightmares
   3. Sleepwalking and Sleeptalking
   4. Nighttime Fears
   5. Bed-Wetting

IMPORTANT TERMS FOR SECTION III

Completion: Fill in the blanks to complete the definitions of key terms for this section of Chapter 8.

1. _____ **object:** Object—commonly a soft, cuddly one—used repeatedly by a child as a bedtime companion.

2. _____: Common sleep disorder of childhood in which a child suddenly awakens from a deep sleep in a state of panic.

3. _____: Frightening dream, occurring toward morning and often vividly recalled.

4. enuresis: _____.

LEARNING OBJECTIVES FOR SECTION III

After reading and reviewing this section of Chapter 8, you should be able to do the following.

1. Describe normal sleep behavior of preschoolers and state how it differs from that of infants and toddlers.

2. List at least three factors that seem to be associated with bedtime struggles.

3. Distinguish between night terrors and nightmares.

4. Identify necessary and effective treatments for sleepwalking, sleeptalking, and nighttime fears.

5. Identify factors that may be involved in bed-wetting and list effective treatments.

Section IV Motor Development

FRAMEWORK FOR SECTION IV

A. Motor Skills
B. Artistic Development

IMPORTANT TERMS FOR SECTION IV

Completion: Fill in the blanks to complete the definitions of key terms for this section of Chapter 8.

1. **scribble:** Early form of drawing (appearing by age 2) in which the chief distinctions are the nature and placement of the _____.

2. **shape stage:** Period in artistic development (at about age _____) when children begin drawing basic shapes—circles, squares, triangles, crosses, X's, and odd forms.

3. _____ **stage:** Period in artistic development (commonly at age 3) in which children combine basic shapes into more complex patterns.

4. **pictorial stage:** Period of artistic development (between ages 4 and 5) in which drawing becomes less abstract and more _____.

LEARNING OBJECTIVES FOR SECTION IV

After reading and reviewing this section of Chapter 8, you should be able to do the following.

1. Outline the development of preschool boys' and girls' increasingly complex large-muscle skills, and state what permits that development.

2. Summarize gender differences in young children's strength, musculature, and motor skills.

3. Give examples of 3-, 4-, and 5-year-olds' growing eye-hand and small-muscle coordination.

4. Outline four stages in young children's drawing, and suggest how adults can best encourage children's artistic development.

Section V   Child Abuse and Neglect

FRAMEWORK FOR SECTION V

A. Causes of Abuse and Neglect
   1. Abusers and Neglecters
   2. Victims
   3. Families
   4. Communities
   5. Cultures
B. Long-Term Effects of Abuse and Neglect
C. Helping Families in Trouble or at Risk
   1. Prevention
   2. Help for the Abused and Their Families

IMPORTANT TERMS FOR SECTION V

Completion: Fill in the blanks to complete the definitions of key terms for this section of Chapter 8.

1. **child _____:** Maltreatment of children involving physical or psychological injury.

2. **_____ syndrome:** Syndrome of child abuse and neglect first identified in 1962.

3. **_____:** Sexual contact between a child and an older person.

4. **_____:** Withholding of adequate care, usually referring to such physical care as food, clothing and supervision.

5. **_____ failure to thrive:** Emotional neglect resulting in a baby's failure to grow and gain weight at home despite adequate nutrition.

LEARNING OBJECTIVES FOR SECTION V

After reading and reviewing this section of Chapter 8, you should be able to do the following.

1. Distinguish between, and give examples of, three forms of maltreatment of children.

2. Compare and contrast typical characteristics of abusers and neglecters.

3. Describe characteristics of a typical abuse victim and a typical abusive family.

4. State ways in which community and culture can contribute to abuse.

5. Discuss the long-term outlook for victims of abuse or neglect.

6. Describe effective ways of preventing or stopping abuse and neglect.

CHAPTER 8 QUIZ

Matching—Numbers: Match each item at the left with the correct number in the right-hand column.

1. Approximate percentage of 5-year-old boys who are bed-wetters _____   3

2. Age at which all primary teeth are normally present _____   4

3. Approximate percentage of children between the ages of 3 and 8 who suffer from night
   terrors or nightmares _____   5

4. Age at which permanent teeth generally begin to appear_____   6

5. Approximate percentage of Americans who cannot maintain an adequate standard of
   living _____   7

6. Number of scribble patterns a 2-year-old typically can draw _____   10

7. Approximate percentage of children between the ages of 5 and 12 who sleepwalk at   15
   least once _____

8. Age at which a child typically can hop four to six steps on one foot _____   17

9. Approximate percentage of children who are left-handed _____   20

10. Age at which a child typically can walk downstairs unaided, alternating feet _____   25

Multiple-Choice: Circle the choice that best completes or answers each item.

1. Which of the following would *not* be a normal change after age 3?
   a. faster growth rate
   b. more slender appearance
   c. increased stamina
   d. decreased appetite

2. Which of the following is *not* among suggestions that, according to your text, may help in dealing with young children who are finicky eaters?
   a. serving finger foods
   b. introducing new foods one at a time
   c. serving casseroles to "hide" rejected foods
   d. giving the child a choice of foods

3. The leading cause of death in childhood in the United States is
   a. contagious diseases
   b. respiratory illnesses
   c. accidents
   d. none of the above

4. It has been found that children in high-quality day care tend to be healthier than children raised at home because of
   a. early detection and treatment of illness
   b. the presence of trained, state-certified personnel
   c. development of immunities as a result of early infections
   d. all of the above

5. Children in poor families are at high risk of
   a. hearing loss
   b. lead poisoning
   c. learning disabilities
   d. all of the above

6. Which of the following is (are) normal for preschoolers?
   a. prolonged bedtime struggles
   b. transitional objects
   c. frequent nightmares
   d. enuresis

7. Night terrors differ from nightmares in that night terrors
   a. usually occur within 1 hour after falling asleep
   b. are often remembered vividly
   c. are experienced more by girls than boys
   d. all of the above

8. According to the text, how can bed-wetting be treated?
   a. Do nothing unless the child sees it as a problem.
   b. Wake a child who begins to urinate.
   c. Administer antidepressant drugs.
   d. all of the above

9. Children between the ages of 3 and 6 can perform increasingly complex motor behaviors because their
   a. brain stem is better developed
   b. muscles, bones, and lungs are stronger
   c. reflexes are quicker
   d. all of the above

10. According to Kellogg, a child's purpose in drawing shapes and designs is to
    a. represent what he or she sees
    b. develop eye-hand coordination
    c. produce aesthetic combinations
    d. please parents and teachers

11. More than 90 percent of child abuse occurs
    a. in day care centers
    b. at home
    c. in parks or other secluded places
    d. in strangers' cars

12. Victims of child abuse are likely to
    a. be hyperactive
    b. be mentally retarded
    c. have been low-birthweight babies
    d. all of the above

13. Which of the following is *not* characteristic of abusive parents?
    a. marital problems and physical fighting
    b. disorganized household
    c. large number of children closely spaced
    d. emotional withdrawal from spouse and children

14. Approximately what proportion of abused children grow up to become abusers themselves?
    a. less than 1 percent
    b. one-third
    c. half
    d. more than 90 percent

15. According to your text, which of the following is *not* generally recommended as a way to stop or prevent child abuse?
    a. separating children from abusive parents
    b. treating abusers as criminal offenders
    c. relieving parents who feel overburdened
    d. teaching parents how to manage their children's behavior

True or False? In the blank following each item, write T (for *true*) or F (for *false*). In the space below each item, if the statement is false, rewrite it to make it true.

1. One way to get a child to eat heartily is to serve a meal immediately after the child has engaged in active play. _____

2. In early childhood, the lungs are not yet fully developed. _____

3. The incidence of contagious childhood diseases has declined steadily since the introduction of immunizations. _____

4. Care of "baby teeth" does not affect dental health because they are not permanent. _____

5. Thumb-sucking that continues past age 6 seems to result from emotional disturbance and should be treated with psychological counseling. _____

6. Enuresis runs in families. _____

7. Girls tend to be more adept than boys at tasks involving small-muscle coordination. _____

8. According to Rhoda Kellogg, adults should encourage children when they begin to draw more recognizable pictures. _____

9. It is possible for a baby to fail to grow and gain weight, despite adequate nutrition. _____

10. Most child abusers have psychotic or malicious personalities. _____

11. A neglectful mother is likely to have had complications during pregnancy. _____

12. Abusive parents are likely to be less sociable than normal parents. _____

13. Approval of spanking as punishment may be related to the incidence of child abuse. _____

14. Children who are sexually abused are likely to be raped or sexually assaulted as adults. _____

15. Apart from physical evidence of sexual abuse, it has few recognizable signs. _____

TOPICS FOR THOUGHT AND DISCUSSION

1. According to your text, it is better to reward a bed-wetter for staying dry at night than to punish the child for bed-wetting. Does that recommendation reflect learning theory as described in Chapter 1 of your text? Would an advocate of the psychoanalytic perspective consider either of these methods effective? Why or why not?

2. In Box 8-2, the authors present one clinician's view that minor childhood illnesses are beneficial in that they promote self-awareness, empathy, and understanding of language. Did you find this view surprising? Convincing?

3. How would you expect differences in preschool boys' and girls' motor development to affect the extent to which, and the ways in which, they play with each other?

4. Recalling cases of child abuse that have been in the news, in what ways do you think the "cycle of abuse" is perpetuated? Who is responsible? How can the cycle be broken?

CHAPTER 8 READING

INTRODUCTION

How do babies who open their mouths so eagerly for every morsel later become such picky eaters? This is a question many exasperated parents ask themselves. Through a cognitive mapping technique, Cheryl Achterberg, Ph.D., assistant professor of nutrition at Pennsylvania State University, has come up with some answers. As in many other areas of a child's world, her answers point up the link between intellectual and physical development—in this instance, between cognitive processes and food choices.

"The Yum-Yuck Syndrome: Why Jenny Won't Eat," by Katherine Fritz, is reprinted from the May 1987 issue of *Human Development Research at Penn State.*

The Yum-Yuck Syndrome: Why Jenny Won't Eat

by Katherine Fritz

Every parent is familiar with the problem: the child who won't eat dinner but is all too eager for dessert.

How do children decide what they'll eat and what they won't, what they like and what they don't? Exasperated parents have asked the question for decades, but Penn State nutrition researcher Cheryl Achterberg says children may not be as haphazard in their choices as they seem. "Children's eating patterns may not be rational, but they certainly aren't random," she says.

Take the case of Jenny, a 4-year-old girl whose growth lagged behind that of her peers because her parents couldn't get her to eat. Through intensive interviewing, Achterberg uncovered a pattern: Jenny hated foods that were brown (meat, gravy, and potatoes, for example) and liked foods that were pink or red (strawberries and tomatoes). Achterberg's advice to the relieved parents: Lay off the hamburger, load up on the spaghetti with tomato sauce.

"I wish they could all be that simple," says Achterberg of the case, part of an earlier study of failure-to-thrive children.

The development of food preferences and eating patterns is a focal point of Achterberg's research. In particular, Achterberg tries to understand the *meanings* that people attach to food—a concept quite different from their *knowledge* about food. "To what extent do the meanings people give to food influence their food choices?" Achterberg asks. "And how does meaning develop? It has something to do with how the brain organizes information. You can know quite a few facts about nutrition, but if they're not connected to other pieces of information, they won't be very meaningful."

The process Achterberg used to understand Jenny's food preferences—first conducting a series of interviews, supplemented by picture cards of different foods, then analyzing the information with a technique called cognitive mapping—enabled her to begin isolating the thinking processes involved in making food choices.

Children seem to attach meaning to food along what Achterberg calls a "yum-yuck dichotomy." The label comes from what one preschooler told her: Food is good if he likes it (yum), and not good if he doesn't like it (yuck). As children get older, their frameworks become more elaborate. "By the time children are 5 or 6," Achterberg says, "most will tell you that foods can be good, bad, or in between. The dichotomy becomes a continuum."

For a study of children's food and nutrition concepts, Achterberg interviewed 3- to 5-year-olds and their parents in a small rural community in upstate New York. The families all were two-parent families, and about half of the parents had had some post-high school education. Achterberg talked first to the children, then to their parents, to see to what extent the views of the two groups were consistent. "That gives us clues about how much the children's views are influenced by their parents, as opposed to school, or television, or some other source."

Achterberg deliberately chose a qualitative rather than quantitative approach for the study. She limited the sample to 27 people (nine families) and conducted more than 80 in-depth interviews—sometimes as many as eight interviews with each child. The research produced more than 500 pages of transcripts.

"We'd start by asking a general, open-ended question about what makes a food good or bad," Achterberg explains. "Then we'd just let the child talk." The interviewer wouldn't direct the conversation except to ask an occasional question for clarification or to ask the child for an example. "After the child had exhausted everything he or she had to say on the subject," says Achterberg, "then we'd go back and pick up another thread. We might say, 'You also said that a food was bad if it had a funny feel to it. Tell me more about that.'"

From the information gathered in interviews, Achterberg would then draw up a cognitive map—a complex spaghetti-like web of connections that approximated the way each child or parent viewed food and nutrition.

She had assumed that parents and children generally would hold the same meanings and concepts about food. But she discovered that the amount of shared meaning varied from one family to the next and from one aspect of nutrition to another, often depending on how much the subject was discussed in that household. "A child might be able to tell you a lot about what makes a food bad for you," she says,

"but very little about what makes a food good for you." Most children, for instance, believed "sugar is bad for you." And one young boy, who was told coffee was bad for children but not why, thought it was because it had sugar. "He'd seen his parents put sugar in their coffee and figured that was what made it bad," Achterberg says. "He didn't know anything about caffeine. Yet his reasoning was sound."

Achterberg often found discrepancies in the meanings that parents and children attached to vitamins. In a society unfamiliar with scurvy, rickets and pellagra, she suspects, vitamins simply aren't discussed. Most of the parents in the study believed that vitamins were "good for you," but didn't understand why. It's no wonder, then, that the children knew even less about vitamins. Says Achterberg, "One child could only say 'vitamins' was a neat word but she didn't know it.

"Vitamins are a concept that not a lot of people attach meaning to. So saying, 'Eat this because it has vitamins,' would not be a good way to get a child to eat."

Psychological, family and social factors all play a role in the meanings attached to food. And notions like "Real men don't eat quiche" apparently start early, Achterberg found. "The children would tell me that soup is children's food, that salads and vegetables are for moms, and steak is for strong men."

Achterberg is now extending the cognitive-mapping approach beyond children to other groups. Several of her graduate students are using the approach to study meanings in sports nutrition; their project involves interviews with gymnasts, long-distance runners, and YMCA coaches. As with the preschoolers, the interviewer starts with a broad question: How does diet affect athletic performance? "We get lots of answers that focus on pre-event meals," Achterberg says. "What to eat before a big game, what happens if you eat too soon before the event. They aren't able to say nearly as much about other aspects of sports nutrition." Achterberg also plans to launch further projects, including one about bulimia and other eating disorders, in which food takes on particularly special meanings.

Ultimately, Achterberg believes her research can lead to better ways of teaching nutrition. "Approaches to nutrition education are often based on rationality," she says. "The assumption has been that the more you know, the more rational your food choices will be. But people don't eat for rational reasons.

"By learning what meanings people attach to food, we can find out where misunderstandings arise. And if we can come to an understanding of why people eat as they do, and why they think about and feel towards food as they do, we wiil have a powerful guide for creating future nutrition education programs."

QUESTIONS ABOUT THE READING

1. Dr. Achterberg is quoted as saying, "Children's eating patterns may not be rational, but they certainly aren't random." On the basis of the examples given in the article, what do you think she meant by this statement?

2. Dr. Achterberg's advice to parents of a preschooler who hated brown foods and liked red ones was to "lay off the hamburger, load up on the spaghetti with tomato sauce." Is this advice consistent with the suggestions given by the authors of your text in Box 8-1? Why or why not? Do you agree with this advice?

3. Dr. Achterberg distinguishes between people's *knowledge* about foods and the *meanings* they attach to them. What is the difference between acquiring knowledge and attaching meaning? Why might different children attach different meanings to the same food?

4. The article states that Dr. Achterberg deliberately chose a qualitative rather than quantitative approach for her study of young children's concepts of foods and nutrition. Which of the research methods described in Chapter 1 did she use? Why do you think she chose this method? Does it appear to have met the purposes of the research? On the basis of the comments by the authors of your text in Chapter 1, what drawbacks does this method have?

5. Dr. Achterberg expressed the hope that her research might aid in creating effective nutrition education programs. On the basis of the findings described in this article, what advice would you give parents who want to teach their children to eat nutritiously?

ANSWER KEY FOR CHAPTER 8

Note: Numbers in parentheses refer to pages in the textbook where answers can be found.

CHAPTER 8 REVIEW

Learning Objectives for Section I

1. (page 287)
2. (287)
3. (288-289)

Learning Objectives for Section II

1. (page 289)
2. (289-290, 291)
3. (290)
4. (290-292)
5. (292-295)
6. (295-296)

Important Terms for Section III

1. transitional (page 297)
2. night terror (298)
3. nightmare (298)
4. bed-wetting (299)

Learning Objectives for Section III

1. (page 297)
2. (297-298)
3. (298)
4. (298-299)
5. (299)

Important Terms for Section IV

1. line (page 302)
2. 3 (302)
3. design (302)
4. representational (302)

Learning Objectives for Section IV

1. (page 300)
2. (301)
3. (301)
4. (301-303)

Important Terms for Section V

1. abuse (page 303)
2. battered child (303)
3. sexual abuse (303)
4. neglect (303)
5. nonorganic (303)

Learning Objectives for Section V

1. (pages 303-304)
2. (304)
3. (305)
4. (305-306)
5. (306)
6. (306-308)

CHAPTER 8 QUIZ

Matching—Numbers

1. 7 (page 299)
2. 3 (295)
3. 25 (298)
4. 6 (295)
5. 20 (294)
6. 17 (302)
7. 15 (298)
8. 4 (301)
9. 10 (301)
10. 5 (301)

Multiple-Choice

1. a (pages 287-289)
2. c (288)
3. c (290)
4. a (293)
5. d (295)
6. b (297-299)
7. a (298)
8. d (299)
9. b (300)
10. c (302)
11. b (304)
12. d (305)
13. d (305)
14. b (306)
15. a (306-308)

True or False?

1. F—A quiet period before a meal is advisable because fatigue or overexcitement can lead to eating problems. (page 288)
2. T (289)
3. F—The incidence of contagious childhood diseases has declined dramatically as a result of immunization, but there are cyclical upsurges when parents, believing that certain diseases have been eliminated, fail to have their children immunized. (289-290)
4. F—Baby teeth affect jaw development, and lifelong dental habits may be set in early childhood. (295)
5. F—Prolonged thumb-sucking seems to be merely a habit and is most effectively treated with a dental appliance. (296)
6. T (299)
7. T (301)
8. F—Adults should let children draw what they like without imposing suggestions; pressure to portray reality leads children to move away from a concern with form and design and often to lose interest in art. (302-303)
9. T (303)
10. F—More than 90 percent of child abusers are not psychotic; and far from being malicious, they often hate themselves for what they do but cannot control themselves. (304)
11. T (304)
12. T (305)
13. T (305-306)
14. T (306)
15. F—Any extreme change in a young child's behavior can be a sign of sexual abuse. (307)

INTELLECTUAL DEVELOPMENT IN EARLY CHILDHOOD

OVERVIEW

Chapter 9 focuses on the rapid development of intellectual skills during the preschool years. In this chapter, the authors:

- Explain how the three major approaches to intellectual development view the advances of early childhood

- Explore how young children think and remember

- Uncover research showing that young children are more competent than psychologists once believed

- Examine personality and social factors—including the family, day care, preschool, and kindergarten—that influence intellectual achievement

- Trace the development of language in early childhood

CHAPTER 9 REVIEW

Section I   Approaches to Intellectual Development

FRAMEWORK FOR SECTION 1

A. Piagetian Approach: The Preoperational Stage
  1. Characteristics of the Preoperational Stage
    a. The Symbolic Function
      (1) Symbols and Signs
      (2) Manifestations of the Symbolic Function
      (3) Development of the Symbolic Function
    b. Achievements of Preoperational Thought
      (1) Understanding of Identities
      (2) Understanding of Functions
    c. Limitations of Preoperational Thought
      (1) Egocentrism
      (2) Centration
      (3) Irreversibility
      (4) Focus on States Rather Than Transformations
      (5) Transductive Reasoning
  2. Evaluating Piaget's Theory: Did Piaget Understand Children's Abilities?
    a. Can Young Children Understand Cause and Effect?
    b. How Egocentric Are Young Children?
    c. How Well Can Young Children Classify?
      (1) Piaget's Stages of Classification
      (2) Recent Research
    d. Can Cognitive Abilities Be Accelerated?
B. Information-Processing Approach: Development of Memory in Early Childhood
  1. Recognition and Recall
  2. Autobiographical Memory
  3. Influences on Children's Memory
    a. General Knowledge
    b. Social Interactions
C. Psychometric Approach: Measuring Intelligence in Early Childhood
  1. Stanford-Binet Intelligence Scale
  2. Wechsler Preschool and Primary Scale of Intelligence (WPPSI)

IMPORTANT TERMS FOR SECTION I

Completion: Fill in the blanks to complete the definitions of key terms for this section of Chapter 9.

1. **preoperational stage:** In Piaget's theory, the second major period of cognitive development (approximately age 2 to age 7), in which children are able to think in _____ but are limited by their inability to use _____.

2. _____: Ability, described by Piaget, to use mental representation, shown in language, symbolic play, and deferred imitation.

3. **symbol:** In Piaget's terminology, a personal mental representation of a(n) _____ experience.

4. **sign:** In Piaget's terminology, a conventional mental representation—such as a word—of a(n) _____.

5. **signifier:** Term used by Piaget for _____ and _____.

6. _____: Term used by Piaget for the real-world object or event represented by a signifier.

7. _____ **imitation:** Ability to observe an action and imitate it after a passage of time.

8. **symbolic play:** Play in which a(n) _____ stands for something else.

9. **language:** Communication system that uses _____ and _____.

10. _____: As used by Piaget, a child's inability to consider another person's point of view.

11. _____: In Piaget's terminology, to think about one aspect of a situation while neglecting others.

12. _____: In Piaget's terminology, to think simultaneously about several aspects of a situation.

13. **conservation:** Piaget's term for awareness that two stimuli which are equal (in length, weight, or amount, for example) remain equal in the face of _____ alteration, so long as nothing has been added to or taken away from either stimulus.

14. _____: Reasoning that shows a particular conclusion to be implied by a general premise.

15. _____: Reasoning which asserts that a general rule can be made on the basis of one or more particular examples.

16. **transduction:** In Piaget's terminology, a child's method of thinking about two or more experiences without relying on abstract _____ .

17. _____: Type of memory that enables a person to correctly identify a stimulus as something previously known.

18. _____: Ability to reproduce material from memory.

19. _____ **memory:** Memory of specific events in one's own life.

20. **Stanford-Binet Intelligence Scale:** Individual intelligence test that includes verbal, nonverbal, _____ , and _____ items.

21. **Wechsler Preschool and Primary Scale of Intelligence (WPPSI):** Individual intelligence test for use with preschool children that includes separate _____ and _____ subtests.

LEARNING OBJECTIVES FOR SECTION I

After reading and reviewing this section of Chapter 9, you should be able to do the following.

1. Summarize what Piaget observed to be the chief difference between children's intellectual abilities at the sensorimotor stage, preoperational stage, and concrete operations stage.

2. Explain the significance of the symbolic function, name three ways in which young children display it, and give an example of each.

3. Define and give an example of each of the following preoperational achievements: understanding of identities and understanding of functions.

4. Give examples of each of the following limitations Piaget observed in preoperational thought: egocentrism, centration, irreversibility, focus on states rather than transformations, transductive reasoning.

5. Explain why Piaget may have underestimated children's thought processes, and name three abilities he seems to have underestimated, according to newer research.

6. Explain under what circumstances cognitive abilities can be accelerated by training.

7. Name two limitations on young children's memory.

8. Distinguish between recognition and recall, and explain why recall is particularly difficult for young children.

9. State at least three characteristics of young children's memory of events in their lives.

10. Identify two important factors in young children's ability to remember.

11. Explain why psychometric tests are more reliable for 4-year-olds than for infants.

12. Name and describe two psychometric intelligence tests used with young children.

Section II Factors in Intellectual Development

FRAMEWORK FOR SECTION II

A. How Does Personality Influence Intellectual Development?
B. How Do Parents Influence Intellectual Development?
  1. The Home Environment
  2. The Father's Role
C. Day Care and Schooling in Early Childhood
  1. Day Care
    a. What Is Good Day Care?
    b. What Are the Benefits of Good Day Care?
  2. Preschool
    a. How Good Preschools Foster Development
    b. The Montessori Method
    c. Compensatory Preschools
      (1) Project Head Start
        (a) Goals of Head Start Programs
        (b) Components of Head Start Programs
      (2) Benefits of Compensatory Programs
        (a) Short-Term Benefits
        (b) Long-Term Benefits
  3. Kindergarten
  4. Educational Television

IMPORTANT TERMS FOR SECTION II

Completion: Fill in the blanks to complete the definitions of key terms for this section of Chapter 9.

1. _____: Program designed to care for young children outside the home.

2. **preschool:** Program designed to provide _____ experiences for young children.

3. **kindergarten:** Traditional introduction to school for 5-year-olds, an optional year of transition between the relative freedom of home or preschool and the _____ of formal schooling.

4. **Project** _____: Compensatory preschool educational program begun in 1965.

LEARNING OBJECTIVES FOR SECTION II

After reading and reviewing this section of Chapter 9, you should be able to do the following.

1. State the relationship between young children's social-emotional and intellectual functioning.

2. Discuss how parents and the home environment influence young children's intellectual development.

3. Describe recent trends in day care, preschool, and kindergarten.

4. Identify two benefits of good day care, and list at least five criteria for choosing a day care center.

5. List ways in which a good preschool can foster children's development, and describe pros and cons of academically oriented preschools.

6. Describe the principal features of the Montessori method.

7. State the goals of compensatory preschool programs, and assess the benefits of Project Head Start.

8. Describe pros and cons of full-day kindergarten.

9. Summarize outcomes of watching *Sesame Street*, and list suggestions for guiding children's television viewing.

Section III Language in Early Childhood

FRAMEWORK FOR SECTION III

A. Words, Sentences, and Grammar
B. Private Speech
C. Social Speech

IMPORTANT TERMS FOR SECTION III

Completion: Fill in the blanks to complete the definitions of key terms for this section of Chapter 9.

1. _____ **speech:** Talking aloud to oneself with no intent to communicate with anyone else.

2. _____ **speech:** Speech intended to be understood by a listener.

LEARNING OBJECTIVES FOR SECTION III

After reading and reviewing this section of Chapter 9, you should be able to do the following.

1. Trace the development of language ability in early childhood.

2. Discuss varying views of the function and value of private speech, list seven types of private speech, and give an example of each type.

3. Outline four stages in the development of social speech, give examples of each, and discuss the relative prevalence of egocentric and social speech in young children.

CHAPTER 9 QUIZ

Matching—Terms and Situations: Match each of the situations described in the left-hand column with the applicable term in the right-hand column.

1. Sherry knows that all babies have mothers. She knows that Stacy is a baby. Therefore, she concludes that Stacy has a mother. _____

2. Andy saw his parents leave for the hospital and saw them bring his baby brother home for the first time. He thinks that they went to the hospital and picked out a baby. _____

3. Scott puts on a lion costume for Halloween. His baby sister cries when she sees him. "Don't worry; I'm still Scott," he says. _____

4. Amy is playing follow-the-leader with her father. Amy is the leader. She crawls under a chair that is too low for him. "C'mon, Daddy!" she calls. _____

5. Billy knows that robins, ducks, and blue jays have wings. He knows that robins, ducks, and blue jays are birds. Therefore he assumes that all birds have wings. _____

6. Ann and her older sister Maria are having lunch. Their mother pours a mug of soup for each. Although the two portions are equal, Maria's mug is taller and narrower than Ann's. "She got more," Ann complains. "Hers is bigger." _____

7. Charles wore his raincoat to preschool one day. It rained. The next day he refused to wear his raincoat. "I don't want it to rain," he explained. _____

8. Rita sees her mother working at a computer. The next day, while playing "office," she "types" on a toy typewriter. _____

9. Jo breaks a ball of clay into two pieces. "Now I have more clay," she says. Her older sister smiles: "If you put it back together, it'll be the same as before." But Jo insists: "No, it's more." _____

10. Jenny has learned that when she drops a slice of bread into the toaster, toast soon pops out. _____

a. deferred imitation

b. understanding of identities

c. understanding of functions

d. egocentrism

e. centration

f. irreversibility

g. focus on states rather than transformation

h. transduction

i. induction

j. deduction

Multiple-Choice: Circle the choice that best completes or answers each item.

1. Most children enter Piaget's preoperational stage at about age
   a. 2
   b. 2½
   c. 3
   d. 4

2. The symbolic function is characterized by
   a. sensory cues
   b. mental representations
   c. abstract thinking
   d. all of the above

3. Which of the folllowing is *not* a manifestation of the symbolic function?
   a. language
   b. deferred imitation
   c. invisible imitation
   d. symbolic play

4. Which of the following is *not* a limitation of preoperational thought identified by Piaget?
   a. egocentrism
   b. focus on states rather than transformations
   c. irreversibility
   d. selective memory

5. According to Piaget, children at the preoperational stage tend to
   a. conserve
   b. decenter
   c. centrate
   d. none of the above

6. Transductive reasoning involves
   a. deduction
   b. induction
   c. logic
   d. none of the above

7. Research indicates that Piaget underestimated preoperational children's ability to
   a. understand causality
   b. distinguish appearance from reality
   c. both a and b
   d. neither a nor b

8. The "naming explosion" and two-category grouping appear to occur at about age
   a. 15 months
   b. 18 months
   c. 2 years
   d. 2½ years

9. Ten beads are arranged in a circle. If they are rearranged in a row, they will be the same 10 beads. This is an example of the principle(s) of
   a. identity
   b. reversibility
   c. compensation
   d. all of the above

10. Early autobiographical memories
    a. typically begin before 3 years of age
    b. are longer-lasting than later memories
    c. are rarely deliberate
    d. all of the above

11. Children's ability to recall improves between ages 2 and 5 because they
    a. gain general knowledge
    b. learn memory strategies
    c. make more effort to remember
    d. all of the above

12. The revised version of the Stanford-Binet Intelligence Scale, prepared in 1985, primarily emphasizes
    a. IQ as an overall measure of intelligence
    b. verbal items
    c. nonverbal items
    d. developed abilities

13. The Home Observation for Measurement of the Environment assesses
    a. mothers' involvement in children's play
    b. how fathers talk to children
    c. how siblings play together
    d. all of the above

14. The proportion of working mothers with children under 6 is
    a. 10 percent
    b. 25 percent
    c. 35 percent
    d. 50 percent

15. Which of the following is *not* necessarily a criterion for good day care?
    a. small groups of children
    b. college-educated caregivers
    c. child-related training of caregivers
    d. sensitivity to children's needs

16. Preschools in the United States serve approximately how many children?
    a. 500,000
    b. 1 million
    c. 2.5 million
    d. 5 million

17. High school students from a deprived background who participated in Project Head Start were more likely than youngsters from similar backgrounds who did not participate to
    a. show permanent gains in IQ
    b. stay in school
    c. do as well in school as average middle-class children
    d. all of the above

18. A typical preschooler watches how many hours of television per day?
    a. less than 2
    b. 3 to 5
    c. about 7
    d. 8 or more

19. Overgeneralization of linguistic rules is a sign of
    a. development of social speech
    b. too much correction by adults
    c. linguistic progress
    d. an academic preschool background

20. Which of the following viewed private speech as inappropriate for young children?
    a. Watson
    b. Piaget
    c. Vygotsky
    d. Kohlberg

True or False? In the blank following each item, write T (for *true*) or F (for *false*). In the space below each item, if the statement is false, rewrite it to make it true.

1. Children first think almost entirely in signs. _____

2. During the preoperational stage, it is common for a child to believe that growth since infancy has made him or her a different person. _____

3. Egocentrism, for Piaget, means selfishness. _____

4. Children at the preoperational stage do not understand that water poured from a pitcher into a glass can be restored to its original state by pouring it back into the pitcher. _____

5. Not until age 7 or 8, according to Piaget, can children classify items into classes and subclasses, using two criteria. _____

6. When a child is on the verge of grasping a new concept, training may accelerate that process. _____

7. A young child recalls items better when they are related to each other. _____

8. The Stanford-Binet Intelligence Scale and the Wechsler Preschool and Primary Scale of Intelligence are group tests often administered in early childhood. _____

9. Children who were happy and well adjusted in preschool tend to do better on first-grade IQ tests than children whose preschool social and emotional adjustment was poor. _____

10. Fathers have more influence on daughters' intellectual development than on sons'. _____

11. Children's language development can be positively affected by high quality day care. _____

12. Children who attend academically oriented preschools tend to excel throughout their school careers. _____

13. The Montessori curriculum is based on a carefully planned environment. _____

14. David Elkind blames parents for pushing children to accelerate their development. __

15. Project Head Start is a compensatory preschool program for poor minority children. _____

16. The neediest children in Project Head Start make the greatest short-term intellectual gains. _____

17. The youngest children in a kindergarten class do less well than the oldest. _____

18. *Sesame Street*, though intended as an educational program, seems to have only entertainment value. _____

19. Private speech accounts for as much as 60 percent of what children say, and the most sociable children tend to use it most. _____

20. Recent research has confirmed Piaget's view that most preschool speech is egocentric. _____

TOPICS FOR THOUGHT AND DISCUSSION

1. Piaget apparently underestimated children's thought processes because he overestimated their language abilities. Have you ever given an incorrect answer to a question you could have answered correctly if the question had been phrased in terms you could understand? What does this sort of experience suggest for teachers and other adults who deal with young children?

2. Freud asked what happens to block early memories; Nelson asked what happens to make early memories endure. On the basis of this example, to what extent do the questions researchers start out with shape the results?

3. Some people believe that it is beneficial to encourage young children to memorize poems or other literary passages. On the basis of the information in this chapter of your text, how would you react to such a practice? What suggestions would you make for helping to develop young children's memory?

4. Considering the significance of parents' influence on intellectual development, what differences would you expect to find between the development of a child raised on a kibbutz in Israel and that of a child raised in a nuclear family? Why do you think there has been a growing emphasis on the role of the family in child rearing on the kibbutz?

5. The authors of your text state that the negative effects of a father's absence from the home may diminish now that single-parent families are common. Does this statement suggest that the significance of the father's role is culturally rather than biologically determined? Do you agree?

6. Why does David Elkind consider it unwise for parents to overestimate their influence on their children's success? Why does Elkind caution working parents who must be away from home all day against "making a virtue out of a necessity"? Can you reconcile these two positions?

7. In view of Elkind's concern about pushing children, how do you think he would react to programs to accelerate the acquisition of such cognitive abilities as conservation?

8. On the basis of the arguments and research presented in Chapter 9 of your text, what is your attitude toward academically oriented and full-day preschool or kindergarten programs for disadvantaged children? For middle-class children?

9. Critics of the Montessori method claim that it is too highly structured, in that the environment and the children's progress in skill development are carefully planned. Advocates claim that the program is planned to let children advance at their own pace. On the basis of what you have read about it, why do you think this method, which was originally designed for poor and retarded children, has become popular in the United States among well-to-do parents of normal children? Would you recommend this program for any particular type of child?

10. Your text suggests, on the one hand, that young children's egocentric speech results primarily from inability to deal with the social aspects of speech (page 343) and, on the other hand, that children who know how to do this sometimes do not care to (page 320). In your experience with young children, which seems to be more often true? Does the authors' statement that adults sometimes speak egocentrically shed any light on the question of why young children do so?

CHAPTER 9 READING

INTRODUCTION

Shirley Jackson was a novelist and short-story writer whose best-known work, "The Lottery," is one of the most famous stories ever written. If you have encountered "The Lottery" in anthologies, you know that it is both mystifying and terrifying. The following story, "Charles," written in 1948, is in a much lighter vein, though it too has an element of mystery.

Charles

by Shirley Jackson

The day my son Laurie started kindergarten he renounced corduroy overalls with bibs and began wearing blue jeans with a belt; I watched him go off the first morning with the older girl next door, seeing clearly that an era of my life was ended, my sweet-voiced nursery-school tot replaced by a long-trousered, swaggering character who forgot to stop at the corner and wave good-bye to me.

He came home the same way, the front door slamming open, his cap on the floor, and the voice suddenly become raucous shouting, "Isn't anybody *here*?"

At lunch he spoke insolently to his father, spilled his baby sister's milk, and remarked that his teacher said we were not to take the name of the Lord in vain.

"How *was* school today?" I asked, elaborately casual.

"All right," he said.

"Did you learn anything?" his father asked.

Laurie regarded his father coldly. "I didn't learn nothing," he said.

"Anything," I said. "Didn't learn anything."

"The teacher spanked a boy, though," Laurie said, addressing his bread and butter. "For being fresh," he added, with his mouth full.

"What did he do?" I asked. "Who was it?"

Laurie thought. "It was Charles," he said. "He was fresh. The teacher spanked him and made him stand in a corner. He was awfully fresh."

"What did he do?" I asked again, but Laurie slid off his chair, took a cookie, and left, while his father was still saying, "See here, young man."

The next day Laurie remarked at lunch, as soon as he sat down, "Well, Charles was bad again today." He grinned enormously and said, "Today Charles hit the teacher."

"Good heavens," I said, mindful of the Lord's name. "I suppose he got spanked again?"

"He sure did," Laurie said. "Look up," he said to his father.

"What?" his father said, looking up.

"Look down," Laurie said. "Look at my thumb. Gee, you're dumb." He began to laugh insanely.

"Why did Charles hit the teacher?" I asked quickly.

"Because she tried to make him color with red crayons," Laurie said. "Charles wanted to color with green crayons so he hit the teacher and she spanked him and said nobody play with Charles but everybody did."

The third day—it was Wednesday of the first week—Charles bounced a see-saw on to the head of a little girl and made her bleed, and the teacher made him stay inside all during recess. Thursday Charles had to stand in a corner during story-time because he kept pounding his feet on the floor. Friday Charles was deprived of blackboard privileges because he threw chalk.

On Saturday I remarked to my husband, "Do you think kindergarten is too unsettling for Laurie? All his toughness, and bad grammar, and this Charles boy sounds like such a bad influence."

"It'll be all right," my husband said reassuringly. "Bound to be people like Charles in the world. Might as well meet them now as later."

On Monday Laurie came home late, full of news. "Charles," he shouted as he came up the hill; I was waiting anxiously on the front steps. "Charles," Laurie yelled all the way up the hill, "Charles was bad again."

"Come right in," I said, as soon as he came close enough. "Lunch is waiting."

"You know what Charles did?" he demanded, following me through the door. "Charles yelled so in school they sent a boy in from first grade to tell the teacher she had to make Charles keep quiet, and so Charles had to stay after school. And so all the children stayed to watch him."

"What did he do?" I asked.

"He just sat there," Laurie said, climbing into his chair at the table. "Hi, Pop, y'old dust mop."

"Charles had to stay after school today," I told my husband. "Everyone stayed with him."

"What does this Charles look like?" my husband asked Laurie. "What's his other name?"

"He's bigger than me," Laurie said. "And he doesn't have any rubbers and he doesn't ever wear a jacket."

Monday night was the first Parent-Teachers meeting, and only the fact that the baby had a cold kept me from going; I wanted passionately to meet Charles's mother. On Tuesday Laurie remarked suddenly, "Our teacher had a friend come to see her in school today."

"Charles's mother?" my husband and I asked simultaneously.

"Naaah," Laurie said scornfully. "It was a man who came and made us do exercises, we had to touch our toes. Look." He climbed down from his chair and squatted down and touched his toes. "Like this," he said. He got solemnly back into his chair and said, picking up his fork, "Charles didn't even *do* exercises."

"That's fine," I said heartily. "Didn't Charles want to do exercises?"

"Naaah," Laurie said. "Charles was so fresh to the teacher's friend he wasn't *let* do exercises."

"Fresh again?" I said.

"He kicked the teacher's friend," Laurie said. "The teacher's friend told Charles to touch his toes like I just did and Charles kicked him."

"What are they going to do about Charles, do you suppose?" Laurie's father asked him.

Laurie shrugged elaborately. "Throw him out of school, I guess," he said.

Wednesday and Thursday were routine; Charles yelled during story hour and hit a boy in the stomach and made him cry. On Friday Charles stayed after school again and so did all the other children.

With the third week of kindergarten Charles was an institution in our family; the baby was being a Charles when she cried all afternoon; Laurie did a Charles when he filled his wagon full of mud and pulled it through the kitchen; even my husband, when he caught his elbow in the telephone cord and pulled telephone, ashtray, and a bowl of flowers off the table, said, after the first minute, "Looks like Charles."

During the third and fourth weeks it looked like a reformation in Charles; Laurie reported grimly at lunch on Thursday of the third week, "Charles was so good today the teacher gave him an apple."

"What?" I said, and my husband added warily, "You mean Charles?"

"Charles," Laurie said. "He gave the crayons around and he picked up the books afterward and the teacher said he was her helper."

"What happened?" I asked incredulously.

"He was her helper, that's all," Laurie said, and shrugged.

"Can this be true, about Charles?" I asked my husband that night. "Can something like this happen?"

"Wait and see," my husband said cynically. "When you've got a Charles to deal with, this may mean he's only plotting."

He seemed to be wrong. For over a week Charles was the teacher's helper; each day he handed things out and he picked things up; no one had to stay after school.

"The P.T.A. meeting's next week again," I told my husband one evening. "I'm going to find Charles's mother there."

"Ask her what happened to Charles," my husband said. "I'd like to know."

"I'd like to know myself," I said.

On Friday of that week things were back to normal. "You know what Charles did today?" Laurie demanded at the lunch table, in a voice slightly awed. "He told a little girl to say a word and she said it and the teacher washed her mouth out with soap and Charles laughed."

"What word?" his father asked unwisely, and Laurie said, "I'll have to whisper it to you, it's so bad." He got down off his chair and went around to his father. His father bent his head down and Laurie whispered joyfully. His father's eyes widened.

"Did Charles tell the little girl to say *that*?" he asked respectfully.

"She said it *twice*," Laurie said. "Charles told her to say it *twice*."

"What happened to Charles?" my husband asked.

"Nothing," Laurie said. "He was passing out the crayons."

Monday morning Charles abandoned the little girl and said the evil word himself three or four times, getting his mouth washed out with soap each time. He also threw chalk.

My husband came to the door with me that evening as I set out for the P.T.A. meeting. "Invite her over for a cup of tea after the meeting," he said. "I want to get a look at her."

"If only she's there," I said prayerfully.

"She'll be there," my husband said. "I don't see how they could hold a P.T.A. meeting without Charles's mother."

At the meeting I sat restlessly, scanning each comfortable matronly face, trying to determine which one hid the secret of Charles. None of them looked to me haggard enough. No one stood up in the meeting and apologized for the way her son had been acting. No one mentioned Charles.

After the meeting I identified and sought out Laurie's kindergarten teacher. She had a plate with a cup of tea and a piece of chocolate cake; I had a plate with a cup of tea and a piece of marshmallow cake. We maneuvered up to one another cautiously, and smiled.

"I've been so anxious to meet you," I said. "I'm Laurie's mother."

"We're all so interested in Laurie," she said.

"Well, he certainly likes kindergarten," I said. "He talks about it all the time."

"We had a little trouble adjusting, the first week or so," she said primly, "but now he's a fine little helper. With occasional lapses, of course."

"Laurie usually adjusts very quickly," I said. "I suppose this time it's Charles's influence."

"Charles?"

"Yes," I said, laughing, "you must have your hands full in that kindergarten, with Charles."

"Charles?" she said. "We don't have any Charles in the kindergarten."

QUESTIONS ABOUT THE READING

1. Did the ending of the story surprise you? If not, at what point did you begin to guess "Charles's" identity? Why do you think Laurie's parents failed to figure it out?

2. Are Laurie's constant descriptions of "Charles's" activities examples of the symbolic function? If so, in what way? Why did Laurie (according to his teacher) become better behaved about the same time that Laurie told his parents "Charles" did?

3. According to Piaget, a boy of kindergarten age normally has an understanding of his own identity. Did Laurie exhibit a lack in this area? Do you think Laurie believed that it was "Charles" who was doing the things Laurie described? If not, why do you think Laurie attributed those actions to "Charles"?

4. This classic story was written more than 40 years ago, before the changes in the kindergarten curriculum and format that are described in Chapter 9 of your text. Did you notice any elements of the story that "date" it? On the basis of Laurie's descriptions of what went on in kindergarten, what sorts of things did he seem to be learning there? Do those things seem to be important? Does this sound like a kindergarten program that David Elkind would approve of?

ANSWER KEY FOR CHAPTER 9

Note: Numbers in parentheses refer to pages in the textbook where answers can be found.

CHAPTER 9 REVIEW

Important Terms for Section I

1. symbols, logic (page 313)
2. symbolic function (313)
3. sensory (313)
4. concept (313)
5. symbols, signs (313)
6. significate (313)
7. deferred (314)
8. object (314)
9. words, grammar (314)
10. egocentrism (315)
11. centrate (316)
12. decenter (316)
13. perceptual (316)
14. deduction (317)
15. induction (318)
16. logic (318)
17. recognition (322)
18. recall (323)
19. autobiographical (323)
20. quantitative, memory (325)
21. verbal, performance (326)

Learning Objectives for Section I

1. (page 313)
2. (313-314)
3. (314-315)
4. (315-318)
5. (318-321)
6. (321-322)
7. (322)
8. (322-323, 324)
9. (323-324)
10. (324-325)
11. (325)
12. (325-326)

Important Terms for Section II

1. day care (page 328)
2. educational (328)
3. structure (328)
4. Head Start (335)

Learning Objectives for Section II

1. (page 326)
2. (326-328)
3. (328)
4. (329-331)
5. (332-333, 337)
6. (333, 335)
7. (335-337)
8. (334, 337-338)
9. (338-340)

Important Terms for Section III

1. private (page 341)
2. social (343)

Learning Objectives for Section III

1. (page 340)
2. (341-342)
3. (343-344)

CHAPTER 9 QUIZ

Matching—Terms and Situations

1. j (page 317)
2. g (316-317)
3. b (314-315)
4. d (315-316)
5. i (318)
6. e (316)
7. h (318)
8. a (314)
9. f (316)
10. c (315)

Multiple-Choice

1. a (page 313)
2. b (313)
3. c (314)
4. d (315-317)
5. c (316)
6. d (318)
7. a (317, 318-319)
8. b (321)
9. a (321)
10. c (323-324)
11. a (324)
12. d (325)
13. a (327)
14. d (329)
15. b (329)
16. c (331)
17. b (336)
18. b (339)
19. c (340)
20. a (342)

True or False?

1. F—Children first think almost entirely in symbols. (page 313)
2. F—By the preoperational stage, children have developed an understanding of their own identity. (314-315)
3. F—Egocentrism is an intellectual limitation, not a moral one, according to Piaget. (316)
4. T (316)
5. T (320)
6. T (321)
7. T (324)
8. F—The Stanford-Binet and the Wechsler are individual tests. (325)
9. T (326)
10. F—Fathers have more influence on sons' intellectual development than on daughters'. (327)
11. T (331)
12. F—Children who attend academically oriented preschools tend to excel during the early years of school but lose their advantage later. (333)

13. T (333)
14. F—Elkind blames accelerated development on social pressures, which victimize both parents and children. (334)
15. F—Project Head Start is for deprived children of any race or ethnic origin. (335)
16. T (336)
17. T (338)

18. F—Frequent viewers of *Sesame Street* improve in cognitive skills and do better in school than children who rarely watch it. (338-339)
19. T (341-342)
20. F—Recent research shows that children's speech is quite social from an early age. (343)

PERSONALITY AND SOCIAL DEVELOPMENT IN EARLY CHILDHOOD

OVERVIEW

Chapter 10 traces several strands of personality development in early childhood. In this chapter, the authors:

■ Present the theoretical perspectives of Freud and Erikson on the significant personality issues during this period

■ Discuss how boys and girls come to identify with adults and how they develop gender identity and adopt "boyish" or "girlish" behaviors

■ Explain how fearfulness, aggression, and altruism develop

■ Examine play as an indicator of social and cognitive development

■ Assess the influence of parenting styles on children's competence

■ Describe young children's relationships with siblings and friends

CHAPTER 10 REVIEW

Section I   Perspectives on Personality in Early Childhood: Psychosexual and Psychosocial Theory

FRAMEWORK FOR SECTION I

A. Sigmund Freud: The Phallic (Early Genital) Stage
   1. The Oedipus Complex
   2. The Electra Complex
   3. Penis Envy
   4. Development of the Superego
B. Erik Erikson: Crisis 3—Initiative versus Guilt
C. Evaluating the Psychosexual and Psychosocial Approaches
   1. Freudian Theory
   2. Eriksonian Theory

IMPORTANT TERMS FOR SECTION I

Completion: Fill in the blanks to complete the definitions of key terms for this section of Chapter 10.

1. **phallic stage:** Stage of the preschool child in Freud's theory of psychosexual development, in which gratification is centered on the _____ area.

2. **Oedipus complex:** In Freud's theory, the process—involving sexual feelings for the _____ , fear of the _____ , and repression of those emotions—by which a boy comes to identify with his _____ .

3. **Electra complex:** In Freud's theory, the process—involving sexual feelings for the _____ , fear of the _____ , and repression of those emotions—by which a girl comes to identify with her _____ .

4. **castration anxiety:** Part of the Oedipus complex in Freud's theory: a boy's fear of castration by his _____ , which leads to repression of sexual feelings for the _____ and identification with the _____ .

5. _____ **envy:** Idea in Freud's theory that a young girl envies the male's _____ and wishes that she had a(n) _____ herself.

6. _____: In Freud's theory, the representation of social values, communicated by parents and other adults.

7. _____ **versus** _____: Third of Erikson's psychosocial crises, in which the child must balance the desire to pursue goals with the moral reservations that prevent carrying them out; successful resolution leads to the virtue of _____ .

LEARNING OBJECTIVES FOR SECTION I

After reading and reviewing this section of Chapter 10, you should be able to do the following.

1. State Freud's explanation for young children's fascination with bodily differences.

2. Explain the following Freudian concepts and their origins: Oedipus complex, castration anxiety, Electra complex, penis envy.

3. Describe the process of introjection and identify the two aspects of the superego.

4. Identify the conflict involved in Erikson's third crisis—initiative versus guilt—and summarize the outcome of a successful or unsuccessful resolution of this crisis.

5. Cite strengths and criticisms of Freud's and Erikson's theories.

Section II Important Personality Developments in Early Childhood

FRAMEWORK FOR SECTION II

A. Emotions and Attitudes
   1. Identification
   2. Sexual Identity
      a. Sex Differences, Gender Roles, and Gender-Typing
         (1) Sex and Gender Differences
         (2) Gender Roles and Gender-Typing
      b. Origins of Differences
         (1) Biological Influences
         (2) Cultural Influences
         (3) Influence of Parents
            (a) How Do Parents Treat Boys and Girls?
            (b) The Father's Role
         (4) Influence of Television
      c. Effects of Gender Prejudice
      d. Acquiring Gender Roles: Theoretical Explanations
         (1) Psychoanalytic Theory
         (2) Social-Learning Theory
         (3) Cognitive-Developmental Theory
         (4) Gender-Schema Theory
   3. Fearfulness
      a. What Do Children Fear, and Why?
      b. Phobias
      c. Preventing and Treating Fears
B. Behaviors
   1. Prosocial Behavior
      a. What Is Prosocial Behavior?
      b. Influences on Prosocial Behavior
      c. Encouraging Prosocial Behavior
         (1) What Parents Do
         (2) Cultural Values
   2. Aggression
      a. The Rise and Decline of Aggression
      b. Triggers of Aggression
         (1) Reinforcement
         (2) Frustration
         (3) Imitation
         (4) Televised Violence
      c. Reducing Aggression
   3. Play
      a. Concepts of Play
      b. Studies of Play
      c. "Pretend" Play

IMPORTANT TERMS FOR SECTION II

Completion: Fill in the blanks to complete the definitions of key terms for this section of Chapter 10.

1. _____: Process by which a person acquires the characteristics of another person or group; one of the most important personality developments of early childhood.

2. _____ **difference:** Actual biological difference between the sexes.

3. _____ **difference:** Psychological difference between the sexes.

4. _____: Behaviors and attitudes that a culture deems appropriate for males and females.

5. _____: Process by which a person learns a gender role.

6. _____: Awareness of one's own sex and the sex of others.

7. **androgens:** General term for the _____ sex hormones.

8. **testosterone:** _____.

9. _____: Having characteristics considered typical of males and other characteristics considered typical of females.

10. **gender** _____: Awareness that one will always be male or female.

11. **gender-**_____ **theory:** Theory that children socialize themselves in their gender roles by developing a concept of what it means to be male or female.

12. _____: Irrational, involuntary fear that is inappropriate to the situation and interferes with normal activities.

13. **systematic** _____: Gradual exposure to a feared object for the purpose of overcoming the fear.

14. _____ **behavior:** Altruistic behavior; selflessness.

15. **dominance hierarchy:** System of social _____ , recognized by all the members of a group, in which some members have power over all other members, some have power over certain other members and are subordinate to others, and some are subordinate to all other members.

16. _____ **play:** Play in which children interact with other children.

17. _____ **play:** Play that reflects the level of the child's intellectual development.

LEARNING OBJECTIVES FOR SECTION II

After reading and reviewing this section of Chapter 10, you should be able to do the following.

1. Explain how identification occurs, according to social-learning theory, and give an example of each of the four processes that establish and strengthen it.

2. Summarize research on gender differences in children.

3. Explain the relationship between gender-typing in early childhood and the development of gender identity.

4. Assess the evidence for biological influences on behavioral differences between the sexes, and explain why biology fails to fully explain these differences.

5. Assess cultural influences on gender roles.

6. Discuss the influence of parents (especially fathers) in encouraging "sex-appropriate" behavior.

7. Discuss the role of television in gender-stereotyping.

8. Describe the effects of gender restrictions.

9. Describe an androgynous person, and list at least four suggestions by Sandra Bem for raising children without gender-role stereotypes.

10. Summarize and evaluate explanations for the development of gender roles, gender-typing, and gender identity according to the psychoanalytic, social-learning, cognitive-developmental, and gender-schema theories.

11. Discuss sources of fears and phobias, and identify methods of prevention and treatment.

12. Identify influences on the development of prosocial behavior, and list five ways in which parents can encourage it.

13. Distinguish between instrumental and hostile aggression, and trace the rise and decline of aggression in early childhood.

14. Discuss four factors that can trigger aggression, and identify successful and unsuccessful techniques for reducing it.

15. Explain the relationship between children's play and their socialization and cognitive development.

16. Name six types of play identified by Mildred Parten, and summarize recent research that has reevaluated nonsocial play.

17. Outline four types of cognitive play identified by Piaget, and explain the significance of pretend play.

Section III   Influences on Personality Development

FRAMEWORK FOR SECTION III

A. How Does the Family Affect Personality Development?
  1. Child-Rearing Practices
    a. Baumrind's Studies: Parents' Styles and Children's Competence
      (1) Three Styles of Parenting
      (2) Why Authoritative Parenting Seems Best
      (3) Evaluating Baumrind's Work
    b. Rewards and Punishment
      (1) Using Rewards: Behavior Modification
      (2) Using Punishment: When Does Punishment Work?
        (a) Timing
        (b) Explaining
        (c) Consistency
        (d) The Person Who Punishes
        (e) The Child's Role
        (f) Side Effects of Punishment
        (g) To Sum Up
    c. Long-Term Effects of Child-Rearing Practices
  2. Brothers and Sisters
    a. How Do Siblings Interact in Early Childhood?
    b. What Do Sibling Relationships Imply about the Future?
B. Relationships with Other Children
  1. Early Friendships
  2. Family Ties and Popularity

IMPORTANT TERMS FOR SECTION III

Completion: Fill in the blanks to complete the definitions of key terms for this section of Chapter 10.

1. _____ **parents:** In Baumrind's terminology, parents whose primary child-rearing values are based on control and obedience.

2. _____ **parents:** In Baumrind's terminology, parents whose primary child-rearing values are self-expression and self-regulation.

3. _____ **parents:** In Baumrind's terminology, parents whose primary child-rearing values blend respect for the child's individuality with a desire to instill social values in the child.

LEARNING OBJECTIVES FOR SECTION III

After reading and reviewing this section of Chapter 10, you should be able to do the following.

1. Compare and evaluate authoritarian, permissive, and authoritative styles of parenting identified by Diana Baumrind.

2. Define behavior modification and compare the effectiveness of rewards and punishments.

3. Differentiate between internal and external rewards, giving an example of each.

4. List and explain six factors that influence the effectiveness of punishment.

5. Compare the long-term effects of specific child-rearing practices with the effect of loving treatment.

6. Describe typical sibling interactions in early childhood and how those interactions influence other relationships.

7. Compare research in the United States and China on characteristics of only children.

8. Identify important features of early friendships, and describe how young children choose friends.

9. Cite factors that influence popularity, and suggest ways to help unpopular children make friends.

CHAPTER 10 QUIZ

Matching—Who's Who: Match each name in the left-hand column with the appropriate description from the right-hand column.

1. Jerome Kagan _____
2. Lawrence Kohlberg _____
3. Erik Erikson _____
4. Sandra Bem _____
5. Jean Piaget _____
6. Karen Horney _____
7. Albert Bandura _____
8. Mildred Parten _____
9. Diana Baumrind _____
10. Sigmund Freud _____

a. originated gender-schema theory
b. traced rise and decline of pretend play
c. described how children identify with models
d. identified styles of child rearing
e. originated concept of penis envy
f. linked gender identity with cognitive development
g. identified classic model for development of social play
h. studied imitation as a trigger for aggression
i. originated concept of womb envy
j. theorized that children need to balance initiative and guilt

Multiple-Choice: Circle the choice that best completes or answers each item.

1. In the ancient Greek myth, Oedipus killed
   a. his mother
   b. his father
   c. himself
   d. a soothsayer

2. In Freud's phallic stage, gratification shifts to the
   a. mouth
   b. anus
   c. nipples
   d. genitals

3. The superego represents
   a. values and ideals
   b. impulses and desires
   c. external control
   d. a strong sense of self

4. Unsuccessful resolution of the crisis of initiative versus guilt may cause
   a. impotence
   b. inhibition
   c. exhibitionism
   d. all of the above

5. Successful resolution of the crisis of initiative versus guilt leads to the virtue of
   a. will
   b. self-control
   c. purpose
   d. spontaneity

6. Identification is an important issue of early childhood for
   a. social-learning theorists
   b. psychoanalysts
   c. both a and b
   d. neither a nor b

7. Children tend to choose models who are
   a. powerful
   b. physically attractive
   c. like themselves
   d. all of the above

8. Gender differences are
   a. biological differences between the sexes
   b. psychological differences between the sexes
   c. behaviors and attitudes deemed appropriate for males and females
   d. all of the above

9. Research on sex and gender differences has found that
   a. aside from anatomy, young boys and girls are more alike than different
   b. brain structure is the same for both sexes
   c. males in all cultures excel in spatial abilities
   d. "tomboys" tend to have genital abnormalities

10. Children from which kind of families tend to be less affected by gender stereotypes than other children?
    a. dual-parent
    b. single-parent
    c. adoptive
    d. extended

11. A typical child, by the time of graduation from high school, is estimated to have watched approximately how many hours of television?
    a. 250
    b. 2500
    c. 25,000
    d. 250,000

12. The psychoanalytic explanation for gender-typing is not widely accepted among research psychologists, because research shows that
    a. young boys are more like their mothers than their fathers
    b. children are influenced by people other than parents
    c. both of the above
    d. neither of the above

13. Gender constancy is usually acquired between the ages of
    a. 1 and 2
    b. 3 and 4
    c. 5 and 7
    d. 8 and 10

14. According to gender-schema theory, gender stereotypes can be eliminated by teaching children to adopt which of the following schemata?
    a. individual-differences schema
    b. cultural-relativism schema
    c. sexism schema
    d. any of the above

15. Children develop the most new fears between the ages of
    a. 6 months and 1 year
    b. 2 and 4
    c. 5 and 7
    d. 8 and 10

16. An effective way to help young children overcome fears is
    a. ignoring their fears
    b. explaining why their fears are unreasonable
    c. removing feared object
    d. encouraging expression of fears

17. The upbringing of Europeans who risked their lives to save Jews during World War II emphasized
    a. fairness
    b. obedience
    c. self-reliance
    d. all of the above

18. In general, aggressive preschoolers are
    a. unsociable
    b. turf guarders
    c. rarely hostile
    d. the least competent

19. Which of the following statements about aggression in young children is *not* true, according to social-learning theory and research?
    a. A frustrated child is more likely to act aggressively than a contented one.
    b. Children who have seen an aggressive adult are more likely to act aggressively.
    c. Televised violence tends to promote aggression.
    d. Spanking is generally an effective way to curb aggression.

20. According to Parten, which of the following shows the most advancement toward social play?
    a. building a block tower alongside another child who is building a block tower
    b. playing with a truck near other children who are building a block tower
    c. watching other children build a block tower
    d. talking to children who are building a block tower

21. Which of the following statements about preschool children's play is *not* true, according to research done since 1970?
    a. Some children's play is more social than others'.
    b. Social play seems to have decreased since the 1920s.
    c. Middle-class children tend to play more socially than less advantaged children.
    d. Nonsocial, or solitary, play is a sign of immaturity.

22. A 3-year-old pushing a toy train and saying "choo-choo" is engaged in what kind of play?
    a. sensorimotor
    b. pretend
    c. sociodramatic
    d. associative

23. According to the text, the most effective style of parenting is
    a. authoritarian
    b. permissive
    c. authoritative
    d. All of the above are equally effective.

24. As compared with children who have siblings, only children tend to be
    a. less sociable
    b. less cooperative
    c. more self-centered
    d. more achievement-oriented

25. Which of the following is more important to 4-year-olds than to 7-year-olds in choosing friends?
    a. physical characteristics
    b. affection
    c. support
    d. common activities

True or False? In the blank following each item, write T (for *true*) or F (for *false*). In the space below each item, if the statement is false, rewrite it to make it true.

1. According to Freud, castration anxiety leads a young boy to identify with his mother. _____

2. According to Freud, a healthy girl should deny her penis envy and learn to be satisfied with her own body. _____

3. According to Freud, a child's ego seeks ways of gratifying impulses without conflicting with moral demands. _____

4. The superego becomes more rigid in adulthood. _____

5. Erikson's crisis of initiative versus guilt reflects a split between the childlike and adult parts of the personality. _____

6. Freud is described as *phallocentric* because of the centrality of the phallic stage in his psychosexual theory. _____

7. When a young boy identifies with a major league baseball player, he believes he can hit a ball the way that player does. _____

8. Behavioral differences between the sexes appear to be largely inborn. _____

9. Children whose mothers work outside the home and whose fathers share housework are unlikely to develop gender stereotypes. _____

10. Male and female embryos look the same until 5 or 6 weeks after conception. _____

11. Parents tend to praise and punish boys more than girls. _____

12. Cross-sex play tends to upset fathers more than mothers. _____

13. Children who watch television a great deal tend to become more gender-typed than children who rarely watch. _____

14. According to Bem, an androgynous personality displays more typically "masculine" traits than typically "feminine" traits.

15. Research shows that children become gender-typed by imitating their parents. _____

16. The gender-schema theory holds that gender-typing can be modified. _____

17. When a childhood fear persists into adulthood, it is called a *phobia*. _____

18. A toddler who grabs a toy from another child is displaying hostile aggression. _____

19. After age 6 or 7, children become more aggressive. _____

20. The effects of televised violence seen by eight-year-olds can endure through the teenage years. _____

21. Children who frequently play by themselves are likely to be unpopular. _____

22. A criticism of Diana Baumrind's work is that it does not take into account how children affect parents. _____

23. It is best to let children reflect on their actions before punishing them. _____

24. Early sibling interactions are primarily competitive. _____

25. Young children's relationships with other children tend to reflect their relationships with their parents. _____

TOPICS FOR THOUGHT AND DISCUSSION

1. Freud's idea that girls cannot be as moral as boys is offensive to many women. Does the fact that it is offensive make the idea wrong? Can you suggest a way to test it?

2. On the basis of Chapter 10, which appears to have a stronger influence on gender differences—biology or culture?

3. Which of the four theories discussed in Chapter 10 of your text seems to best explain gender role acquisition? Why? Can you select elements from more than one theory to produce a more complete explanation?

4. If television can help abolish gender stereotypes, how should such programming be designed? What aspects of male and female personality should be portrayed?

5. The authors of your text state that children's fears are influenced by changing social conditions. Do children today seem to have fears similar to or different from those you or your parents from their childhood?

6. Research suggests that violent television programs promote or reinforce aggressive behavior, even years later. If this is so, should violence should be banned from children's programs? From programs aired at times when children are likely to see them?

7. Since aggression tends to decline after early childhood, should parents of young children simply let it take its course? How would authoritarian, permissive, and authoritative parents be likely to answer this question?

8. Were you surprised that children of permissive parents tend to be less exploratory than children of authoritarian parents? Does the authors' explanation (page 377 in your text) make sense to you? Why or why not?

9. Discrepancies between Parten's findings and more recent studies of children's play have been explained as a possible result of environmental and social class differences between the groups of children studied. Could similar differences help explain why some of Piaget's findings (discussed in Chapter 9) have not held up in recent research?

CHAPTER 10 READING

INTRODUCTION

This selection, condensed from "Paradoxes of Parenthood: On the Impossibility of Raising Children Perfectly," by Sophie Freud, deals with a key topic discussed in Chapter 10 of your textbook: the effects of parenting styles and child-rearing practices on children's development. The essay also touches on several other important themes of the chapter, including gender-typing and the effectiveness of rewards and punishments.

Sophie Freud's essay appears in a collection called *No Way: The Nature of the Impossible.* The editors of the book note that she is a professor of social work at Simmons College School of Social Work in Boston; that she teaches and writes about human development, psychological theories, and the psychology of women; and that she "continues to be an imperfect mother to three adult children."

Paradoxes of Parenthood: On the Impossibility of Raising Children Perfectly

by Sophie Freud

I entered young parenthood with the certainty that I would rear my children in the best possible way. I felt myself to be loving and generous and infinitely patient. I would read the right books and follow their advice most faithfully. Under my guidance my children would become mentally healthy, happy, and productive human beings. I would avoid all the mistakes my parents had made. I had unbounded confidence in my own ability to become a perfect parent.

Little did I realize at that distant time what hubris (arrogance) was involved in these presumptuous goals.

My thoughts on this subject are meant to explain to young parents why the road ahead, however well paved with the best intentions, will be a thorny one. My thoughts are also meant to comfort myself and other middle-aged parents who tried both too hard and yet not hard enough to be a good enough parent and to convince us that it was not our fault if we failed in the impossible task of rearing our children perfectly.

Parents are asked to provide discipline *and* acceptance; firm guidance *and* encouragement toward autonomy; a commitment to high values *and* a willingness to compromise and conform to societal expectations. I shall argue that the parental role involves a series of incompatible demands, which defy satisfactory resolution.

Elusive Goals

With respect to values, I think our ancestors had a clearer vision than we have. Until quite recently we had few questions about the desirability of premarital chastity, lifelong fidelity to one marital partner, valor in battle, patriotism that included a willingness to die for one's country, obedience to and respect for one's elders, religious faith, self-sacrifice, ambition, and achievement through very hard work. Yet all of these values have now been questioned and at times violently rejected, not just by isolated nonconformists but by significant groups in the society. Parents who hope to do a perfect job will have to sift and choose among competing values and decide which ones they will at least try to transmit to their children.

Not long ago it was taken for granted that boys and girls would adopt different values. Now many people, but certainly not the majority of Americans, would advocate androgynous values, with equal standards of sensitivity, assertiveness, courage, and warmth for both boys and girls, women and men. I know mothers who set out to raise androgynous sons but were defeated in their attempt to do so. When the little boys started to play with dolls in kindergarten, they were taunted by other boys and they cried. They had also been told not to fight. Clearly they had been raised to be sissies. The mothers did not want their sons to be outcasts. They told them to stop playing with dolls and pointed out how much fun it was to ride a nice red fire truck. The fathers did not want their sons to be teased. They showed their sons how to punch anyone who teased them.

It is hard for parents to imbue their children with values that are rejected by the culture of the majority; their wish to teach their children certain values may conflict with their even more urgent intent to help their children secure a safe and respected place in the society in which they will live. We live in such a rapidly changing society that even pragmatic values become unpredictable. The generation of women to which I belong was raised to the tune of "Cinderella and the Prince"; they "lived happily ever after," only to find themselves at midlife obsolescent, bewildered, and often alone.

Yet, let us assume that we could agree on *what* to teach our children. The question then arises of *how* we teach it.

Teaching and Learning

Loevinger has pinpointed a major problem in the area of teaching values.[1] She suggests that learning takes place in three major ways: through cognitive understanding, through watching models, and through rewards and punishments. The problem is that parents may choose to teach by one method and children may perversely choose to learn by a different method. As a result, what is learned may be other than what was intended. Parents may choose to punish their children for a misdeed, acting on a reward-and-punishment theory, while children might decide in this instance to learn in a modeling framework and conclude that power rests with whoever is stronger. Or, alternatively, a parent may *explain* to a child what she has done wrong, and the child, adopting a reward-and-punishment framework, may conclude that misbehavior will bear no consequences beyond words.

All our behavior can be seen as forms of communication with various levels of messages, including the levels of content and relationship. Those who observe us, or listen to us, can attend at whatever level they choose or happen to notice, and often that level is not the one we intended to be noticed or even one we were aware of transmitting. A scolding may be viewed at the relationship level as "caring" or "paying attention" and thus become a reward. Praise may be perceived as pressure for future performance and thus felt as a threat.

The Right Discipline

Many parents continue to imagine that "the right discipline" is the key to parenting success. They have somehow lost that key and turn to experts to find it again. Thus, it is ironic and instructive that two prominent contemporary writers, both of them parents and educators, give us completely contradictory advice. Alice Miller, in three consecutive books,[2] accuses parents through the centuries of having been bent on breaking their children's wills, humiliating them, robbing them of any sense of control over their lives, and destroying their spirit, their curiosity, and their vitality, all for the sake of shaping obedient, conforming, nonfeeling adults. Miller has contempt for every form of "Erziehung" (a German word conveying socialization, pedagogy, discipline, and education), viewing it as inevitably coercive and manipulative. She argues that only if the child and the care giver each respect the other as a separate human being, and each allow the expression of and recognize the other's authentic feelings, will the development of a humane and whole and vital human being be assured.

Marie Winn, on the other hand, is alarmed at the premature exposure of children to the ugly realities of adult life.[3] She deplores the permissiveness of the current generation of parents, viewing lack of rules, structures, and firm expectations as destructive and dangerous neglect and an abdication of the protective obligations of parents. In direct contrast to Miller, Winn locates the problem in too little parental control. She appears nostalgic for the "benign dictatorship" of parents of olden days and calls for more adult authority and less egalitarianism.

Both these authors are passionate and convincing in their arguments. Where does this leave a well-meaning young mother or father in search of the key to perfect parenthood?

The New Good Enough Mother

We congratulate Winnicott[4] for asking mothers to be merely "good enough" rather than perfect. In contrast to the very best mother, the merely good enough mother is not always attentive. Sometimes she is casual, or she is preoccupied and turns her back to attend to her own needs. Sometimes she is in a hurry and imposes her own agenda, overlooks subtle cues, and becomes unreliable and unpredictable. Too much predictability might even create stagnation in a relationship. I like to think we need unpredictability in a framework of predictability. Flaws in caretaking introduce novelty and new learning. The child needs to learn that his mother is still there, even if she does turn her back, and that both goodness and badness belong to one and the same mother. The good enough mother might ultimately be better than the very best mother, since it is one of the paradoxes of

parenthood that loving too well ultimately means not loving well enough.

Overloving Parents

We have learned that children are more often damaged by too much loving than by too little. Overloving implies overinvolvement with the child in the expectation that the child will give meaning and reason to one's own life. It involves possessiveness, anxious overprotection, and inability to see the child's needs as separate and different from one's own needs.

Even child abuse may be a form of overloving. Parents who are indifferent to a child who cries may close the doors or turn on the TV. It is only when there is intense involvement with the child and her crying is heard as a personal accusation that she may need to be beaten into silence.

Parental intrusiveness takes many different forms; in any of these forms, it can endanger a child's healthy growth and development.

Who Is in Charge?

Although Miller and Winn come to different conclusions, they both zero in on the parent's psychic vulnerability: the dilemma of having to discipline children while also needing their love and approval. We have come upon another paradox: parents' ability to discipline their children is based on a positive loving bond between parent and child, yet discipline forever threatens disruption of that bond.

The parent-child relationship can be viewed as the prototype of a "complementary relationship"[5] in which two partners have unequal social power but intermeshing needs. Indeed, during the formative period of her life, the child depends on the parent for her very survival, as well as for her physical, emotional, and social welfare. It seems clear, at least at first sight, that the parent is in the dominant position in this relationship. Yet, the parent's self-definition as a good parent—or even as a good person, since the parenting role is quite central for most people—is a crucial aspect of his or her identity. Whether one has succeeded in "being a good parent" in one's own eyes, as well as in the eyes of other people, is usually judged on the basis of the child's ongoing welfare and happiness *and* of the relationship that is maintained with the child.

Thus the child's dependency on the parents for physical and emotional welfare is matched by the parents' dependency on their children for self-regard.

I view the parent role as one of "responsibility without authority" and every administrator knows that this creates a no-win situation. Parents are held responsible and hold themselves responsible for their children's ongoing life and ultimate fate.

As parents we tend to ignore the innate emotional and intellectual dispositions of our children. We also tend to ignore the larger sociocultural context, which constrains, distorts, and shapes our ability to be wise and loving parents. We insist that regardless of circumstances, it is our parental responsibility to raise our children perfectly. Responsibility is the essence of parenthood. Yet, responsibility ought to entail authority and control; and the more responsibility one feels, the more control one wishes to have. I believe the problem of parental control and over-control, which easily merges into oppressive intrusiveness, arises from this dilemma.

"I have to protect you against your own mistakes," a friend of mine used to say to her children. "I have to control you for your own good." She would hound them into doing their homework, bribe them into good academic performance, coerce them into practicing their musical instruments, shame them into learning foreign languages. She would only show them affection if they met her expectations. Her children have become accomplished and successful professionals. Yet their sense of self-worth depends on their achievements, and although they pursue these relentlessly, it continues to remain elusive. They will never forgive her for loving them conditionally and for having been such a controlling mother.

Another friend of mine believed in the importance of self-regulation above all. She was extremely respectful of her children's decisions. She allowed them to discontinue their hobbies whenever the efforts seemed to outweigh the rewards. She allowed them to drop out of school where they learned meaningless things and to follow their own stars. I don't know what became of her children. We quarreled because I reproached her for being an uncaring and neglectful parent.

Letting Go

How can parents fill the requirements of a role in which they must learn to release control while responsible for the success of the enterprise? We should not delegate our own unfinished life tasks to our children; yet children need some firm guidance, lest they lose their way.

The dilemma of simultaneously fostering attachment and separation is perhaps the most difficult parental task. It involves promoting individuation and autonomy, apparently essential life goals, while also offering the child an experience of attachment that is profound and meaningful enough to evoke a lifelong capacity to love, to feel, and to care.

I referred earlier to parents' double wish to see their child succeed and to maintain an affectionate bond. The second part of this wish faces us with yet another paradox of parenthood: disenchantment with and rebellion against parents is a necessary aspect of the relationship; the relationship is flawed if it remains conflict-free and apparently harmonious.

The process of disillusionment with formerly idealized parents is a necessary developmental step of adolescence, and some form of self-assertive differentiation should be an ongoing aspect of the good enough parent-child relationship. We would be worried about a two-year-old who does not oppose parental demands and develop her own growing willfulness; we would be concerned about a school child who never values her teacher's or her peer's opinions above those of her parents.

The most permissive and tolerant parents are in the worst position. Their children have to go to greater lengths to be critical, disapproving, and provocative. Moreover, such parents may have such good will that they may even wish to help their children become rebellious(!), an effort doomed by its own internal contradiction.

Separation and loss, with its necessary mourning, is built into the very core of the parental role. The goal of the parent-child relationship from the very beginning involves a gradual separation and loosening of bonds. Parental love must be demonstrated by not loving too much and by introducing a measure of detachment into a relationship that is totally involving. The most devoted parent will send her child out into the world, applaud the child's new attachments, and recede into the background. Success in the area of the child's well-being might mean defeat in holding onto a close and primary bond.

Failed Intent

It will be forever impossible to be a perfect parent, because our actions do not always match our intent. Our internalized parents interfere with our intention to be the most enlightened and responsible parents. We tend to project these internalized figures upon our children, eventually repeating, in some form, old and familiar relationship patterns.

Conclusion

We must learn to respect impossibilities. The very idea that we are in charge of our own perfections, let alone that of our children, is grandiose and presumptuous. The goal of becoming a perfect parent carries the seeds of guilt, blame, disappointed expectations, and defeat.

I think, on reflection, that it is *possible* to become a perfect parent by tolerating, forgiving, and transcending imperfections, our own and those of our children. We shall become perfect parents by accepting the impossibility of such a goal.

Notes

1. J. Loevinger, "Patterns of Child Rearing as Theories of Learning," *Journal of Abnormal and Social Psychology,* *59:* 148-150 (1959).

2. A. Miller, *Prisoners of Childhood,* Basic Books, New York, 1981; idem, *For Your Own Good,* Farrar, Strauss & Giroux, New York, 1983; idem, *Thou Shalt Not Be Aware,* Farrar, Strauss & Giroux, New York, 1984.

3. M. Winn, *Children without Childhood,* Pantheon Books, New York, 1981.

4. See, for example, D. W. Winnicott, *The Family and Individual Development,* Basic Books, New York, 1965.

5. P. Watzlawick, J. Beavin, and D. Jackson, *Pragmatics of Human Communication,* W. W. Norton, New York, 1967.

QUESTIONS ABOUT THE READING

1. Sophie Freud argues that perfect parenting is impossible because parents are faced with "incompatible demands." Is her argument convincing? In your own words, how would you summarize these incompatible demands?

2. Two diametrically opposed views of discipline are presented in this essay: Alice Miller's and Marie Winn's. Would you consider it accurate to equate Miller's view with the permissive style of parenting and Winn's with the authoritarian style, or do you think that this is an oversimplification?

3. Baumrind's research, described in Chapter 10 of your text, led her to conclude that authoritative parenting works better than authoritarian or permissive parenting. Which (if any) of the following positions do you think Sophie Freud might take? (a) "Authoritative parenting is probably as close to perfection as we can hope to get—and certainly much closer than authoritarian or permissive parenting." (b) "Given the incompatible demands of the parental role, none of the three parenting styles is likely to work very well." (c) "If parenting is characterized by love and intelligence, any one of the three styles might produce the "good enough" parent." Would you yourself take any of these positions?

4. Sophie Freud seems less optimistic than Sandra Bem about the possibility of raising androgynous children. What do you think?

5. Is Sophie Freud's discussion of the ambiguous effects of reward and punishment consistent with the treatment in your text? What about her discussions of parental love and control?

6. Do you agree that child abuse may be "a form of overloving"? Why or why not?

ANSWER KEY FOR CHAPTER 10

Note: Numbers in parentheses refer to pages in the textbook where answers can be found.

CHAPTER 10 REVIEW

Important Terms for Section I

1. genital (page 349)
2. mother, father, father (349)
3. father, mother, mother (349)
4. father, mother, father (349)
5. penis, penis, penis (350)
6. superego (350)
7. initiative, guilt, purpose (351)

Learning Objectives for Section I

1. (page 349)
2. (349-350)
3. (350-351)
4. (351)
5. (351-352)

Important Terms for Section II

1. identification (page 352)
2. sex (354)
3. gender (354)
4. gender roles (354)
5. gender-typing (354)
6. gender identity (355)
7. male (355)
8. male sex hormone (355)
9. androgynous (360)
10. constancy (361)
11. schema (362)
12. phobia (365)
13. desensitization (365)
14. prosocial (366)
15. ranking (368)
16. social (372)
17. cognitive (372)

Learning Objectives for Section II

1. (pages 352-353)
2. (354-355)
3. (355)
4. (355-357)
5. (357)
6. (357-359)
7. (359)
8. (359-360)
9. (358, 360, 362-363)
10. (360-363)
11. (363-365)
12. (366-367)
13. (367-368)
14. (368-371)
15. (371-372)
16. (372-374)
17. (374-375)

Important Terms for Section III

1. authoritarian (page 376)
2. permissive (376)
3. authoritative (376)

Learning Objectives for Section III

1. (pages 376-378)
2. (378-380)
3. (378)
4. (379)
5. (380)
6. (381)

7. (382, 383)
8. (382-384)
9. (384-385)

CHAPTER 10 QUIZ

Matching—Who's Who

1. c (page 353)
2. f (361)
3. j (351)
4. a (362)
5. b (374-375)
6. i (352)
7. h (369)
8. g (372)
9. d (376)
10. e (350)

Multiple-Choice

1. b (page 349)
2. d (349)
3. a (350)
4. d (351)
5. c (351)
6. c (352-353)
7. a (353)
8. b (354)
9. a (354-357)
10. b (359)
11. c (359)
12. c (360-361)
13. c (361)
14. d (363)
15. b (364)
16. d (365)
17. a (367)
18. b (367-368)
19. d (368-371)
20. a (372-373)
21. d (372-374)
22. b (374-375)
23. c (377)
24. d (382)
25. a (384)

True or False?

1. F—According to Freud, castration anxiety leads a young boy to identify with his father. (page 349)
2. F—According to Freud, denial of penis envy leads to neurosis in adulthood. (350)
3. T (350)
4. F—The superego becomes less rigid in adulthood. (351)
5. T (351)
6. F—*Phallocentricism* means regarding male behavior as the norm. (352)
7. T (353)
8. F—Research suggests that behavioral differences between the sexes can be changed and are not necessarily inborn. (355)
9. F—Children typically acquire the gender stereotypes of their culture, even when those stereotypes are inconsistent with their parents' behavior. (355)
10. T (355)
11. T (357)
12. T (358)
13. T (359)
14. F—An androgynous personality contains a balanced combination of the typical characteristics of both sexes. (360)
15. F—When children are tested on masculinity and femininity, they are no more like their parents than like a random set of parents. (361)
16. T (362)
17. F—A phobia is an irrational fear, which can be present in either a child or an adult. (365)
18. F—A toddler who grabs a toy from another child is displaying instrumental, not hostile, aggression. (367-368)
19. F—After age 6 or 7, children become less aggressive. (368)
20. T (370)
21. F—Some kinds of nonsocial play are associated with social competence and popularity. (374)
22. T (377)
23. F—The less time between an action and its punishment, the better. (379)
24. F—Early sibling interactions are primarily prosocial, not competitive. (381)
25. T (385)

PHYSICAL DEVELOPMENT IN MIDDLE CHILDHOOD

OVERVIEW

Chapter 11 follows a child's growth and development during the elementary school years. In this chapter, the authors:

- Point out factors that influence height and weight in middle childhood
- Discuss childhood obesity, its possible causes, and treatment
- Describe the principal health and safety concerns of middle childhood
- Explain how children's understanding of health and illness develops
- Trace the development of motor skills for boys and girls, and discuss the stigma attached to left-handedness

CHAPTER 11 REVIEW

Section I Growth during the School Years

FRAMEWORK FOR SECTION I

A. Height and Weight
  1. Variations in Growth
  2. Predicting Height
  3. Abnormal Growth
B. Nutrition and Growth
  1. Malnutrition
  2. Obesity
     a. What Is Obesity, and How Common Is It?
     b. What Causes Obesity?
     c. Treating Childhood Obesity

IMPORTANT TERMS FOR SECTION I

Completion: Fill in the blanks to complete the definitions of key terms for this section of Chapter 11.

1. _____: Girl's first menstruation.

2. **obesity:** Overweight condition marked by a skin-fold measurement in the _____ percentile (thicker than the skin fold of _____ percent of children of the same age and sex).

LEARNING OBJECTIVES FOR SECTION I

After reading and reviewing this section of Chapter 11, you should be able to do the following.

1. Summarize the growth patterns of boys and girls in middle childhood and their average changes in height and weight.

2. Identify factors that account for variations in growth.

3. Explain why prediction of adult height is uncertain.

4. State considerations in treating children whose growth is below normal.

5. Describe how nutritional needs change during middle childhood.

6. Describe long-term effects of malnutrition in infancy on children's personality and behavior.

7. Identify trends in the prevalence of obesity, list four possible causes of this condition, and describe an effective treatment.

Section II Health and Safety

FRAMEWORK FOR SECTION II

A. Health Concerns
   1. Minor Medical Conditions
   2. Vision and Visual Problems
   3. Dental Health and Dental Problems
   4. Stuttering
   5. Tics
   6. High Blood Pressure
   7. Type A Behavior
B. Safety Concerns: Accidental Injuries
   1. Which Children Are Most Likely to Be Hurt?
   2. How Are Children Most Likely to Be Hurt?

IMPORTANT TERMS FOR SECTION II

Completion: Fill in the blanks to complete the definitions of key terms for this section of Chapter 11.

1. **stuttering:** Involuntary _____ or prolongation of syllables.

2. **tic:** Involuntary, repetitive muscular movement; also called _____ *movement disorder.*

3. **Type _____:** Personality type which includes traits such as aggressiveness, impatience, anger, hostility, and competitiveness and when present in adults is correlated with coronary disease.

4. **Type _____:** Personality type that is easygoing and relaxed.

LEARNING OBJECTIVES FOR SECTION II

After reading and reviewing this section of Chapter 11, you should be able to do the following.

1. Summarize the incidence of various minor medical conditions in middle childhood.

2. Explain cognitive changes in children's understanding of health and illness.

3. Describe normal changes in vision in middle childhood and tell what vision problems may develop at that time.

4. Assess the the current state of dental health and dental care among school-age children.

5. Outline causes and treatments for stuttering, tics, and high blood pressure.

6. Distinguish between Type A and Type B personalities, and discuss the stability of Type A behavior from childhood through adulthood.

7. Explain why today's schoolchildren are less healthy than children of the previous generation and what can be done to improve their health.

8. Explain why accidental injury is a great concern in middle childhood; point out which children are at the greatest risk and where, and how accidents can be prevented.

Section III Motor Development

FRAMEWORK FOR SECTION III

A. Motor Skills in Middle Childhood
B. Handedness

IMPORTANT TERM FOR SECTION III

Completion: Fill in the blank to complete the definition of the key term for this section of Chapter 11.

1. **handedness:** _____ for using one hand rather than the other; determination may be difficult, because not everyone prefers one hand for every task.

LEARNING OBJECTIVES FOR SECTION III

After reading and reviewing this section of Chapter 11, you should be able to do the following.

1. Trace the development of motor skills from age 6 to age 12, and point out differences between boys and girls.

2. Discuss what is known about the causes of right- and left-handedness and the basis, if any, for prejudice against left-handedness.

CHAPTER 11 QUIZ

Matching—Numbers: Match each of the items in the left-hand column with the correct number in the right-hand column.

1. Height (in inches) of average 9-year-old boy or girl _____   6
2. Average number of calories (in hundreds) needed daily in middle childhood _____   7
3. Percentile of skin-fold measurement indicating obesity _____   8
4. Percentile of skin-fold measurement indicating superobesity _____   10
5. Age at which first molars typically erupt _____   12
6. Age at which second molars typically erupt _____   13
7. Approximate percentage of schoolchildren who stutter _____   24
8. Age at which typical child can balance on one foot without looking _____   53
9. Age at which typical child can grip with 12 pounds of pressure _____   85
10. Age at which typical child can do a 3-foot standing high jump _____   95

Multiple-Choice: Circle the choice that best completes or answers each item.

1. The average annual weight gain (in pounds) in middle childhood is
   a. 1 to 2
   b. 3 to 4
   c. 5 to 7
   d. 8 to 10

2. Girls generally begin their growth spurt at about age
   a. 9
   b. 10 to 12
   c. 13 or 14
   d. 15

3. Which of the following statements about middle childhood is *not* true?
   a. Girls retain more fatty tissue than boys.
   b. Risk of accidents decreases.
   c. Colds and sore throats are prevalent.
   d. Efficiency of motor activity improves.

4. Eight-year-olds tend to be tallest in which of the following parts of the world?
   a. southeast Asia
   b. Oceania
   c. South America
   d. eastern Australia

5. A pediatrician is likely to recommend growth-hormone therapy only if a child is *all but which* of the following?
   a. unusually short
   b. unusually tall
   c. deficient in the hormone
   d. emotionally upset about his or her height

6. Children who were malnourished during infancy tend to be passive and unsociable because
   a. as infants, they were too weak to attract the mother's attention
   b. their mothers do not care about them
   c. they have learned not to depend on other people
   d. all of the above

7. Which of the following apparently does *not* tend to lead to obesity?
   a. genetic predisposition
   b. late weaning during infancy
   c. watching television
   d. being in a low socioeconomic group

8. Egocentric explanations for illness
   a. are abnormal in children older than 7
   b. are a defense against feelings of helplessness
   c. make children superstitious about germs
   d. all of the above

9. The improvement in American schoolchildren's dental health can be attributed to
   a. improved eating habits
   b. less fear of the dentist
   c. fluoridated drinking water
   d. all of the above

10. Symptoms of Tourette's syndrome are
    a. muscular and vocal tics; outbursts of obscenities
    b. aggression, impatience, and competitiveness
    c. migraine headaches and nearsightedness
    d. cavities and tooth decay

11. The childhood characteristic most likely to predict Type A behavior in adulthood is
    a. difficult temperament
    b. striving for achievement
    c. aggressiveness
    d. none of the above

12. The leading cause of disability and death in children over 1 year of age is
    a. heart disease
    b. obesity
    c. injury
    d. viral infection

13. Most childhood accidents occur in
    a. automobiles or the home
    b. school
    c. team or individual sports
    d. playgrounds

14. Differences between boys' and girls' motor abilities appear to be due to differences in
    a. strength and endurance
    b. interest and motivation
    c. expectations and participation
    d. skill and training

15. Left-handed people tend to be
    a. allergy-prone
    b. good at spatial tasks
    c. dyslexic
    d. all of the above

True or False? In the blank following each item, write T (for *true*) or F (for *false*). In the space below each item, if the statement is false, rewrite it to make it true.

1. White children are usually bigger than nonwhite children of the same age and sex. _____

2. Fat children tend to mature late. _____

3. The adolescent growth spurt makes it difficult to predict children's adult height. _____

4. Obesity is more common in the western United States than in the northeast or midwest. _____

5. Behavior modification has been effective in treating obesity. _____

6. Children who contract a particular minor medical condition once are likely to contract it again. _____

7. Children under 6 years old tend to be nearsighted. _____

8. Tooth decay can be prevented by the use of adhesive sealants on chewing surfaces. _____

9. Stuttering is more common in girls than in boys. _____

10. Childhood tics usually persist into adulthood. _____

11. Hypertension, or high blood pressure, is often associated with obesity. _____

12. Children identified as Type A are prone to heart attacks in adulthood. _____

13. Children with no siblings are less likely to be injured than children who have siblings. _____

14. At age 6, girls are superior to boys in accuracy of movement. _____

15. According to SAT tests given to 12- and 13-year-olds, a disproportionately high percentage of intellectually gifted students are left-handed. _____

TOPICS FOR THOUGHT AND DISCUSSION

1. What are the dangers of judging health and screening for abnormalities on the basis of average figures for physical growth? What specific problems might arise—for example, with respect to diagnosing malnutrition or deciding on the advisability of administering growth hormones?

2. Why do you think magical explanations for illness sometimes last well into childhood? Might there be a conflict between children's cognitive development and their emotional needs?

3. The authors of your text suggest that youngsters who, in early childhood, adjust well to going to the dentist become more resistant to dental visits in middle childhood because they are modeling their parents' behavior. Does this strike you as a likely explanation for this phenomenon? If not, can you suggest another explanation?

4. Can you suggest a hypothesis to explain why the relationship between the prosocial and antisocial aspects of Type A behavior reverses itself between childhood and adulthood, and can you suggest a way of testing your hypothesis?

5. There seems to be room for more research on the topic of handedness and its connection to physical or intellectual abilities. How would you design such research? What questions would you ask? What methods and types of experiments would you utilize?

6. In view of the lack of evidence to back up the prejudice against left-handedness, why do you think such prejudice has been so widespread?

CHAPTER 11 READING

INTRODUCTION

Although fat children often are the butt of jokes, being fat is no laughing matter. According to your text, obesity among schoolchildren has increased dramatically: "there are more fat children in the United States than ever before." These children are vulnerable to a variety of physical, social, and emotional problems. Furthermore, overweight children tend to become overweight adults, inviting such serious health problems as heart disease, cancer, and diabetes. This article by Sally Squires, reprinted from the *Washington Post*, takes a close look at the causes of and treatments for this major health hazard among our nation's youngsters.

Baby Fat: A Weigh to Poor Health

by Sally Squires

At the best of times, they are called pleasingly plump. Or chubby. And it's said in polite, hushed tones that they haven't yet outgrown their "baby fat."

At the worst of times, they are taunted by classmates. They earn nicknames like Tubby or Fatso. They're the Fat Alberts and the Porkies—labels that leave their psyches smarting well into adulthood.

But for the estimated 10 percent to 30 percent of U.S. children ages 8 to 18 who are overweight, being fat is more than a social inconvenience.

Their extra pounds mean they are vulnerable to a host of physical ailments that can shave years from their lives—through premature heart disease, cancer, high blood pressure and diabetes.

Experts once advised parents to wait and let their overweight children "grow out of" their so-called baby fat. Today, pediatricians and others are taking a more aggressive approach, bolstered by scientific studies that show that being an overweight child lays the foundation for becoming an overweight adult—and increases the risk of dying early from heart attacks, strokes and other ailments.

"As late as 1974, people were concerned that if you did anything to change a child's diet, you would end up with a malnourished kid," said Robert Klesges, a psychologist at Memphis State University.

"But that has changed dramatically in the last 10 years."

What concerns experts most is that obesity seems to be on the rise in the United States, particularly among children.

"We've shown over the past 15 years that obesity in children 6 to 11 years has increased 54 percent among U.S. children," said Dr. William Dietz, a pediatrician and director of Clinical Nutrition at the New England Medical Center in Boston. "Among youngsters 12 to 17 years obesity has increased 39 percent in the past 15 years."

In a consensus statement on obesity, the National Institutes of Health reported in 1985 that it "views with concern the increasing frequency of obesity in children and adolescents. Obese children should be encouraged to stay within normal [weight] limits."

Yet experts are still struggling to define what is normal and what isn't. Most now agree that obese children are those who are 20 percent or more above the ideal weight for their height, age and sex. Overweight children are generally children who are 10 percent to 19 percent above their ideal weight for height, age and sex.

But if the definitions aren't totally clear, the research is.

"Overweight children are at greater risk of becoming overweight adults than lean children are," said Leonard Epstein, an obesity researcher at the University of Pittsburgh School of Medicine. A growing number of studies have shown, Epstein said, that "a large number of overweight children do not outgrow being overweight."

Consider that:

At age 6 months, about one-third of obese infants are destined to become overweight adults, a study by researchers at the University of Rochester showed.

By age 7, four of every 10 obese children become overweight adults.

At ages 10 through 13, about 70 percent of overweight children can count on carrying their extra pounds with them into adulthood.

Exactly which heavy children will go on to be heavy adults is not always clear, but there are some intriguing clues that suggest a variety of factors—

such as region of the country, family income, family size—help determine who will become a fat adult.

For example, children from small families are more prone to putting on unwanted pounds than youngsters from large families. An only child has twice the chance of becoming heavy as does a child with three or more brothers or sisters.

Children from urban areas are more likely to be overweight than their rural counterparts, although no one knows why. Obesity experts believe the difference is the result of less exercise and more opportunities for eating. City children rarely have yards in which to play. Their activities are likely to be confined indoors and burn up fewer calories that may help to contribute to extra pounds.

Youngsters who live in colder climates—the Northeast and the Midwest—also run a higher risk of added pounds than children who live in the South and the West. The reason, experts say, is that during the winter, people put on weight for extra warmth and lead more sedentary lives because of the inclement weather.

Income also plays a role in determining which children are likely to be fat for life. Lower-income families are more apt to have youngsters with weight problems than upper-income families. Children from middle-income households fall in between.

But the single most important predictor of whether a child is at risk for becoming obese is the parents' weight.

Researchers such as Dr. Albert Stunkard of the University of Pennsylvania are documenting scientifically what many people always have suspected: that being fat—and being lean—seems to run in families.

In a study of Danish adults who had been adopted into other families as children, Stunkard and his colleagues found that the body weight of adoptees much more closely matched the body weight of their biological rather than adoptive parents. The findings point to the important role that the genes may play in obesity.

Other studies underscore the point. One of the most widely cited among obesity researchers is a report that found 80 percent of the children with two obese parents will become obese adults, while about 40 percent of the children with one obese parent will become fat, and only 20 percent of children whose parents are normal weight will be obese as adults.

Based on these results, some people have suggested that the battle is pointless. What's the use of trying to fight obesity, they say, if it's been preordained?

Helping Your Child Lose Weight

Childhood obesity experts offer these tips to parents of overweight children:

Don't put your child on a diet without first checking with your pediatrician or family physician. It's important that children be medically evaluated before starting any weight loss program.

If you place your overweight youngster on a diet, be sure to follow through. Studies suggest that losing a few pounds and then putting it back on again right away can be harmful. This yo-yo effect can even make it more difficult for children, and adults, to lose weight because the body can respond by acting as though it is being starved.

When you choose a weight-loss program for your children, be sure it allows a gradual weight loss, one of just a half-pound to a pound per week for children 6 and older. For those younger than 6, it may simply be best for them not to gain any more weight until they grow taller.

If you place one child on a diet, make sure the whole family helps. That means getting rid of all the fattening foods from the cupboards and the refrigerator.

Limit television watching to a half hour or less a day, obesity experts suggest. The more children languish in front of the television, the fewer calories they burn.

Encourage youngsters to move around and play outdoors. In short, do anything to increase the number of calories they burn. Walking is one of the best exercises for heavy children. The best bet, say experts, is when a parent walks regularly with a child.

"That's a wrong idea," Stunkard said. What these new results do, he added, is "give people the possibility of informed prevention, not just a shotgun approach."

It means that families with a history of obesity "will really have to work on trying to prevent obesity in their kids." And once those children are adults, they, too, will have to "remain eternally vigilant against gaining weight."

The struggle is worth it, experts say, for like their adult counterparts, overweight children pay a stiff emotional and physical price for their added pounds. "The more severe a problem a child has, the less likely that he or she will be able to grow out of it," Dietz said.

"The biggest factor for overweight and obese children is the psychological problems," said Dr. Dorothy Richmond, a pediatrician who specializes in treating eating disorders at Georgetown University Medical School. "Those problems have more immediate effects than the medical problems, and they're much more common."

The psychological suffering for fat children often translates to behavior problems: trouble in school; shyness; hyperactivity; being withdrawn or depressed.

Fat children are teased about their weight by their peers. They are the last chosen to play on the team. The style of clothes that is so important to adolescents often isn't even an option. "You don't get designer jeans in the superhusky sizes," said Richmond.

But being fat also takes a physical toll, she added. "They have a whole host of minor complaints: back pain, foot pain, inability to do exercise, shortness of breath."

The very obese child may have trouble sleeping at night because the chest can't expand normally.

"Carbon dioxide builds up in the blood, and they feel sleepy and may fall asleep in class," Richmond said. Extra pounds also can cause sleep apnea—the temporary cessation of breathing—which forces them to wake up numerous times during the night to breathe.

Being overweight in childhood often sets the stage for a lifetime battle with excess pounds and an increased risk of heart disease, diabetes, cancer and orthopedic problems.

Obese children often suffer from "high blood pressure, abnormal glucose tolerance tests—an indication of greater risk for diabetes—and high blood cholesterol levels," Dietz said. "By treating children who are overweight, we are really preventing severe adult disease and avoiding the medical and social complications of obesity in childhood."

The other benefit of helping fat children lose weight is that it can change their self-image and make them feel better about themselves.

"The self-confidence that emerges from these children once they have lost weight just amazes me," said Debra DeVos, whose daughter lost 25 pounds through the Stoplight Diet, a program developed at the University of Pittsburgh. "You see grades excelling, you see children wanting to interact with peers. The aura of self-confidence just reeks from them."

QUESTIONS ABOUT THE READING

1. The authors of your text suggest that children make fatness an object of ridicule because "American society equates thinness with beauty." Why, in the light of that societal value, is obesity becoming so prevalent? What lifestyle changes discussed in various sections of Chapter 11 might be relevant?

2. This article gives a definition of obesity based on variation above the "ideal weight" for a child's height, age, and sex. Your text gives a different definition, based on skin-fold measurement. Which definition seems more useful, and why?

3. The article cites a finding of a University of Rochester study that one-third of obese infants become overweight adults—a finding that seems contrary to other research reported in Chapter 5 of your text. Can you think of any factors that might be investigated by researchers trying to reconcile these results?

4. Are the risk factors for obesity identified in the article largely consistent with those identified in your text?

5. Why is a gradual weight-loss program important? Can you explain in your own words why the "yo-yo effect" in dieting can be harmful? Why might it be best for children under 6 simply "not to gain any more weight until they grow taller"?

ANSWER KEY FOR CHAPTER 11

Note: Numbers in parentheses refer to pages in the textbook where answers can be found.

CHAPTER 11 REVIEW

Important Terms for Section I

1. menarche (page 396)
2. 85th, 85 (399)

Learning Objectives for Section I

1. (pages 395, 396)
2. (395-396)
3. (396-397)
4. (397)
5. (397)
6. (398-399)
7. (399-401)

Important Terms for Section II

1. repetition (page 404)
2. stereotyped (405)
3. A (405)
4. B (406)

Learning Objectives for Section II

1. (pages 401-402)
2. (402)
3. (402)
4. (402-404)
5. (404-405)
6. (405-406)
7. (407)
8. (407-409)

Important Term for Section III

1. preference (page 411)

Learning Objectives for Section III

1. (pages 409-411)
2. (411-412)

CHAPTER 11 QUIZ

Matching—Numbers

1. 53 (page 396)
2. 24 (397, 398)
3. 85 (399)
4. 95 (399)
5. 6 (403)
6. 13 (403)
7. 10 (404)
8. 7 (409)
9. 8 (409)
10. 12 (409)

Multiple-Choice

1. c (page 395)
2. b (395)
3. b (395)
4. d (396)
5. b (397)
6. a (398)
7. b (400)
8. b (402)
9. c (403)
10. a (405)
11. a (406)
12. c (407)
13. a (408)
14. c (411)
15. d (412)

True or False?

1. F—Nonwhite children are usually somewhat bigger than white children of the same age and sex. (page 396)
2. F—Fat children tend to mature early. (396)
3. T (397)
4. F—Obesity is more common in the northeast and midwest. (399)
5. T (401)
6. T (401)
7. F—Children under 6 tend to be farsighted. (402)
8. T (403)
9. F—Stuttering is 3 times more common in boys than in girls. (404)
10. F—Most tics go away before adolescence. (405)
11. T (405)
12. F—Type A behavior, which is associated with heart attacks in adults, is not consistent from childhood to adulthood. (406)
13. T (408)
14. T (409)
15. T (412)

INTELLECTUAL DEVELOPMENT IN MIDDLE CHILDHOOD

OVERVIEW

Chapter 12 focuses on a number of important issues concerning intellectual development in middle childhood. In this chapter the authors:

■ Look at the intellectual development of school-age children from the Piagetian, information-processing, and psychometric perspectives

■ Outline stages in the development of moral reasoning in relation to cognitive development

■ Describe advances in memory and language abilities

■ Discuss controversies surrounding the design and use of IQ tests, particularly for minority children

■ Examine the role that school plays in children's lives and how schools meet the special needs of children with disabilities

■ Suggest how giftedness, creativity, and talent can be nurtured

CHAPTER 12 REVIEW

Section I Approaches to Intellectual Development

FRAMEWORK FOR SECTION I

A. Piagetian Approach: The Stage of Concrete Operations (about 7 to 11 Years)
1. Conservation
   a. Testing Conservation
   b. Development of Different Types of Conservation
   c. Effects of Experience on Conservation
2. Moral Development: Three Theories
   a. Piaget: Constraint and Cooperation
   b. Selman: Role-Taking
   c. Kohlberg: Levels of Moral Reasoning
      (1) Kohlberg's Moral Dilemmas
      (2) Kohlberg's Levels and Stages
      (3) Evaluating Kohlberg's Theory
         (a) Cross-Cultural Validity
         (b) Validity for Females
         (c) The Role of Experience
         (d) Testing Procedures and the Meaning of Results
B. Information-Processing Approach: Development of Memory in Middle Childhood
1. Memory Capacity
2. Strategies for Remembering
   a. Rehearsal
   b. Categorization
   c. Elaboration
   d. External Aids
3. Metamemory
C. Psychometric Approach: Measuring Intelligence in Middle Childhood
1. Psychometric Intelligence Tests for Schoolchildren
2. Implications of Intelligence Tests
   a. Cross-Cultural Testing
      (1) Culture-Free and Culture-Fair Tests
      (2) Intelligence Testing of Black Children
   b. Changes in Performance on Intelligence Tests

IMPORTANT TERMS FOR SECTION I

Completion: Fill in the blanks to complete the definitions of key terms for this section of Chapter 12.

1. **concrete operations:** Piaget's third stage of cognitive development, during which children develop the ability to think logically about the here and now, but not about _____.

2. **conservation:** Piaget's term for awareness that two stimuli which are equal (in length, weight, or amount, for example) remain equal in the face of perceptual _____ , so long as nothing has been added to or taken away from either stimulus.

3. **horizontal decalage:** In Piaget's terminology, the development of different types of _____ at different ages; thus a child can _____ substance before weight, and substance and weight before volume.

4. **morality of _____:** In Piaget's theory, the first stage of moral reasoning, in which a child thinks rigidly about moral concepts; also called *heteronomous morality*.

5. **morality of _____:** In Piaget's theory, the second stage of moral reasoning, in which a child has moral flexibility; also called *autonomous morality*.

6. **role-taking:** In _____'s terminology, assuming another person's point of view.

7. **preconventional morality:** Kohlberg's first level of moral reasoning, in which the emphasis is on external control, obedience to the rules and standards of others, and the desire to avoid _____.

8. **morality of conventional role conformity:** Second level in Kohlberg's theory of moral reasoning, in which children want to please other people and have _____ the standards of authority figures.

9. **morality of** _____: Third level of Kohlberg's theory of moral reasoning, in which people follow internally held moral principles and decide between conflicting moral standards.

10. _____ **memory:** Awareness of images and _____ that disappears quickly unless it is transferred into short-term memory.

11. **short-term memory:** _____ memory, which has a limited capacity; the content fades rapidly unless it is stored or actively preserved through rehearsal. Compare _long-term memory_.

12. **long-term memory:** Stored memories; the capacity seems unlimited and the duration of a memory may be _____. Compare _short-term memory_.

13. **rehearsal:** Strategy to keep an item in short-term memory through conscious _____.

14. _____: Process of organizing material in one's mind into related groupings to aid in remembering.

15. **elaboration:** Linking items to be remembered by creating a(n) _____ about them or a visual image of them.

16. _____: Knowledge of the process of memory.

17. **Wechsler Intelligence Scale for Children (WISC-R):** Individual intelligence test for children that includes _____ and _____ subtests.

18. _____ - _____ **School Ability Test:** Group intelligence test for children.

19. **System of** _____ **(SOMPA):** Battery of measures designed to take environmental factors into account in assessing intelligence.

LEARNING OBJECTIVES FOR SECTION I

After reading and reviewing this section of Chapter 12, you should be able to do the following.

1. List six capabilities children achieve in the stage of concrete operations.

2. Explain the concept of conservation and how it is tested.

3. Outline the sequence in which different types of conservation typically develop, and cite factors that affect the age at which they develop.

4. Explain the link between moral values and cognitive development.

5. Identify and describe Piaget's two stages of moral reasoning.

6. List Selman's five stages of role-taking.

7. Outline Kohlberg's three levels and six stages of moral reasoning, and give a typical answer to a moral dilemma at each stage.

8. Cite four types of criticisms of Kohlberg's theory.

9. Identify three types of memory, and describe four common strategies for remembering.

10. Trace progress in schoolchildren's understanding of their own memory processes.

11. Summarize the pros and cons of intelligence testing.

12. Name three commonly used intelligence tests for school-age children.

13. Explain the problem of cultural bias in designing intelligence tests.

14. Assess factors affecting differences between intelligence test scores of black and white children.

15. Point out reasons for the high achievement of Japanese and Chinese schoolchildren.

16. Explain why a child's performance on intelligence tests can change.

17. List at least five ways to teach children thinking skills.

Section II Development of Language in Middle Childhood

FRAMEWORK FOR SECTION II

A. Grammar: The Structure of Language
B. Language and Communication
C. Children's Humor

IMPORTANT TERMS FOR SECTION II

Completion: Fill in the blanks to complete the definitions of key terms for this section of Chapter 12.

1. **syntax:** Way in which words are organized into phrases and _____.

2. _____: Knowledge of communication processes.

LEARNING OBJECTIVES FOR SECTION II

After reading and reviewing this section of Chapter 12, you should be able to do the following.

1. Trace the development of schoolchildren's use and understanding of grammar (including syntax).

2. Explain the significance of metacommunication.

3. Summarize the relationship between humor and cognitive development.

Section III The Child in School

FRAMEWORK FOR SECTION III

A. Recent Trends in Education
B. Teachers
   1. Teachers' Influence
   2. Teachers' Expectations: The Self-Fulfilling Prophecy
C. Schoolchildren with Special Needs
   1. Children with Disabilities
      a. Mentally Retarded, Learning-Disabled, and Hyperactive Children
         (1) Mental Retardation
         (2) Learning Disabilities
         (3) Hyperactivity
      b. Educating Children with Disabilities
   2. Gifted, Creative, and Talented Children
      a. Giftedness
         (1) Defining and Identifying Giftedness
         (2) The Lives of Gifted Children
         (3) Educating Gifted Children
      b. Creativity
         (1) Defining and Identifying Creativity
         (2) Fostering Creativity
      c. Talent: Recognizing and Encouraging Talented Children

IMPORTANT TERMS FOR SECTION III

Completion: Fill in the blanks to complete the definitions of key terms for this section of Chapter 12.

1. _____ **prophecy:** Prediction of behavior that biases people to act as though the prophecy were already true.

2. **mental** _____: Below-average intellectual functioning.

3. **dyslexia:** Inability or difficulty in learning to _____.

4. _____ **(LDs):** Disorders that interfere with specific aspects of learning and school achievement.

5. _____ **disorder (ADHD):** Syndrome characterized by inattention, impulsivity, and considerable activity at inappropriate times and places.

6. **mainstreaming:** Integration of
_____ and
_____ children in the same
classroom.

7. _____: One or more of the
following: superior general intellect,
superiority in a single domain (like
mathematics or science), artistic talent,
leadership ability, or creative thinking.

8. _____: Ability to see things in a
new light, to see problems that others fail to
recognize, and to come up with new, unusual,
and effective solutions.

9. **convergent thinking:** Thinking aimed at
finding the one _____ answer to a
problem.

10. _____ **thinking:** Creative
thinking; the ability to discover new, unusual
answers to a problem.

11. _____ **Tests of Creative Thinking:**
Test battery developed for use with
schoolchildren that measures creativity with
words, pictures, and sounds and words.

LEARNING OBJECTIVES FOR SECTION III

After reading and reviewing this section of Chapter
12, you should be able to do the following.

1. Summarize recent trends in American
education.

2. Cite findings about teachers' influence on
students' success, and explain the role of the
self-fulfilling prophecy.

3. Describe how parents can help children
achieve in school, and list at least five
suggestions for helping children read better.

4. Describe the incidence, causes, effects, and
treatment of mental retardation, learning
disabilities, and hyperactivity.

5. Present the pros and cons of mainstreaming
students with disabilities.

6. Compare various ways in which giftedness is
defined and identified.

7. Summarize findings about the life success and
social adjustment of gifted children.

8. Compare the two major approaches to
educating gifted children.

9. Explain how creativity differs from academic intelligence, and describe how it can be identified and fostered.

10. Describe ways of recognizing and encouraging talent that have led to outstanding achievement.

CHAPTER 12 QUIZ

Matching—Who's Who: Match each name in the left-hand column with the appropriate description at the right.

1. Jean Piaget _____
2. Robert Selman _____
3. Lawrence Kohlberg _____
4. Carol Gilligan _____
5. Robert Sternberg _____
6. Carol S. Chomsky _____
7. Helen Keller _____
8. Thomas Edison _____
9. Stephen A. Baccus _____
10. Lewis Terman _____

a. held that women define morality differently from men
b. tested children's understanding of syntax
c. had dyslexia
d. identified the phenomenon of horizontal decalage
e. was considered a child prodigy; graduated from law school at age 16
f. identified levels of moral reasoning from responses to moral dilemmas
g. initiated a longitudinal study of gifted children
h. was deaf and blind at a time when education for the handicapped was not readily available
i. criticized IQ tests for failure to measure important aspects of intelligence
j. held that moral development is linked to role-taking

Multiple-Choice: Circle the choice that best completes or answers each item.

1. Which of the following can be performed more easily during Piaget's stage of concrete operations than during the preoperational stage?
   a. understanding conservation
   b. classifying objects
   c. distinguishing between reality and fantasy
   d. all of the above

2. The last type of conservation to develop is
   a. volume
   b. weight
   c. substance
   d. none of the above; they all develop at about the same time

3. According to Piaget, the factor that most strongly affects the development of conservation is
   a. intelligence
   b. maturation
   c. experience
   d. cultural background

4. In Piaget's theory of moral reasoning, children reach the stage of morality of cooperation when they can
   a. think less egocentrically
   b. accept adult standards and rules
   c. judge an act by its consequences
   d. all of the above

5. In Selman's theory, reciprocal awareness typically develops at about what age?
   a. 3 to 4
   b. 5 to 7
   c. 8 to 10
   d. 11 to 13

6. According to Kohlberg, a person's level of moral reasoning is related to
   a. training by parents
   b. education
   c. cognitive level
   d. emotional maturity

7. In Kohlberg's third stage, maintaining mutual relations, children obey rules because they want to
   a. avoid punishment
   b. be rewarded
   c. do their duty
   d. please and help others

8. Which of the following has *not* been a criticism of Kohlberg's theory?
   a. Research has failed to confirm his proposed sequence of stages.
   b. Men tend to score higher than women.
   c. People from nonwestern cultures score lower than westerners.
   d. The link between hypothetical and actual behavior is not clear.

9. The capacity of which kind of memory increases rapidly in middle childhood?
   a. sensory
   b. short-term
   c. long-term
   d. all of the above

10. Which of the following is an external aid to memory?
    a. categorization
    b. elaboration
    c. writing
    d. rehearsal

11. The most widely used individual intelligence test is the
    a. Wechsler Intelligence Scale for Children
    b. Stanford-Binet Intelligence Test
    c. Otis-Lennon School Ability Test
    d. System of Multicultural Pluralistic Assessment

12. Test developers have been unable to devise culture-free intelligence tests because
    a. tests require the use of language
    b. "common" experiences are affected by cultural values
    c. it is impossible to eliminate culture-linked content
    d. all of the above

13. Which of the following statements about performance on intelligence tests is true?
    a. Because intelligence is inborn, an individual's IQ is fairly stable; thus test performance, in general, has remained approximately constant.
    b. Motivation, personality, and experience can contribute to a rise or fall in an individual's IQ; but, on the average, test performance has remained approximately constant.
    c. Motivation, personality, and experience can contribute to a rise or fall in an individual's IQ; test performance, in general, has improved in recent years.
    d. Motivation, personality, and experience can contribute to a rise or fall in an individual's IQ; test performance, in general, has declined in recent years.

14. Which of the following sentence constructions would a 6-year-old be most likely to use?
    a. "She knew that the teacher was going to call on her."
    b. "These cookies were baked yesterday."
    c. "If you let me use your truck, then I'll let you use my shovel."
    d. "I have looked all over for my ball, and I can't find it."

15. According to research, which of the following parents is most likely to have a child who is a high achiever?
    a. Alice, who expects her daughter to do well in school and puts pressure on her to do so
    b. Brenda, who expects her son to do well but puts no pressure on him
    b. Curt, who puts pressure on his son to do well but doesn't really expect him to
    d. David, who expects his daughter to do well and punishes her when she falls short

16. The Education for All Handicapped Children Act requires placement of handicapped children, whenever possible, in
    a. residential programs
    b. special schools
    c. special classes
    d. regular classes

17. Identification of giftedness is usually based on
    a. an IQ score of 130 or higher
    b. outstanding ability in a specific area like math or science
    c. creativity
    d. all of the above

18. Which of the following of Gardner's "intelligences" is measured by traditional intelligence tests?
    a. musical
    b. spatial
    c. bodily-kinesthetic
    d. none of the above

19. Gifted children tend to have social and emotional problems if their IQs are higher than
    a. 120
    b. 140
    c. 160
    d. 180

20. Tests of creativity attempt to measure
    a. convergent thinking
    b. divergent thinking
    c. subjective thinking
    d. artistic talent

True or False? In the blank following each item, write T (for *true*) or F (for *false*). In the space below each item, if the statement is false, rewrite it to make it true.

1. According to Piaget, the ability to think abstractly develops in the stage of concrete operations, which coincides with middle childhood. _____

2. Piaget discovered the principle of conservation while working with epileptic children. _____

3. Piaget's stage of morality of constraint coincides roughly with his stage of concrete operations. _____

4. Selman influenced Piaget and Kohlberg. _____

5. Some people never reach Kohlberg's third level, morality of autonomous moral principles. _____

6. When sixth-graders try to remember something, they are more likely to categorize the information than to repeat it over and over. _____

7. Black Americans on average score 15 points lower on IQ tests than white Americans. _____

8. According to studies, the explanation for the high achievement of Asian children is that they start out with a slight cognitive advantage. _____

9. The ability to think is inborn and cannot be taught. _____

10. Children's understanding of syntax continues to develop until the age of 9 or later. _____

11. Five-year-olds often are unaware that when they do not understand directions they cannot do a job well. _____

12. Children who continually make up jokes and puns are seen by teachers as troublemakers. _____

13. One reason for the "back to basics" trend in education was a drop in students' SAT scores in the 1970s. _____

14. Schoolchildren's achievement tends to match their teachers' expectations. _____

15. All but about 15 percent of retarded people can acquire skills up to the sixth-grade level. _____

16. With proper guidance, a child can outgrow a learning disability such as dyslexia. _____

17. Advocates of enriching rather than accelerating gifted children's education believe that skipping exposes children to too much pressure. _____

18. Creativity and intelligence are highly correlated. _____

19. There is little or no evidence that tests of creativity, such as the Torrance Tests of Creative Thinking, are valid. _____

20. According to a study of high achievers done in Chicago, a "longitudinal" approach to the training of talent is more effective than a "cross-sectional" approach. _____

TOPICS FOR THOUGHT AND DISCUSSION

1. Piaget initially thought that he had discovered a method for distinguishing intellectual development in epileptics from that of normal children—until he expanded his conservation experiments to include nonepileptic children. He is quoted in your text (Box 12-1) as saying, "A biologist would have to verify; a philosopher would not have checked." What do you think Piaget meant by this remark?

2. What areas of agreement and disagreement do you find in the theories of moral development proposed by Piaget, Selman, and Kohlberg?

3. Is criticism of Kohlberg's theory of moral development by Carol Gilligan and others similar to criticisms of intelligence testing for cultural bias? If these criticisms are valid, do they make both the theory and the tests useless? Can you suggest any additional ways to deal with these difficulties, besides those mentioned in your text?

4. Do you think that the "back to the basics" trend is likely to produce predominantly convergent or divergent thinkers?

5. The authors of your text favor a definition of giftedness that includes artistic talent as well as creativity. The researchers who conducted the Chicago study mentioned in Chapter 12 seem to have defined talent quite broadly, since the study included pianists, sculptors, athletes, mathematicians, and neurologists. How would you define *talent*? How does it differ from creativity? Does a discussion of talent belong in a chapter on intellectual development?

6. Box 12-3 presents suggestions for teaching children to think, and Box 12-4 presents suggestions for helping children read better. Recalling John Holt's comments about the teaching of reading (in Chapter 6 of this Study Guide), do you think that Holt would approve or disapprove of the suggestions in these boxes?

CHAPTER 12 READING

INTRODUCTION

"John Scott is a sixteen-year-old college freshman who has given us an unusual opportunity to bring you a very personal, sensitive story," wrote the editors of *Instructor* magazine in introducing the author of the following selection.

"Don't Make Me Walk When I Want to Fly," reprinted from the magazine's January 1977 issue, is an autobiographical account by a boy who was identified as gifted early in his school career. Although he was clearly an achiever, his recollections of his school experiences give some clues about obstacles that may cause some gifted children to have social problems or to fail to make the most of their abilities.

Because he was writing for an audience of elementary school teachers, Scott's comments center on how his schooling affected him; but he also assesses the influences of his family and his home environment. His views on the nurturance of gifts and talents are refreshing and revealing and also may have application to children who are not considered gifted.

As you read this selection, keep in mind that different schools have different kinds of educational programs for gifted students, and practices in some schools have changed since the article was written.

Don't Make Me Walk When I Want to Fly: An Open Letter from a Gifted Child

by John Scott

My name is John. I'm 16, and I have two younger brothers, Mark and Todd. On our school records, a green clip identifies all of us as *Ex Chs*, which for years mystified me, but which you know stands for Exceptional Child—the smarty pants variety.

My parents were told that my IQ is in the 160s and that my brothers weren't far behind. School was easy, and I was in the top five percent on SAT scores. Maybe I'm innately bright, but I have another theory as to why I became an *Ex Ch*.

Here's how I explain myself. I was born right after my grandfather's death, and my grandmother became a great influence in my life. At first it was almost full time. She spent her waking hours reading, showing, telling, taking me places—the latter starting when I was less than one year old.

Influence number two was almost as potent. My aunt is a reviewer of children's books. From the day I was born, boxes of books arrived at my grandmother's house. I can honestly say that I can't remember when I couldn't read. My grandmother thinks I recognized words at two, and it's probably true, for both my brothers did. Anyway, I spent hours on my grandmother's lap following along as she read, and I guess I learned automatically.

The other major contributors to my early life were my mother and father. My dad is a carpenter, and early he taught me how to use tools, how to measure exactly, how to be thrifty and neat in what I made. Under him, I developed precise skills. He's also an outdoor man and spent many hours with my brothers and me gardening, hiking, and camping. I learned innumerable lessons from my father, who is a truly great guy in a thousand ways.

My mother gave me order and oughtness in a low-key sort of way. I can never remember not folding my clothing neatly at night. Changing my clothes after school was automatic, and they got hung up, too. My brothers and I shared a room and each guy made his own bed—a hard, fast rule. Even on weekends when we got up ahead of our parents to watch cartoons, no one dared look at TV if his bed wasn't made. From my mother I also learned the rules of politeness—how to meet grown-ups, how to accept gifts. Don't knock it. This training gave me a lot of confidence.

It wasn't until I went to kindergarten that I realized I knew more or thought more complexly than other kids. Sunday school had been sort of vague. I would sit and read the Sunday school papers, but I honestly didn't know that the other kids couldn't read them.

In kindy I was a marked kid. I handed out papers for the teacher, read stories to the other kids, and once I even marked papers for the first-grade teacher. I didn't learn much except an important lesson that I've been learning ever since: One's peers are suspicious and resentful of you when you do things more quickly or better than they do. I soon found ways to hide or play down what I know, and I find myself still doing it today.

Since this is a letter for teachers, I want to tell you mostly what happened in school. Unlike many schools, it *did* try to take care of *Ex Chs* in a variety of ways.

Skipping

I'm sorry to report that I got skipped twice. After my kindergarten performance, the first-grade teacher didn't want me. (Maybe it was those papers that I marked.) Anyway, the principal convinced my parents I should start the next year in second grade.

At first I found myself behind the others in both motor and formal skills. I didn't write as small and neatly as they did, and had to do a lot of practicing at home for the first couple of months. Also, the kids who had been in first grade knew how to do their workbook exercises and they had less trouble sitting at their desks for long periods of time. Yet, I soon noticed that my classmates, whom I was in awe of because they were older, made some pretty simple judgments and decisions which the teacher accepted. I learned to keep quiet.

My second skipping came after I was in fourth grade for two months. I felt the teacher wanted to get rid of her *Ex Ch* so she pushed me off on the fifth-grade teacher. It was the best break of my elementary years. I'll tell you why later—but I paid for it in high school.

Absolutely, I don't recommend skipping for *Ex Chs*. It may be an immediate solution, but it's a long-range detriment. It's no fun being 13, 14, and 15 in tenth, eleventh, and twelfth grades.

Enrichment

If schools don't skip *Ex Chs,* then they have to provide more of the stuff that's called enrichment. Schools aren't set up for innovative enrichment—they could learn a lesson from my grandmother—but I'll describe what happened. A student interested in science or math was accommodated fairly easily. There were kits for them to build, experiments to do, advanced workbooks in math, and so on. Unfortunately, I was interested in books, social situations, aesthetics, and languages; so I was more of a problem. The school didn't have kits for me.

For example, in the summer between second and third grades, I met a Spanish boy. That fall I asked the principal if I could learn Spanish, but he turned me down because there was no teacher to help me, and he wouldn't let me do it on my own. I think the prospect of a seven-year-old third grader learning Spanish independently may have been too much for him to accept.

Language and Communication

My fifth-grade teacher was an elderly lady near retirement. She was a jewel, and I cried at her funeral last year. She may have had no training in what to do with an *Ex Ch,* but she was a natural. First, she talked to me about anything and everything. She introduced me to old-fashioned diagraming which I found to be great fun. We played games, with her trying to concoct a sentence that I couldn't diagram. She brought me Latin books and I would stay after school and talk Latin to her. Latin was the only other language she had ever learned, but from that experience I learned that I have a knack for languages. Today, I speak fairly fluent Spanish, French, and German, having learned the first two in high school and teaching myself the latter with the use of tapes, records, and self-study books.

She gave me Lamb's *Tales from Shakespeare,* then took me to see Hamlet and I became a disciple of the Bard . . . and was she ever sneaky! She insisted I train my memory and gave me passages of Shakespeare to memorize. I fell for it, seeing myself as the next John Gielgud. Today I'm grateful. Memorizing is not only a wonderful tool, it gives comfort and support in lonely moments.

She built my vocabulary by introducing me to complex words, and in our private conversations we used them freely—you never heard such talk! You may have sensed that she and I were almost clandestine in our special relationship. In front of others she treated me like them and I understood. Fifth grade was my happiest year, and I never had a better teacher.

Special Efforts

While I was in fifth grade, a new young principal who cared about *Ex Chs* came to our school. He set out to identify us and give us special things to do. Some of his projects were what I called, *so-whats,* but my brothers loved them. I didn't, but I respected him so much that I did them anyway. For example, he taught us how to estimate the height of a flagpole by measuring its shadow. He showed us how to estimate the number of bricks used to build our school. Today I amuse myself in boring situations by doing *so-whats.* In high school courses that were dull, I'd figure how many bricks would be needed to box in the room. Doodling is another good *so-what.* I find I can keep myself out of a lot of trouble by doodling.

The principal organized chess games and encouraged games such as Monopoly and 3-D checkers. He liked games and I think we all learned from playing them.

Special Projects

By the time I was in sixth grade, the principal had convinced someone in authority that there should be a resource teacher to set up special projects for *Ex Chs.* He meant well, but we were better off when he was taking care of us.

Don't think me a snob, but the person who thinks up *Ex Ch* projects better be a former *Ex Ch.* Our resource teacher wasn't and didn't have much of a sense of humor. In October I was assigned a research project on Columbus. (Original idea, wasn't it?) The whole thing was pretty boring, but I did it and got into a lot of trouble. As part of the assignment was to do a piece of original writing, I wrote a funny (to me) soap-opera skit. My plot was that Isabella and Christopher were having an affair. Ferdinand discovered it and sent Chris off on the high seas. Further, Ferdy got his revenge by using Isabella's money to finance the project. The teacher went into shock and called my parents.

Responsibility

My brothers and I were encouraged to earn our own money. I started with a paper route and soon had both brothers involved. We had it down pat, both distribution and collection. We paid our father a dollar to drive us to deliver Sunday papers.

Once we mastered paper delivery, we began looking for a way to earn greater profits. Since we had our own tools, which our father had taught us how to care for and use, we opened a gardening service. Throughout junior and senior high school we had all the lawns we could care for. Of course there were some family donations but most of the $3,100 I had in my savings account when I graduated from high school I had earned.

Aesthetics

Starting in sixth grade (my parents had reservations, and I told none of my friends) I enrolled in ballet class. Today I don't want to be a ballet dancer and I'm through my John Gielgud period, but the ballet class was a great experience. I enjoyed the expressive movement, the music, the costumes, and even learned how to do some choreography.

I experimented on my grandmother's piano and took enough lessons to give me a limited facility. My tastes in music differ from my brothers'; so my father helped me fix my own equipment in the headboard of my bed, and I listen with earphones.

The Future

As maybe you can guess, I hope to be a writer and am studying toward that end in college. I think I would also like to teach literature or languages in college.

In conclusion, I'd have to say that I came out of elementary school relatively unscathed. No teacher was ever really mean to me, and my fifth-grade teacher and the principal were great—I group them with my parents and grandmother in a special closed set.

But elementary school could have been a lot better. I spent a lot of time standing still, doodling, and pretending. Undoubtedly, the teachers had a lot of other children who needed their attention more than I did.

I want to finish with an idea and a question. The idea is, if you have an *Ex Ch* in your room, remember he has problems of his own. Be supportive, even protective, and never put him down in front of his peers. Help him fly when the world around him is walking.

The question—would you have wanted me in *your* room?

QUESTIONS ABOUT THE READING

1. Scott attributes his giftedness not to "innate brightness" but to the influence of his grandmother, the books he received from his aunt, and the primarily social skills he learned from his father and mother. Do you think he is sincere in this disclaimer of innate brightness, or is it an example of his tendency to "hide" his gifts? Does his account support the relative weight given to hereditary and environmental influences on intelligence in various chapters of your text?

2. Which practices followed in Scott's upbringing were similar to those recommended in Box 12-4 of your text? Which were different? Which might be useful with "average" children?

3. Scott says he was "a marked kid" from kindergarten on, and he continues to find ways to "hide or play down" what he knows. Why does outstanding academic ability tend to "mark" a child in this way, while outstanding athletic or musical ability does not? Are there ways in which our culture could avoid the potential waste of gifts due to peer resentment?

4. In what ways was Scott's fifth-grade teacher different from his other teachers? In what ways was she like his grandmother? In what ways was she like the "Miss A" described in your text? Are the same qualities likely to make a teacher successful with gifted students as with disadvantaged students? If so, does this suggest that in some respects the needs of gifted students are not so special after all?

5. Terman's study suggested that skipping grades is not harmful to bright children; yet Scott, who skipped twice, does not recommend the practice. Other studies show that skipping (or some other form of acceleration) seems valuable for some gifted children but not for others. If you had been Scott's parent and his teacher recommended skipping, what factors would you have taken into consideration in deciding whether or not to approve the move? What other options might you have suggested or investigated?

6. Some critics of enrichment programs for gifted students claim that they consist largely of what Scott calls "so-whats." What does this expression mean? Do you think Scott means that these activities were useless? What other, more useful kinds of enrichment activities might such a program provide?

7. Scott sums up his elementary school experience by saying that he came out of it "relatively unscathed." How would you sum up your own school experience?

8. What do you think the title of the article means? If you were in charge of organizing an educational program for gifted students, what guidelines might you glean from this article?

ANSWER KEY FOR CHAPTER 12

Note: Numbers in parentheses refer to pages in the textbook where answers can be found.

CHAPTER 12 REVIEW

Important Terms for Section I

1. abstractions (page 419)
2. alteration (419)
3. conservation, conserve (420)
4. constraint (421)
5. cooperation (422)
6. Selman's (423)
7. punishment (424)
8. internalized (424)
9. autonomous moral principles (424)
10. sensory, sensations (428)
11. working (428)
12. permanent (428)
13. repetition (428)
14. categorization (429)
15. story (429)
16. metamemory (429)
17. verbal, performance (431)
18. Otis-Lennon (431)
19. Multicultural Pluralistic Assessment (435)

Learning Objectives for Section I

1. (page 419)
2. (419-420)
3. (420-421)
4. (421)
5. (421-422)
6. (423)
7. (424-426)
8. (426-427)
9. (428-429)
10. (429-430)
11. (430)
12. (431)
13. (431-433)
14. (433-435)
15. (434)
16. (435)
17. (436)

Important Terms for Section II

1. sentences (page 437)
2. metacommunication (438)

Learning Objectives for Section II

1. (page 437)
2. (438)
3. (438-439)

Important Terms for Section III

1. self-fulfilling (page 442)
2. retardation (443)
3. read (444)
4. learning disabilities (444)
5. attention-deficit hyperactivity (445)
6. handicapped, nonhandicapped (446)
7. giftedness (447)
8. creativity (450)
9. "right" (450)
10. divergent (450)
11. Torrance (450)

Learning Objectives for Section III

1. (pages 439-440)
2. (440-443)
3. (441)
4. (443-446)
5. (446-447)
6. (447-448)
7. (448-449)
8. (449)
9. (450-451)
10. (451-453)

CHAPTER 12 QUIZ

Matching—Who's Who

1. d (page 420)
2. j (423)
3. f (424)
4. a (427)
5. i (430)
6. b (437)
7. h (443)
8. c (444)
9. e (447)
10. g (448)

Multiple-Choice

1. d (page 419)
2. a (420)
3. b (420-421)
4. a (421-422)
5. c (423)
6. c (424)
7. d (425)
8. a (426-427)
9. b (428)
10. c (429, 430)
11. a (431)
12. c (431)
13. c (435)
14. a (437)
15. a (441)
16. d (446)
17. a (447)
18. b (448)
19. d (449)
20. b (450)

True or False?

1. F—The ability to think abstractly does not develop until adolescence. (page 419)
2. T (420)
3. F—The stage of morality of constraint coincides roughly with Piaget's preoperational stage. (421)
4. F—Selman was influenced by Piaget and Kohlberg. (424)
5. T (424)
6. T (430)
7. T (433)
8. F—There appears to be no cognitive difference between Asian and American children. (434)
9. F—Research shows that children can be taught to think more effectively. (435, 436)
10. T (437)
11. T (438)
12. F—According to one study, children with a keen sense of humor tend to be competent in the classroom and to be seen positively by their teachers. (439)
13. T (440)
14. T (442-443)
15. T (443)
16. F—Learning disabilities are not outgrown, but people can compensate for them. (445)
17. T (449)
18. F—Studies have found only modest correlations between creativity and intelligence. (450)
19. T (451)
20. T (452)

PERSONALITY AND SOCIAL DEVELOPMENT IN MIDDLE CHILDHOOD

OVERVIEW

Chapter 13 describes the rich, expanding social world of middle childhood and the personality changes a child experiences during these years. In this chapter, the authors:

- Outline the way a child's self-concept develops and compare four theoretical explanations for this important personality development

- Summarize how schoolchildren spend their time

- Describe the functions and influence of the peer group

- Examine the bases of friendship and popularity

- Point out changes in parent-child and sibling relationships

- Look at the impact on children of parents' employment, divorce, and remarriage

- Describe common childhood emotional disturbances and their treatment

- Identify factors contributing to stress and resilience and suggest ways to help children cope with stress

CHAPTER 13 REVIEW

Section I The Self-Concept

FRAMEWORK FOR SECTION I

A. Developing a Self-Concept
   1. Beginnings: Self-Recognition and Self-Definition
   2. Coordination of Self-Regulation and Social Regulation
   3. Self-Esteem
      a. Self-Esteem in Middle Childhood
      b. Parenting Styles and Self-Esteem
B. Theoretical Perspectives on the Self-Concept in Middle Childhood
   1. Sigmund Freud: The Latency Period
   2. Erik Erikson: Crisis 4—Industry versus Inferiority
   3. Social-Learning Theory
   4. Cognitive-Developmental Theory

IMPORTANT TERMS FOR SECTION I

Completion: Fill in the blanks to complete the definitions of key terms for this section of Chapter 13.

1. **self-_____:** Sense of self, which guides one in deciding what to do in the future.

2. **self-_____:** Realization, beginning in infancy, of separateness from other people, eventually allowing reflection on one's own actions in relation to social standards.

3. **self-_____:** Ability to recognize one's own image.

4. **self-_____:** Physical and psychological characteristics one considers important to describe oneself.

5. **_____ self:** Person's concept of what he or she is like; compare _____ self.

6. **_____ self:** Person's concept of what he or she wishes to be like; compare _____ self.

7. **self-_____:** Favorable self-evaluation or self-image.

8. **_____ period:** In Freud's terminology, a period of relative sexual calm that occurs during middle childhood after the Oedipus complex has been resolved.

9. **industry versus inferiority:** In Erikson's theory, the fourth crisis that children face; they must learn the _____ of their culture or risk developing feelings of inferiority.

10. **self-_____:** According to the information-processing approach, a set of "knowledge structures" which guide and organize the processing of information about the self and help children decide how to act.

LEARNING OBJECTIVES FOR SECTION I

After reading and reviewing this section of Chapter 13, you should be able to do the following.

1. Describe the self-concept and its development from infancy to middle childhood.

2. Show how self-regulation and social regulation interact, and name four tasks facing schoolchildren in developing a self-concept.

3. Describe elements of self-esteem and how parenting styles influence its development.

4. Compare interpretations of the development of the self-concept in middle childhood according to Freud's psychosexual theory, Erikson's psychosocial theory, social-learning theory, and cognitive-developmental theory

Section II Aspects of Personality Development in Middle Childhood

FRAMEWORK FOR SECTION II

A. Everyday Life
 1. How Do Children Spend Their Time?
 2. With Whom Do Children Spend Their Time?
B. The Child in the Peer Group
 1. Functions and Influence of the Peer Group
  a. Positive Effects
  b. Negative Effects: Conformity
 2. Who Is in the Peer Group?
  a. How Do Peer Groups Generally Form?
  b. How Can Interracial Peer Groups Be Encouraged?
   (1) Integration
   (2) School-Based Programs
 3. Friendship
 4. Popularity
  a. The Popular Child
  b. The Unpopular Child
   (1) Why Are Some Children Unpopular?
   (2) How Can Unpopular Children Be Helped?

C. The Child in the Family
 1. Parents and Children: Relationships and Issues
  a. Discipline
  b. Control and Coregulation
  c. Variations in Parenting
 2. How Parents' Work Affects Children
  a. Mothers' Work
   (1) The Mother's Psychological State
   (2) Working Mothers and Family Interactions
   (3) Working Mothers and Children's Values
   (4) How Children React to Mothers' Working
    (a) Infants, Toddlers, and Preschoolers
    (b) School-Age Children
    (c) Adolescents
  b. Fathers' Work
   (1) The Father's Psychological State
   (2) Fathers' Work and Children's Values
   (3) Other Factors
 3. Children of Divorce
  a. How Do Children React to Divorce at Different Ages?
  b. What "Tasks" Face Children of Divorce?
  c. What Are the Long-Term Effects of Divorce on Children?
  d. What Factors Influence Children's Adjustment to Divorce?
   (1) Parenting Styles and Parents' Attitudes
   (2) Remarriage of the Mother
   (3) Relationship with the Father
   (4) Parents' Accessibility
 4. One-Parent Families
  a. What Stresses Does the One-Parent Family Place on Children?
  b. How Does the One-Parent Family Affect Schooling?
  c. What Are the Long-Term Effects of the One-Parent Family?
 5. Stepfamilies
 6. Sibling Relationships

IMPORTANT TERMS FOR SECTION II

Completion: Fill in the blanks to complete the definitions of key terms for this section of Chapter 13.

1. _____: Negative attitudes toward certain groups.

2. _____: Teaching children character, self-control, and moral behavior.

3. **coregulation:** _____ stage in the control of behavior in which parents exercise general supervision and children exercise moment-to-moment self-regulation.

LEARNING OBJECTIVES FOR SECTION II

After reading and reviewing this section of Chapter 13, you should be able to do the following.

1. Summarize how and with whom school-age children spend their time.

2. Compare the importance of the various relationships in children's lives.

3. Identify positive and negative effects of a peer group.

4. Explain how peer groups form, and how racial prejudice can be overcome.

5. List and gives examples of Selman's five stages of friendship.

6. Describe some characteristics of popular and unpopular children, and suggest ways to help unpopular children gain social acceptance.

7. Identify changes and variations in the kinds of issues that arise between parents and school-age children, the methods of discipline parents use, and the degree of control they exercise.

8. Describe how mothers' and fathers' employment affects children.

9. List guidelines to determine when children are ready for self-care.

10. Describe how divorce affects children and how they can be helped to adjust.

11. Identify short-term and long-term effects of being raised in a one-parent family.

12. Describe the stepfamily and its effects on children.

13. Identify direct and indirect ways in which siblings influence each other.

Section III Emotional Disturbances in Childhood

FRAMEWORK FOR SECTION III

A. Three Types of Emotional Disturbances
1. Acting-Out Behavior
2. Anxiety Disorders
   a. Separation Anxiety Disorder
   b. School Phobia
3. Childhood Depression
B. Treatment Techniques
1. Psychological Therapies
   a. Individual Psychotherapy
   b. Family Therapy
   c. Behavior Therapy
   d. Evaluating Psychological Therapies
2. Drug Therapy

IMPORTANT TERMS FOR SECTION III

Completion: Fill in the blanks to complete the definitions of key terms for this section of Chapter 13.

1. _____ **behavior:** Misbehavior (for example, lying or stealing) spurred by emotional difficulties.

2. **separation anxiety disorder:** Condition involving excessive anxiety for at least 2 weeks, concerning separation from people to whom a child is _____.

3. **school** _____: Unrealistic fear of school, probably reflecting separation anxiety.

4. **affective disorder:** Disorder of _____ , such as depression.

5. **childhood depression:** Affective disorder characterized by inability to have fun or to concentrate, and by an absence of normal emotional _____.

6. **psychotherapy:** Treatment technique in which a therapist generally helps patients gain _____ into their personalities and relationships and helps them interpret their feelings and behaviors.

7. **family therapy:** Treatment technique in which the whole family is treated together and is viewed as the _____.

8. **behavior therapy:** Treatment approach using principles of learning theory to alter behavior; also called *behavior* _____.

9. **drug therapy:** Administration of drugs to treat _____.

LEARNING OBJECTIVES FOR SECTION III

After reading and reviewing this section of Chapter 13, you should be able to do the following.

1. Explain why acting-out behavior occurs, and state what forms it may take.

2. Describe symptoms and treatment of separation anxiety disorders, particularly school phobia.

3. List signs of childhood depression.

4. Compare individual psychotherapy, family therapy, behavior therapy, and drug therapy.

Section IV Stress and Resilience

FRAMEWORK FOR SECTION IV

A. Sources of Stress
B. The Hurried Child
C. Coping with Stress: The Resilient Child

IMPORTANT TERMS FOR SECTION IV

Completion: Fill in the blanks to complete the definitions of key terms for this section of Chapter 13.

1. _____ **maltreatment:** Action or failure to act that damages children's behavioral, cognitive, emotional, or physical functioning; emotional abuse.

2. _____ **children:** Children who bounce back from unfortunate circumstances that would have a highly negative impact on the emotional development of most children.

LEARNING OBJECTIVES FOR SECTION IV

After reading and reviewing this section of Chapter 13, you should be able to do the following.

1. List several sources of childhood stress and some typical childhood fears.

2. Explain Elkind's concept of the "hurried child."

3. Discuss the impact and prevention of psychological maltreatment.

4. Identify five factors that seem to contribute to resilience in children.

CHAPTER 13 QUIZ

Matching—Aspects of the Developing Self-Concept:
Match each situation in the left-hand column with
the appropriate term in the right-hand column.

1. George cut down a small cherry tree with a hatchet. When asked who did it, he realized that it was he, George. _____

2. Susan and her friend are looking through photos in their school yearbook. Susan excitedly points to a face in the crowd at a football game. "Look! That's me!" she cries. _____

3. At the beginning of the school year, Mark's first-grade teacher asks the children in the class to tell something about themselves. When it is Mark's turn, he says, "I have blond hair, I have a dog, and I like to draw." _____

4. Caren looks at herself in the mirror. "I'm getting fat," she says. _____

5. While bicycling with a friend, Caren sees an ice cream vendor in the park. "I'd love to have an ice cream bar, but I shouldn't," she says. "I want to be thinner." _____

6. "Come on," says Caren's friend. "One little ice cream bar won't hurt." Caren shakes her head: "No, I'm not going to have one." _____

7. Elissa is happily playing house with her dolls when her 3-year-old brother comes along and wants to play with the dolls, too. Elissa is momentarily annoyed but tells her brother, "OK, you can be the father." _____

8. Dana is playing tennis. Trying to put away an overhead shot, she hits the ball into the net. "That's OK," she tells herself, "I'll make the next one." _____

9. Tim and his buddies are hanging around a music store, which is having a sidewalk sale. While the clerk is distracted, some of the boys take cassettes out of a bin and put them in their pockets. Tim, seeing his friends doing this, grabs a cassette even though he knows he shouldn't. _____

10. Jeremy comes home from school and finds a note from his mother: "Please remember to water the plants and clean up your room." Jeremy is tired and would rather watch television right away, but because of his mother's reminder, he does his chores first. _____

a. self-esteem
b. coregulation
c. self-awareness
d. self-regulation
e. conformity
f. self-definition
g. ideal self
h. self-recognition
i. coordination of self-regulation and social regulation
j. real self

Multiple-Choice: Circle the choice that best completes or answers each item.

1. The sequence of development toward self-knowledge and self-regulation is
   a. self-recognition; self-awareness; self-definition; real and ideal self
   b. self-awareness; self-recognition; self-definition; real and ideal self
   c. real and ideal self; self-awareness; self-definition; self-recognition
   d. self-definition; self-awareness; self-recognition; real and ideal self

2. Coopersmith's criteria for self-esteem include
   a. significance and competence
   b. strength and kindness
   c. internal control and consistent demands
   d. all of the above

3. According to Freud, the development of self-concept in middle childhood is made possible by limitation of the dominance of the
   a. id
   b. ego
   c. superego
   d. parents

4. The virtue that arises from successful resolution of Erikson's crisis of industry versus inferiority is
   a. productivity
   b. self-confidence
   c. competence
   d. industriousness

5. Which of the following is *not* an example of a self-schema?
   a. "I am a good athlete."
   b. "I am a hard worker."
   c. "I have trouble making friends."
   d. "I don't like Tracy."

6. According to the Institute for Social Research (1985), about how many hours does the average American child have available per week for leisure activity?
   a. 15 or less
   b. 20 to 30
   c. 40
   d. 55

7. The relationships that generally involve most conflict during middle childhood are those with
   a. parents
   b. siblings
   c. peers
   d. teachers

8. Which of the following is *not* a positive effect of the peer group?
   a. providing emotional security
   b. testing values
   c. permitting independence
   d. fostering coregulation

9. At which of Selman's levels of friendship would a child say, "He wouldn't let me watch television at his house, so he's not my friend anymore"?
   a. undifferentiated
   b. unilateral
   c. reciprocal
   d. mutual

10. The most effective disciplinary methods for school-age children stress
    a. rewards
    b. punishment
    c. reasoning
    d. parental control

11. In comparison with children of a full-time homemaker, school-age children of a working mother generally
    a. have higher IQs
    b. live in more structured homes
    c. show poorer social adjustment
    d. all of the above

12. There are about how many school-age "self-care children" of working parents in the United States today?
    a. fewer than 1 million
    b. 2 million
    c. 10 million
    d. 20 million

13. For which of the following would headaches, vomiting, lying, and stealing be typical reactions to parents' divorce?
    a. preschoolers
    b. elementary school children
    c. young adolescents
    d. older adolescents

14. Which of the following statements about children's adjustment to divorce is true, according to research?
    a. The best custody arrangement for both boys and girls is generally with the mother.
    b. Boys whose mothers reject them tend to express anger against their fathers.
    c. Boys tend to have more adjustment problems than girls when their mothers remarry.
    d. Boys with authoritative parents usually have fewer behavior problems than those with authoritarian or permissive parents.

15. About what proportion of American children live in one-parent families?
    a. nearly half
    b. 1 in 4
    c. 1 in 10
    d. 1 in 20

16. In what percent of American families does the mother have custody of the children after a divorce or separation?
    a. slightly more than 50
    b. 60
    c. 75
    d. 90

17. The combination of siblings likely to quarrel most is
    a. two brothers
    b. two sisters
    c. a brother and sister
    d. none of the above; all quarrel equally

18. School-phobic children tend to be
    a. boys
    b. low achievers
    c. overly dependent on their mothers
    d. all of the above

19. Behavior modification is based on principles of which theoretical approach?
    a. psychosexual
    b. psychosocial
    c. learning
    d. cognitive-developmental

20. Michael Rutter has studied characteristics of what kind of child?
    a. invulnerable or resilient
    b. "hurried"
    c. maltreated or abused
    d. school-phobic

True or False? In the blank following each item, write T (for *true*) or F (for *false*). In the space below each item, if the statement is false, rewrite it to make it true.

1. One of a child's tasks in developing a self-concept is to learn how society works. _____

2. Social-learning theorists believe that the resolution of the Oedipus conflict allows for development of the self-concept in middle childhood. _____

3. Disadvantaged children tend to watch television more than other children. _____

4. School-age children spend very little time with their parents, and peer relationships are most important in their lives. _____

5. School-age youngsters who are headed for serious trouble tend to be those who are peer-oriented. _____

6. Racial prejudice is found mainly among white children. _____

7. According to Selman, because children at the undifferentiated level of friendship are egocentric, they think exclusively about what they want from a relationship. _____

8. Popular children generally refrain from asking for help. _____

9. Issues between school-age children and their parents tend to center on schoolwork, friends, and chores. _____

10. Parents' approach to child rearing generally changes as children grow older. _____

11. Almost 7 out of 10 married women with children under 18 are in the work force. _____

12. Young middle-class boys may be adversely affected by their mothers' employment. _____

13. Teenage children of working mothers often have social problems. _____

14. Working-class fathers tend to encourage obedience and conformity in their children more than middle-class fathers do. _____

15. Young children often believe that they were responsible for their parents' divorce. _____

16. The final task children face, in their adjustment to divorce, is accepting its permanence. _____

17. Children whose parents have joint custody generally adjust to divorce better than those who are in sole custody of one parent. _____

18. Family income is an important factor in the effect of divorce on children. _____

19. A stepfamily typically consists of a father, his children, and a stepmother. _____

20. Elder siblings tend to be bossy. _____

21. Younger siblings tend to be good at sensing other people's needs. _____

22. Ten-year-olds normally make up stories, or lie to avoid punishment. _____

23. A child who seems happy and well adjusted but suddenly refuses to go to school is likely to be exhibiting characterological school phobia. _____

24. Social and academic incompetence are believed to be causes of childhood depression.

25. A good psychotherapist will show a child that feelings of hostility toward a parent are harmful. _____

26. In family therapy, the person whose problem causes the family to seek treatment is sometimes the healthiest member. _____

27. Drug therapy is treatment for drug addiction. _____

28. Therapy for specific problems (like phobias and hyperactivity) tends to be more effective than therapy aimed at improving social adjustment in general. _____

29. School is a source of insecurity for many children. _____

30. According to research, some children seem to be born with resilient, "stress-proof" personalities. _____

TOPICS FOR THOUGHT AND DISCUSSION

1. Most theoreticians and researchers see the development of a child's self-concept as a social phenomenon. How would Freud explain this? Erikson? Piaget? A social-learning theorist?

2. Siblings, the child's first "peer group," play an important role in the development of the self-concept. What differences, then, might you expect to find in the self-concept development of only children and of children with siblings?

3. *Prejudice* is defined in your text as "negative attitudes toward certain groups." How else can this term be defined? In the context of this chapter—the discussion of children in peer groups—why is the authors' definition appropriate?

4. The authors of your text state that some degree of conformity to group standards is healthy in both children and adults. Do you agree? If so, in what respects is conformity healthy or unhealthy? Can you think of examples that are not mentioned in your text?

5. Some research suggests that a woman who is satisfied with her work is likely to be a more effective parent but a man who is deeply satisfied with his work may become so engrossed in it that he may, in effect, withdraw from family life. Might gender-typing (discussed in Chapter 10) help to explain this difference?

6. Do you agree with David Elkind that children today are put under too much pressure to succeed and grow up? Can you think of examples? As a parent, what might you do to avoid raising a "hurried child"? (Note: Elkind's views on "pushing" preschool children can be found in Box 9-4 of your text.)

7. Why do you think there has been little research on hereditary factors in stress and resilience? What difficulties would there be in designing a study on this subject? Can you suggest a way to do so?

CHAPTER 13 READING

INTRODUCTION

About one in seven schoolchildren is either a bully or the victim of a bully, according to the following article, "Schoolyard Menace." How do bullies get that way? How do they choose their victims? Who suffers more—the bully or the victim? What can be done to stop a bully?

This selection is relevant to several themes discussed in Chapter 13 of your text and also to the discussions of aggression (Chapter 10) and child abuse (Chapter 8). The author, Marjory Roberts, is a reporter for *Psychology Today*, where the article (which has been somewhat condensed here) first appeared in February 1988.

Schoolyard Menace

by Marjory Roberts

I can still remember him in vivid detail: the edge in his voice as he taunted his victims, the delight in his face, even his name, though I won't say it here. I always gave him a wide berth and so avoided his aggression, but other kids, not so lucky, were his constant victims. You probably remember him, too, by a different name. He's the schoolyard bully.

Like first loves and favorite teachers, bullies occupy a spot in everyone's memory. And like all people who leave an indelible impression, the name, the face and the emotions that bully stirred up years ago may still come to mind, full force, years later.

That bully is no longer the mean-spirited child you remember, but research suggests that he's still taunting, still bullying his way through life. He may now abuse his wife in place of the schoolyard victim, and he's likely to have committed any one of a number of crimes. He was a lousy student in school and he's an unsuccessful adult today. Odds are he's raising a bully of his own.

It's no wonder bullies have a place in so many memories, since approximately one in seven schoolchildren is either a bully or a victim, according to psychologist Dan Olweus, a Swedish researcher who has been studying bullies for almost 20 years. Olweus estimates that in this country the problem affects almost five million elementary and junior high school students.

The bully is not the child who occasionally pushes or shoves a classmate. But bullies are not so seriously antisocial as to be diagnosed with a "conduct disorder," the clinical categorization of the seriously disturbed child. Instead, bullies are a subset of aggressive kids who seem to derive satisfaction from harming others, physically or psychologically. Such aggression is a way of life for them, Olweus says, and they don't pick a fair fight.

"A bully is the king of the mountain, and the victim is almost always weak," says Harry Berkowitz, a fourth-grade teacher at Quarton Elementary School in Michigan.

Bullies are usually boys, though girl bullies do exist. Like boys, they are impulsive and dominant, but rather than attacking their victims physically, they are apt to harass them verbally or simply exclude them from the group, according to Olweus. For the most part, they bully other girls, he says. Aggressive girls have been socialized like boys, says psychologist Leonard Eron of the University of Illinois. They probably grew up in a boy's world of rough-and-tumble games, playing sports and concealing their feelings. These girls might not face the same bleak futures as their male counterparts, Eron adds, but as adults, they do tend to have psychological problems and to punish their children harshly, thus contributing to a new generation of bullies.

Even so, the bullies of memory are boys—fearsome boys. The underlying problem, many researchers agree, results from some combination of parental influence, aspects of a child's home environment and a hot-headed temperament. "Too little love and care and too much freedom in childhood . . . contribute strongly to the development of an aggressive personality," Olweus says.

Trouble begins when parents pay little attention to their chilren or reject them altogether, according to studies by Olweus and others. "Parents of aggressive kids really don't know what their kids are doing," Eron says. "They don't know the kinds of things their kids worry or dream about." These parents also tend to punish their children harshly or physically. "Physical violence generates violence," Olweus says.

Psychologist Nathaniel Floyd agrees. Living with parents who abuse them teaches children that aggression and violence are effective ways to reach a goal, he says.

Floyd speculates that the defenseless kids who end up as victims remind bullies of their own defenselessness against abuse at home and the shame and humiliation it causes them. Bullies, he believes, feel threatened by their victims' vulnerability. "In every bully, there is the shadow of the little kid who was once abused himself," Floyd says. They bully "as if to say, 'You're the victim, not me.' "

Children may, however, contribute to the level of aggression in their families. Psychologist Gerald Patterson of the Oregon Social Learning Center and colleagues have studied families in which children resort to aggression because it seems the only way to get along at home. "People teach one another when they interact," Patterson explains. A family may learn that coercion works, for example, when a sibling squabble erupts: A young girl teases her brother, he retaliates by punching her and she quits taunting him. Thus he learns that aggression works. Then the mother steps in and in turn hits her son as punishment. Temporary peace and quiet may result, but each family member has had a lesson in the value of physical force. Thus as both initiator and victim of aggression, children may unintentionally train their parents to punish them severely or even to abuse them.

Television is another environmental culprit. It repeatedly presents kids with athletes, movie stars and politicians who achieve success with aggression, Eron says. And rather than releasing "pent-up hostility," watching displays of aggression appears to provoke further aggression.

Aside from their often troublesome home lives, some aggressive children may have difficulty interpreting the intentions of their classmates, another body of research reveals. In a 1980 study, Vanderbilt University psychologist Kenneth Dodge gave aggressive and nonaggressive boys a brief hypothetical story to read. Each boy imagined that a classmate spilled a lunch tray all over his back. Dodge asked them whether the classmate had hostile or benign intentions and how they would respond if this really happened to them. The aggressive boys read hostile intent into the story 50 percent more frequently than

Braking Bullies

Solving problems always comes down to a matter of force for bullies; alternative strategies simply don't occur to them. Researchers are trying to introduce bullies to less violent tactics in hopes that they might learn more acceptable ways of dealing with their peers.

Psychologist John Lochman of the Duke University Medical Center and coworkers put aggressive boys in groups of five and lead them through 18 weekly sessions, teaching them to substitute assertiveness for aggression in solving problems. The kids role-play and watch videotapes of other children learning to understand and interpret situations that make them angry. The program aims to help children cope with anger, Lochman says, so that they do not respond impulsively when something riles them. Last year, for example, one former bully learned to move beyond his habitually aggressive first reaction by telling himself to "chill out" or "not to let [another child] get to me."

The 1981 to 1982 groups went through six "booster" sessions the following school year, and Lochman compared them to aggressive boys who did not go through the program. Three to four years after he worked with these boys, they had better problem-solving skills than did the others, lower rates of drug and alcohol use and higher self-esteem.

Psychologist Nathaniel Floyd, who works in the Westchester County, New York, school system, helps bullies examine what they find provocative about their victims, and he trains them to control their need to bully.

Floyd teaches victims to be assertive and explains bullies' values, so that victims can better understand their adversaries' motives. Both bullies and victims sign "behavioral contracts" that establish areas in which they need to change. Bullies agree to respect other children, property and teachers, while victims agree to control their whining and attention-seeking. Teachers run group lessons on nonviolent problem-solving, cooperation and teamwork. After six years of work and observation with such children, Floyd has anecdotal reports that suggest his program is a success.

Psychologist Robert Selman of Harvard University and his associates have paired aggressive and nonaggressive kids in 8 to 10 hour-long sessions designed to teach the values of collaboration. The teams work out solutions to make-believe and real-life problems each week. They define the problem, come up with three possible solutions, choose the best one and evaluate it for any "stumbling blocks that could make [it] fail." Like Lochman, Selman hopes to teach these children that they can solve a problem without using force or violence. "Aggressive kids often jump to a solution for a problem they haven't thought through," Selman notes. Though he does not realistically expect the program to change children's personalities, he says it can at least give them "a stop-and-think approach to social problem-solving." Ultimately, Selman feels that aggressive children may need more than a short-term negotiation course to get at the root of the problem.

---

did the others, and they had aggressive retaliation in mind more often.

Other research by Dodge and coworkers shows that such children are always ready to defend themselves, regardless of whether a classmate really means to taunt or harm them and especially when they feel threatened. "They make errors in presuming hostility where none exists," explains Dodge, who has observed this pattern of paranoid misinterpretation even in 7-year-olds. Consequently, other children grow to dislike their aggressive classmates, and their originally unfounded suspicions become a self-fulfilling prophecy.

"Aggressive children also seem to have a perceptual blind spot for their own level of aggression," says psychologist John Lochman of the Duke University Medical Center. In one study, he had boys previously rated as aggressive or nonaggressive listen to a story about two kids who bump into each other in the hall and begin to yell and fight. The boys identified which child had caused the fight, speculated about what the characters were thinking and

feeling and prescribed a way to resolve the incident. Lochman then paired one aggressive and one non-aggressive boy, telling them that when they talked over their reactions to the story, they should defend their opinion. Afterwards, they rated their own and their partner's level of aggressiveness.

Lochman found that aggressive boys underestimated their own aggressiveness. They also described their partners as the aggressor more frequently than did nonaggressive boys. "Aggressive boys had distorted perceptions," Lochman says. "These kids overperceive hostility in their peers."

They are way off the mark, according to what is known about the victims of bullying. The kids bullies pick on, also mostly boys, are anxious, sensitive and quiet, Olweus says. "As a rule, they don't have a single good friend at school," he says. "Victims seem to signal to others that they are insecure and worthless individuals who will not retaliate if they are attacked or insulted." Floyd, who has worked with hundreds of bullies and victims in Westchester

County, New York, believes that bullies find specific kinds of children annoying and intolerable. Typically, they target kids who complain, seek attention and seem emotionally needy and physically weak, Floyd explains. "Bullies love to say that such kids are really 'asking for it,' " he explains. "They have become bullies by overcoming these more sensitive characteristics."

Potential victims apparently sense their status, and they walk school corridors in fear. In a 1983 study by the National Association of Secondary School Principals, many students surveyed named "fear of bullies" as one of their most serious concerns. Sometimes, these kids attempt to avoid relentless bullying by skipping school or feigning illness, and in a few cases victims have committed suicide, killed their tormentor or sued their school.

If the victims' school days are unhappy, their tormentors face grim prospects for the days, months and years ahead. Such children often carry their aggression with them into a relatively unsuccessful adulthood, according to data Eron and his colleagues collected in a 22-year study. They are more likely than their less aggressive classmates to abuse their spouses, the study showed, and they tend to punish their children more severely, in effect raising a new generation of bullies. And their antisocial behavior may extend beyond home: Eight-year-old bullies have a 1-in-4 chance of having a criminal record by their 30th birthday, compared to other boys' odds of 1 in 20.

These boys' aggressiveness seems to get in the way of their intellectual development, Eron says. His 22-year study showed that aggression in childhood predicted poorer intellectual achievement later. "Aggressive children may be so obstreperous," Eron explains, "that teachers and classmates avoid them, seriously limiting their learning opportunities."

American schools have made little attempt to combat the bully problems. For the most part, concerned school personnel wage small-scale battles—largely on their own. "I let bullies know that what they're doing is wrong and unacceptable," says Robert Maher, assistant principal of Lakeland High School in New York. "But that's only between 7:30 and 4. Most of the problems we see in high school didn't begin in high school. We're dealing with a finished product." And the problem is compounded, he says, because kids don't tell parents or teachers about bullies for fear of retaliation.

In 1983, the Norwegian Ministry of Education began a nationwide campaign against bullying, largely under Olweus's guidance. "There is a network

of action," he says, that includes teachers, parents and students. At school, his plan requires close supervision of children and clearly laid-out rules against bullying that are consistently enforced. The program also involves parents in discussion groups on the subject, and it entreats adults and classmates to support and protect victims. Olweus has found that bully and victim problems occur 50 percent less frequently in the 42 Norwegian schools that followed these guidelines for over two school years.

Clearly, the problem has at least one feasible solution. With enough concerned educators and parents in this country, and a workable plan of action, perhaps a future generation of American schoolchildren won't grow up with a bully etched forever in memory.

QUESTIONS ABOUT THE READING

1. Hostile aggression is common in early childhood but normally diminishes by middle childhood. What intellectual factors might contribute to bullies' arrested personality development? For example, do bullies seem to be unusually egocentric for their age? Can you suggest a reason, other than the one given in the article, why bullies tend to do poorly in school and in adulthood?

2. The article says that bullies often underestimate their own aggressiveness and overestimate their peers'. On the basis of the discussion of self-concept in Chapter 13 of your text, what might be the source of these misconceptions? Would you expect that bullies have high or low self-esteem?

3. Most bullies are boys. Would you be more inclined to attribute this fact to boys' tendency toward difficult temperament, or to differences in socialization between boys and girls?

4. What factors trigger bullies' aggression, according to the article? Are they the same as the factors in aggression discussed in Chapter 10 of your text?

5. Why do bullies find weak, sensitive, and friendless children especially annoying and intolerable?

6. Some authorities quoted in the article seem to equate harsh physical punishment with child abuse. Do you agree? What other parental behaviors increase the likelihood that a child will become a bully?

7. Do you think American schools should mount a concerted campaign against bullying, as Norwegian schools have done?

ANSWER KEY FOR CHAPTER 13

Note: Numbers in parentheses refer to pages in the textbook where answers can be found.

CHAPTER 13 REVIEW

Important Terms for Section I

1. concept (page 459)
2. awareness (459)
3. recognition (459)
4. definition (459)
5. real, ideal (459)
6. ideal, real (459)
7. esteem (460)
8. latency (462)
9. skills (462)
10. schema (463)

Learning Objectives for Section I

1. (pages 459-462)
2. (460)
3. (461-462)
4. (462-464)

Important Terms for Section II

1. prejudice (page 468)
2. discipline (473)
3. transitional (474)

Learning Objectives for Section II

1. (pages 464-466)
2. (465-466)
3. (466-467)
4. (468-469)
5. (470-471)

6. (471-472)
7. (473-475)
8. (476-480)
9. (479)
10. (480-485)
11. (485-487)
12. (487-488)
13. (488-489)

Important Terms for Section III

1. acting-out (page 489)
2. attached (490)
3. phobia (490)
4. mood (491)
5. reactions (491)
6. insight (492)
7. client (492)
8. modification (492)
9. emotional disorders (493)

Learning Objectives for Section III

1. (page 489)
2. (490-491)
3. (491-492)
4. (492-493)

Important Terms for Section IV

1. psychological (page 494)
2. resilient (495)

Learning Objectives for Section IV

1. (pages 493-494)
2. (494-495)
3. (495)
4. (495-497)

CHAPTER 13 QUIZ

Matching—Aspects of the Developing Self-Concept

1. c (page 459)
2. h (459)
3. f (459)
4. j (459)
5. g (459)
6. d (459, 460)
7. i (460)
8. a (460-461)
9. e (466-468)
10. b (474)

Multiple-Choice

1. b (page 459)
2. a (461)
3. a (462)
4. c (462)
5. d (463)
6. d (464)
7. b (466)
8. d (466)
9. b (470)
10. c (473-474)
11. b (477-478)
12. b (479)
13. b (481)
14. d (484)
15. b (485)
16. d (485)
17. a (488)
18. c (490-491)
19. c (492)
20. a (496)

True or False?

1. T (page 460)
2. F—Freudian psychoanalysts believe that the resolution of the Oedipus conflict allows for development of the self-concept in middle childhood. (462)
3. T (465)
4. F—Although school-age children spend little time with their parents, their relationships with parents remain most important. (465)
5. F—"Peer-oriented" children tend to engage in minor antisocial behavior, but youngsters headed for serious trouble tend to be those who do not get along with peers. (467)
6. F—Studies during the 1960s and 1970s found antiblack bias among both white and black children. (468)
7. T (470)
8. F—Popular children generally ask for help when they need it. (471)
9. T (473)
10. F—Although issues and disciplinary methods change as children get older, parents' basic approach to child rearing generally does not. (474)
11. T (476)
12. T (477-478)
13. F—Teenage children (especially daughters) of working mothers tend to be better adjusted socially than other teenagers. (478)
14. T (480)
15. T (481, 483)
16. F—The final task children face in their adjustment to divorce is achieving realistic hope about their own intimate relationships. (482)
17. F—Joint custody does not seem to help children adjust to divorce and may worsen the situation when the divorce has been bitter. (484)
18. T (486)
19. F—A stepfamily is typically composed of a mother, her children, and a stepfather. (487)
20. T (488)
21. T (488)
22. F—Children who continue to tell tall tales or lie frequently after the age of 6 or 7 may be acting out emotional problems. (489)
23. F—A child who seems happy and well adjusted but suddenly refuses to go to school is likely to be exhibiting neurotic school phobia. (490)
24. F—It is unknown whether incompetence causes depression or vice versa. (491)
25. F—A good psychotherapist will show acceptance of a child's feelings and of the child's right to have them. (492)
26. T (492)
27. F—Drug therapy is the treatment of emotional disorders with drugs. (493)
28. T (493)
29. T (494)
30. F—There has been little research on hereditary factors in handling stress; it is not clear whether resilience is mostly innate or developed. (496)

PHYSICAL DEVELOPMENT IN ADOLESCENCE

OVERVIEW

Chapter 14 sketches the enormous physical changes that occur during adolescence. In this chapter, the authors:

■ Point out possible causes and effects of variations in the timing of puberty

■ Outline the characteristic physical changes that take place in males and females during adolescence and discuss the psychological impact of these changes

■ Examine causes, implications, prevention, and treatment of eating disorders, drug abuse, sexually transmitted diseases, and abuse and neglect

■ Describe trends and patterns in suicide among teenagers and suggest methods of prevention

---

CHAPTER 14 REVIEW

Section I Adolescence: A Developmental Transition

FRAMEWORK FOR SECTION I

A. The Timing of Puberty
B. The Secular Trend

IMPORTANT TERMS FOR SECTION I

Completion: Fill in the blanks to complete the definitions of key terms for this section of Chapter 14.

1. **adolescence:** Developmental transition period between childhood and _____.

2. **puberty:** Process that leads to sexual maturity and the ability to _____.

3. **estrogen:** _____ sex hormone.

4. _____ **trend:** Trend noted by observing several generations; in child development, a trend toward earlier attainment of adult height and sexual maturity, which began a century ago and appears to have ended in the United States.

LEARNING OBJECTIVES FOR SECTION I

After reading and reviewing this section of Chapter 14, you should be able to do the following.

1. Identify difficulties in precisely demarcating adolescence.

2. Tell what happens during puberty, and state its duration and average age of onset in boys and girls.

3. List the typical sequence of physiological changes in adolescent girls and boys.

4. Decribe the secular trend in age of attaining adult height and sexual maturity, and identify its most likely cause.

Section II Puberty: The Physical Changes of Adolescence

FRAMEWORK FOR SECTION II

A. What Physical Changes Take Place during Adolescence?
   1. Adolescent Growth Spurt
   2. Primary Sex Characteristics
   3. Secondary Sex Characteristics
   4. Menarche: The Beginning of Menstruation
      a. Timing of Menarche
      b. Effects of Exercise on Menstruation
B. What Is the Psychological Impact of Physical Changes?
   1. Feelings about Menarche and Menstruation
   2. Feelings about Physical Appearance

IMPORTANT TERMS FOR SECTION II

Completion: Fill in the blanks to complete the definitions of key terms for this section of Chapter 14.

1. **adolescent growth spurt:** Sharp increase in _____ and _____ that precedes sexual maturity.

2. _____ **sex characteristics:** Organs directly related to reproduction, which enlarge and mature in early adolescence; compare _____ *sex characteristics.*

3. _____ **sex characteristics:** Physiological signs of sexual maturation (such as breast development and growth of body hair) that do not involve the sex organs; compare _____ *sex characteristics.*

4. **menarche:** Girl's first _____.

LEARNING OBJECTIVES FOR SECTION II

After reading and reviewing this section of Chapter 14, you should be able to do the following.

1. Describe the four major physical changes that occur during adolescence.

2. Discuss the psychological impact of these changes.

3. Compare psychological effects of early and late maturation in boys and in girls.

Section III Health Issues in Adolescence

FRAMEWORK FOR SECTION III

A. Nutrition
  1. Adolescents' Nutritional Needs
  2. Eating Disorders
    a. Obesity
    b. Anorexia Nervosa and Bulimia Nervosa
      (1) Anorexia Nervosa
      (2) Bulimia Nervosa
      (3) Treating Anorexia and Bulimia
B. Use and Abuse of Drugs
  1. Trends and Patterns of Drug Abuse
  2. Alcohol
  3. Tobacco
  4. Marijuana
C. Sexually Transmitted Diseases
  1. What Are STDs?
  2. Implications for Adolescents
D. Abuse and Neglect during Adolescence
E. Death in Adolescence
  1. Death Rates and Causes of Death
  2. Suicide
    a. Trends and Patterns of Suicide
    b. Who Is at Risk?

IMPORTANT TERMS FOR SECTION III

Completion: Fill in the blanks to complete the definitions of key terms for this section of Chapter 14.

1. **obesity:** Overweight condition marked by a skin-fold measurement in the _____ percentile.

2. _____ **nervosa:** Eating disorder, seen mostly in young women, characterized by self-starvation.

3. _____ **nervosa:** Eating disorder in which a person regularly eats huge quantities of food (binges) and then purges the body by taking laxatives or inducing vomiting.

4. **sexually transmitted disease (STD):** Disease spread by sexual contact; also called _____ *disease.*

LEARNING OBJECTIVES FOR SECTION III

After reading and reviewing this section of Chapter 14, you should be able to do the following.

1. List some important nutritional needs of adolescents.

2. Describe three common eating disorders and their treatment.

3. Identify trends and patterns of drug use and abuse by adolescents.

4. State why teenagers use alcohol, tobacco, and marijuana, and describe the effects of each.

5. Identify symptoms, effects, and treatment of the most prevalent sexually transmitted diseases, discuss reasons for their high incidence among adolescents, and list suggestions for prevention.

6. Describe the nature and incidence of abuse and neglect of adolescents.

7. Name the three leading causes of death in adolescence, and differentiate death rates and causes by sex and race.

8. Describe trends and patterns of suicide among adolescents; list factors that increase the risk of suicide, warning signs, and suggestions for prevention.

CHAPTER 14 QUIZ

Matching—Health Issues: Match each term in the left-hand column with the appropriate description at the right.

1. Genital herpes _____
2. Anorexia nervosa _____
3. AIDS _____
4. Alcohol _____
5. Chlamydia _____
6. Obesity _____
7. Gonorrhea _____
8. Tobacco _____
9. Genital warts _____
10. Bulimia nervosa _____
11. Syphilis _____
12. Marijuana _____

a. eating disorder producing tooth decay and gastric irritation
b. failure of the immune system, transmitted through interpersonal exchanges of bodily fluids
c. drug most often abused by children and adolescents
d. eating disorder associated with risk of heart disease
e. drug linked with lung cancer
f. eating disorder characterized by extreme thinness and distorted body image
g. most prevalent STD in the United States
h. small, painless growths
i. drug that can impede memory
j. STD that can lead to paralysis, convulsions, brain damage, and sometimes death
k. highly contagious, painful blisters with no known cure
l. second most common STD in the United States

Multiple-Choice: Circle the choice that best completes or answers each item.

1. The end of adolescence is
   a. easier to determine than its beginning
   b. harder to determine than its beginning
   c. legally defined as age 18 in the United States
   d. mainly a physiological phenomenon

2. Clitoridectomy is
   a. female sexual maturity
   b. male sexual maturity
   c. female circumcision
   d. male circumcision

3. The average age at which boys enter puberty is
   a. 10
   b. 12
   c. 13
   d. 14

4. The adolescent growth spurt often results in
   a. awkwardness
   b. disproportionate body parts
   c. nearsightedness
   d. all of the above

5. Which of the following are primary sex characteristics?
   a. pubic hair
   b. ovaries
   c. breasts
   d. all of the above

6. The first sign of puberty in girls is usually
   a. menstruation
   b. budding of the breasts
   c. underarm hair
   d. oily skin, leading to acne

7. The average age of menarche
   a. has been dropping steadily for the past 100 years
   b. has remained stable since the 1940s
   c. varies in different climates
   d. is relatively early among athletes, dancers, and swimmers

8. According to research, early-maturing girls are more likely than later-maturing girls to
   a. have a good body image
   b. be sociable and poised
   c. react positively to menarche
   d. become well-adjusted adults

9. A sign of bulimia is
   a. loss of hair
   b. abnormal thinness
   c. constant talk about food
   d. each of the above

10. The drug estimated to take the most lives is
    a. tobacco
    b. alcohol
    c. crack
    d. heroin

11. The leading cause of death among 15- to 24-year-old Americans is
    a. suicide
    b. homicide
    c. alcohol-related motor accidents
    d. drug overdoses

12. The most widely used illicit drug in the United States is
    a. hashish
    b. cocaine
    c. heroin
    d. marijuana

13. About how many Americans are estimated to be carriers of AIDS?
    a. 40,000
    b. 270,000
    c. 1.5 million
    d. 5 million

14. Which sexually transmitted disease has the following symptoms: reddish-brown sores on the mouth or genitalia in the first stage, and then a widespread skin rash?
    a. herpes
    b. gonorrhea
    c. syphilis
    d. AIDS

15. The highest teenage suicide rate is among
    a. white males
    b. white females
    c. black males
    d. black females

True or False? In the blank following each item, write T (for *true*) or F (for *false*). In the space below each item, if the statement is false, rewrite it to make it true.

1. Normally, the time of onset of puberty in both boys and girls varies by about 4 years. _____

2. Girls normally enter puberty about 2 years earlier than boys. _____

3. At puberty, the production of male and female hormones is triggered by the pituitary gland. _____

4. The age at which youngsters reach adult height and sexual maturity is genetically determined. _____

5. The first menstruation means that a girl can become pregnant. _____

6. Most American women remember menarche negatively. _____

7. Adults who felt attractive as teenagers tend to have high self-esteem. _____

8. Anorexia nervosa is the most common eating disorder in the United States. _____

9. Antidepressant drugs are used to treat anorexia and bulimia. _____

10. Use of marijuana first became common during the 1960s. _____

11. AIDS is caused by a bacterial infection. _____

12. Adolescents are more likely to be neglected than abused. _____

13. Boys attempt suicide more often than girls. _____

14. Young people who attempt suicide are likely to have had prenatal problems or suffered respiratory distress at birth. _____

15. Extensive press reports of suicides seem to induce more suicides. _____

TOPICS FOR THOUGHT AND DISCUSSION

1. Sol Gordon says that teenaged boys are "programmed to have sex" and that girls therefore must be taught to protect themselves against pregnancy. If so, would you hypothesize that such male "programming" comes from differences in socialization or differences in biological development? If boys had a more androgynous upbringing (as described in Chapter 10), would you expect the pressure for early sexual experience to diminish? Why or why not?

2. The causes of both anorexia and bulimia are unknown. How might you design further experiments to test existing hypotheses about the causes of these disorders?

3. Do you think that there is a connection between the prevalence of alcohol abuse by adolescents and the existence of a legal drinking age?

4. Both adolescents and adults expose themselves to the health risks discussed in this chapter: drugs, sexual diseases, and eating disorders. Why, then, are these issues particularly important in adolescence?

5. Your text, in Box 14-5, cites an example of a therapist who asked a pregnant teenager contemplating suicide to rank her options. Considering both the proper role of a psychotherapist and the other suggestions for preventing suicide given in the box, what should the therapist have done if the girl had ranked suicide as her best option?

CHAPTER 14 READING

INTRODUCTION

The physical side of adolescence can be psychologically uncomfortable for teenagers. Yet they are often reluctant to discuss such subjects as bodily changes, sex, and drugs with their parents. The following article by Carol Weston, condensed from the July 26, 1988, issue of *Woman's Day*, suggests how parents can help.

The Worries Teens Won't Share with Their Parents

by Carol Weston

"*I hide things from my parents because I don't want to upset them*," says Kim, 15. "*I don't think of it as lying; I think of it as protecting them.*"

Such remarks are typical of teenagers' feelings about discussing sensitive subjects with their parents.

After all, adolescence is the time for establishing an independent identity. "It can be difficult to accept," explains Dr. Wade Silverman, a psychologist in Atlanta, "but the older children get, the more they are influenced by peers and the less by parents."

As the author of two books for teens (*Girltalk* and *Girltalk about Guys*), I've received hundreds of letters from adolescents who found it easier to confide in a total stranger than in their parents.

"*My friend and I are 13,*" wrote one girl, "*and she has a totally flat chest. Is there something wrong?*" A 14-year old boy admits, "*I know things are supposed to be happening to my body now, but how do I know if I'm really normal?*"

Parents know their children will eventually make peace with their bodies, but adolescents find it painful to be behind or ahead of the pack. They tend to be extremely self-conscious about their changing bodies and complexions. They need information and reassurance, yet are often too embarrassed to bring up the subject.

If you've noticed that your daughter keeps asking for notes to be excused from gym or that all your son's friends are shaving but he doesn't have his first whisker, you might broach the subject—with compassion. Empathy and compliments go a long way toward making teens feel more comfortable with themselves. Don't tease your daughter about the "bumps on her chest" or your son about his "frog voice." Remind them that different rates of development are perfectly normal and that many of their classmates are too absorbed with their own body changes to be overly critical of anyone else's.

"I'd never tell my parents how much I drink," says Chris, 17. "Since alcohol's not a problem for me, why let it be a source of friction?"

While parents can't monitor every drop their kids drink, they *can* be good role models, expressing their feelings about alcohol abuse and pointing out the dangers of driving while under the influence. Signing the SADD (Students Against Driving Drunk) Contract for Life—an agreement that stipulates if the teen calls home, the parent will pick him or her up, no questions asked—is a smart move and a conversation-opener. (To obtain a copy, contact your child's school or write SADD, P.O. Box 800, Marlboro, MA 01752.)

Other good ways to bring up the subject? "Mention someone else's alcohol problem," suggests Elizabeth Winship, author of the nationally syndicated teen advice column *Ask Beth.* "Or say something about the drinking laws to instigate a conversation in which you aren't blaming or prying."

"I would not tell my parents about using drugs," says Rob, 15. "They'd ground me or throw me into some therapy center with a bunch of addicts."

While the majority of teenagers don't abuse drugs, most parents *under*estimate how likely their children are to use illegal substances and *over*estimate how likely the kids are to confide in them. According to an Emory University Medical School study of 600 high school seniors and parents in the Atlanta area, only 3 percent of parents said their kids had used marijuana within the last month, while 28 percent of students admitted they had. Over half the parents said teenagers would talk to them about drug abuse, but only 20 percent of the seniors said they'd turn to parents first.

Parents should read up on substance abuse so they can recognize the signs, from the paraphernalia to behavior changes. If you discover your teen is involved in drugs, Dr. Silverman says, it's important to communicate that you love him but will not tolerate certain behavior. You could say, for instance, "You're a wonderful son and we love you, but we can't accept your use of drugs. If this happens again, we'll have to take action." Whether that means grounding, withholding allowance or consulting a psychologist depends on the situation

"I don't tell my parents anything about my sex life," says Adam, 17. "It would be too awkward, and besides, it's none of their business. It doesn't affect how we get along."

Parents can't control their teenager's sex life, but they *can* provide a warm, loving home so he or she isn't desperate to find love elsewhere. They can also encourage the postponement of sexual activity. Tell your child that sex always changes things—it means risking pregnancy, sexually transmitted diseases and often a reputation. No one should be pressured into sex. Remind your son of his right to say no too; he may act macho but secretly be worried and unready for sex.

Try to avoid point-blank questions, which invite deceit and defensiveness. Instead of asking, "Are you having sex?" mention a pregnancy statistic or ask your adolescent's opinion about abortion. Let a sexy commercial, television show or movie be your springboard for conversation.

Don't assume your daughter is sexually active just because she wears makeup or short skirts. If you accuse her of sleeping around with no evidence, she may figure that since she's getting the blame anyway, she might as well begin doing it.

"I'm confused about the Pill. How long before and after sex do you take it?" asked one typical letter.

Two out of three sexually active teenagers do not use birth control regularly, and over one million teen girls wind up pregnant each year. Some are reluctant to use contraceptives because that implies premeditated sex; they prefer to think they were "swept away" by desire. Others don't understand the connection between sex and pregnancy.

Many parents shy away from teaching youngsters about sexual responsibility, but that can be dangerous. It's OK to explain that you are opposed to teen sex and that discussing the subject makes you uncomfortable, but you must provide the facts about contraception. Ignorance can be disastrous.

As you try to grow closer to your teenager, be careful not to invade his or her privacy. When your teen is being particularly uncooperative or uncommunicative, don't overreact. Most adolescents eventually straighten out.

During your adolescent's rebellious years, take comfort in the fact that you're not the only frustrated, confused or alienated parent. Hang in there; things usually do get easier. In the meantime, try to remember that even when teenagers are at their most exasperating, they still love and need you.

QUESTIONS ABOUT THE READING

1. Do the questions of the teenagers quoted in the article "ring true"—that is, do they remind you of concerns and feelings you and your friends had during adolescence?

2. On the basis of your own experience, do you think that the advice given in the article would be effective? What advice would you give to parents of teenagers concerning bodily changes, use of alcohol and drugs, and sexual activity?

ANSWER KEY FOR CHAPTER 14

Note: Numbers in parentheses refer to pages in the textbook where answers can be found.

CHAPTER 14 REVIEW

Important Terms for Section I

1. adulthood (page 504)
2. reproduce (505)
3. female (508)
4. secular (508)

Learning Objectives for Section I

1. (page 505)
2. (506-507)
3. (508)
4. (508-509)

Important Terms for Section II

1. height, weight (page 509)
2. primary, secondary (510)
3. secondary, primary (511)
4. menstruation (512)

Learning Objectives for Section II

1. (pages 509-513)
2. (513-515)
3. (514)

Important Terms for Section III

1. 85th (page 516)
2. anorexia (517)
3. bulimia (518)
4. venereal (524)

Learning Objectives for Section III

1. (page 516)
2. (516-519)
3. (519-521)
4. (521-524)
5. (524-527)
6. (527-528)
7. (528)
8. (528-531)

CHAPTER 14 QUIZ

Matching—Health Issues

1. k (pages 524, 525)
2. f (517)
3. b (524)
4. c (521)
5. g (524, 525)
6. d (516)
7. l (524, 525)
8. e (522)
9. h (525)
10. a (518)
11. j (525)
12. i (523)

Multiple-Choice

1. b (page 505)
2. c (506)
3. b (507)
4. d (510)
5. b (506, 510)
6. b (508, 511)
7. b (512)
8. d (514)
9. a (518)
10. a (520)

11. c (522)
12. d (523)
13. c (524)
14. c (525)
15. a (528)

True or False?

1. F—Normally, the time of onset of puberty in both boys and girls varies by 6 to 7 years. (page 506)
2. T (507)
3. T (508)
4. F—The age at which youngsters reach adult height and sexual maturity has been dropping, apparently as a result of higher living standards, though the leveling of this trend suggests some genetic limits. (509)
5. F—Early menstrual periods usually do not include ovulation; many girls cannot conceive for 12 to 18 months after their first menstruation. (512)
6. T (513)
7. T (515)
8. F—Obesity is the most common eating disorder in the United States. (516)
9. T (519)
10. F—Marijuana has been used all over the world for centuries; for example, in China and India since before the birth of Christ. (519, 523)
11. F—AIDS is caused by a viral infection. (524, 526)
12. T (528)
13. F—Girls attempt suicide more often than boys, but boys' suicide attempts are more often successful. (528)
14. T (529)
15. T (530)

INTELLECTUAL DEVELOPMENT IN ADOLESCENCE

OVERVIEW

Chapter 15 examines the progress in adolescents' intellectual development. In this chapter, the authors:

■ Describe the dramatic change in cognitive development that comes with the achievement of abstract and hypothetical thinking

■ Name some egocentric attitudes and behaviors that appear in adolescence

■ Explore the effects of advanced cognitive development and cultural differences on moral reasoning

■ Describe aspects of the high school experience and the role it plays in adolescent development

■ Outline factors that influence adolescents' career planning

CHAPTER 15 REVIEW

Section I Aspects of Intellectual Development

FRAMEWORK FOR SECTION I

A. Cognition
  1. Cognitive Maturity: Piaget's Stage of Formal Operations
     a. The Nature of Formal Operations
        (1) Seeing New Possibilities
        (2) The Pendulum Problem
     b. What Brings About Cognitive Maturity?
     c. Assessing Cognitive Development: Limitations of Piaget's Theory
  2. Egocentrism in Adolescents' Thought
     a. Finding Fault with Authority Figures
     b. Argumentativeness
     c. Self-Consciousness
     d. Self-Centeredness
     e. Indecisiveness
     f. Apparent Hypocrisy
B. Moral Development
  1. Kohlberg's Theory
     a. Kohlberg's Levels of Morality
     b. How Do Adolescents at Different Levels React to Kohlberg's Dilemmas?
        (1) Preconventional Level
           (a) Stage 1
           (b) Stage 2
        (2) Conventional Level
           (a) Stage 3
           (b) Stage 4
        (3) Postconventional Level
           (a) Stage 5
           (b) Stage 6
  2. Cultural Aspects of Moral Development

IMPORTANT TERMS FOR SECTION I

Completion: Fill in the blanks to complete the definitions of key terms for this section of Chapter 15.

1. **formal operations:** In Piaget's terminology, the final stage of cognitive development, characterized by the ability to think _____.

2. _____: Observer who exists only in the mind of an adolescent and is as concerned with the adolescent's thoughts and behaviors as the adolescent is.

3. **personal** _____: Conviction, typical in adolescence, that one is special, unique, and not subject to the rules that govern the rest of the world.

LEARNING OBJECTIVES FOR SECTION I

After reading and reviewing this section of Chapter 15, you should be able to do the following.

1. Describe the capabilities characteristic of Piaget's stage of formal operations, as illustrated by the pendulum problem.

2. State the necessary conditions for achievement of cognitive maturity, according to Piaget.

3. Cite some limitations of Piaget's theory.

4. List six egocentric attitudes or behaviors typical of adolescents, according to Elkind.

5. Explain where and how most adolescents fit into Kohlberg's levels of moral reasoning.

6. Discuss how cultural standards can influence moral development.

Section II   High School

FRAMEWORK FOR SECTION II

A. The High School Experience
B. Family Influences on Achievement in High School
   1. Influence of Parents
      a. Parents' Interest
      b. Relationships with Parents
      c. Parenting Styles
   2. Effects of Socioeconomic Status
C. Dropping Out of School
   1. Who Drops Out?
   2. Why Do They Drop Out?
   3. What Happens to Dropouts?
   4. Can Dropping Out Be Prevented?

LEARNING OBJECTIVES FOR SECTION II

After reading and reviewing this section of Chapter 15, you should be able to do the following.

1. Summarize recent trends in high school education.

2. Compare stresses involved in making the transitions from elementary school to junior high to high school with the stresses involved in going from elementary school directly to high school.

3. Cite ways in which parents influence achievement in high school.

4. State the relationship between socioeconomic status and achievement in high school.

5. Discuss factors that influence students to drop out of high school, summarize the consequences of dropping out, and describe a successful dropout prevention program.

Section III   Developing a Career

FRAMEWORK FOR SECTION III

A. Stages in Vocational Planning
B. Influences on Vocational Planning
   1. How Do Parents Affect Vocational Plans?
   2. How Does Gender Affect Vocational Plans?

LEARNING OBJECTIVES FOR SECTION III

After reading and reviewing this section of Chapter 9, you should be able to do the following.

1. Outline the three classic stages in vocational planning.

2. Summarize the influences of parents and gender on adolescents' vocational planning.

3. Discuss the advantages and disadvantages of part-time work for teenagers.

CHAPTER 15 QUIZ

Matching—Numbers: Match each item in the left-hand column with the appropriate number from the right-hand column. (Note: Decimals have been rounded up to the nearest whole number.)

1. Percentage of people aged 16 to 20 who can solve the pendulum problem, according to one study _____

2. Percentage of Americans 25 and older who are high school graduates _____

3. High school dropout rate (percent) for 1980 sophomore class _____

4. Approximate age by which Piaget's stage of formal operations is usually attained _____

5. Percentage of Upward Bound graduates who go on to 4-year colleges _____

6. High school dropout rate (percent) for Native Americans _____

7. Percentage of Americans 25 and older who have finished 4 years of college _____

8. Percentage of male high school dropouts who were looking for work in 1982 _____

9. Percentage of doctors' sons who choose medicine as a career, according to one study _____

10. High school dropout rate (percent) for Asian-Americans _____

5
12
15
20
23
27
44
53
77
80

Multiple-Choice: Circle the choice that best completes or answers each item.

1. An adolescent who can think abstractly, imagine possibilities, and test hypotheses is in Piaget's stage of
   a. concrete operations
   b. scientific operations
   c. logical operations
   d. formal operations

2. A successful solution of the pendulum problem depends upon
   a. careful observation
   b. trial and error
   c. inductive reasoning
   d. varying one factor at a time

3. Piaget's definition of cognitive maturity has been criticized for failure to consider
   a. nonscientific aspects of intelligence
   b. women's perspective
   c. cultural factors
   d. socioeconomic factors

4. Although Frank, aged 17, knows that drinking and driving is dangerous, he does it anyway. When his mother remonstrates, he tells her, "Get off my back, Mom—I'll be OK!" In Elkind's terminology, this is an example of
   a. argumentativeness
   b. the personal fable
   c. finding fault with authority figures
   d. apparent hypocrisy

5. Most adolescents are at which of Kohlberg's levels of morality?
   a. preconventional
   b. conventional
   c. postconventional
   d. unconventional

6. According to Kohlberg, people indicate their stage of development by
   a. their response to a moral dilemma
   b. the length of time they spend thinking about a moral dilemma
   c. the reasoning behind their response to a moral dilemma
   d. the kinds of moral dilemmas they consider

7. In the past decade, high schools have given increased emphasis to
   a. academics
   b. athletics
   c. social life
   d. vocational training

8. Parents whose children do well in high school tend to be those who
   a. encourage children to look at both sides of an issue
   b. teach children not to argue with adults
   c. "ground" children who get low grades
   d. believe that children should be responsible for their own lives

9. High school students with the lowest grades tend to have parents whose parenting style is
   a. authoritative
   b. authoritarian
   c. permissive
   d. inconsistent

10. Single parents tend to be
    a. authoritative
    b. authoritarian
    c. permissive
    d. inconsistent

11. The major influence(s) on adolescent achievement in high school is (are)
    a. socioeconomic status
    b. home atmosphere
    c. parents' educational levels
    d. all of the above

12. Upward Bound is a program for high school dropouts, emphasizing
    a. vocational training
    b. job placement
    c. a wilderness experience
    d. college-preparatory courses

13. Amy, who is 18, wants to be a teacher. She is applying to colleges with strong education programs and is working as a teaching aide at a local preschool. Which period of vocational development does she appear to be in?
    a. fantasy
    b. tentative
    c. realistic
    d. active

14. A student who works more than 3 hours a day after school is more likely than a student who does not work part time to
    a. develop good work habits
    b. learn to handle money responsibly
    c. earn more money in later life
    d. drop out of school

15. Women who choose nontraditional careers tend to be
    a. only children
    b. eldest children
    c. middle children
    d. youngest children

True or False? In the blank following each item, write T (for *true*) or F (for *false*). In the space below each item, if the statement is false, rewrite it to make it true.

1. Adolescents sometimes exhibit egocentric thinking. _____

2. According to the Piagetian perspective, adolescents' idealism is a sign of cognitive immaturity. _____

3. Most adults have reached cognitive maturity. _____

4. A high level of cognitive development goes hand in hand with an equally high level of moral development. _____

5. A person at Kohlberg's postconventional level of morality can choose between two socially accepted moral standards. _____

6. According to Kohlberg, moral thinking is influenced by culture. _____

7. The average high school graduate today is better educated than an average graduate of 25 years ago. _____

8. The transition to high school tends to be more stressful for youngsters who go to junior high than for those who enter high school directly after 8 years of elementary school. _____

9. Students who earn high grades tend to have parents who are highly involved and interested in their schooling. _____

10. Teenagers whose parents are experiencing marital conflict tend to have low grades. _____

11. Conflict with mothers seems to have less impact on school performance than conflict with fathers. _____

12. Girls are more likely than boys to drop out of high school. _____

13. Students with poorly educated parents are more likely to drop out of high school than children whose parents are well educated. _____

14. Dropouts are more likely than high school graduates to lose their jobs, if they can get jobs at all. _____

15. A majority of dropouts regret leaving school. _____

16. Most high school seniors have a clear idea of how to reach their career goals. _____

17. About half of all high school juniors and seniors have paid jobs. _____

18. Both boys and girls are strongly influenced in their career choices by their fathers' occupations. _____

19. Boys generally are better than girls at algebra. _____

20. Gender differences in cognitive abilities seem to have declined since the early 1970s. _____

TOPICS FOR THOUGHT AND DISCUSSION

---

1. In research on both Piaget's and Kohlberg's theories, why is the answer a child gives to a problem less important than the way the answer is arrived at?

2. Do you agree with the criticism of Piaget's view of intelligence as too narrow? Thinking back to the description of Piaget's background in Chapter 1, can you suggest possible reasons for the kinds of tasks he chose to assess cognitive maturity?

3. Studies based on Kohlberg's theory of moral reasoning show that most adolescents are at a level where they have internalized standards of adult authorities, conform to social conventions, and define right conduct in terms of obedience to law. Yet, according to Elkind, teenagers take risks such as experimenting with illicit drugs because they believe they are not subject to the rules that govern the rest of the world. How would you explain this apparent contradiction?

4. How would a proponent of the view that intelligence is inborn react to the information given in Chapter 15 about the influence of parents on adolescents' academic achievement?

5. Socioeconomic status has been found not to be a major factor in school achievement; home atmosphere is. Yet it is generally assumed that socioeconomic status strongly affects achievement. Can you suggest an explanation consistent with the findings?

6. Your text refers to the 6-3-3 pattern (6 years of elementary school, 3 years of junior high, and 3 years of high school) as typical. Years ago, the 8-4 pattern, in which youngsters went directly from eighth grade to high school, was the typical one. On the basis of the research discussed in Box 15-2, would you favor a return to this earlier pattern? Why or why not? Are there factors that should be considered besides those discussed in your text?

7. How would Freud explain the influence a father's occupation exerts on his son's career choice? How would a social-learning theorist explain it?

8. Can you suggest ways to help adolescents make more realistic career plans?

CHAPTER 15 READING

INTRODUCTION

Can young people be helped to reach higher levels on Kohlberg's ladder of moral reasoning? This report from the April 9, 1989, education section of *The New York Times* describes a practical application of Kohlberg's ideas—an experiment in participatory democracy at an inner-city high school in the Bronx. Before reading the article, you may want to review the presentation of Kohlberg's theory in Chapter 12 of your text, which is more complete than the discussion in Chapter 15.

Morality Lessons? Hear! Hear!

by Douglas Hand

Theodore Roosevelt High School on Fordham Road in the Bronx is a medieval-looking building in one of the city's more depressed neighborhoods. There, the unofficial rule of conduct for students, as one youngster put it, is: "Don't look at somebody wrong or they'll beat you up."

Of its more than 3,000 students, 56 percent are Hispanic, 34 percent are black, and 10 percent Asian, drawn from 26 immigrant groups in the South and West Bronx. Nearly all come from families with incomes below the poverty line. Said Paul Shapiro, the principal, "My kids have all the problems of the South Bronx—broken homes, drugs, health problems, teen-age pregnancy."

It was a challenging setting for the "just community," a controversial experiment in self-governing and participatory democracy. For the last three years, Roosevelt High School has been home to two such groups—communities not of scholars but of students whose discussions of their own conduct and that of classmates, gently guided by teachers, are supposed to foster moral growth, a sense of community and a common understanding of how to act in the larger society.

According to administrators, teachers and students at Roosevelt, the experiment is working. "Students, over all, did become better people—less violent, more involved," said Caesar Previdi, who was principal from 1980 through 1986 and is now principal at Martin Luther King Jr. High School in Manhattan. Early on, he said, students applied skills developed in the just community—the ability to frame arguments, for example—in the classroom.

The program at Roosevelt consists of classes in which students and teachers spend several hours each week discussing, referring to committees and voting on issues of class members' social life and behavior; the majority rules. "The democracy is intense," said Ramon Holguin, 17 years old. "I like it."

Rosa Arroyo, 18, noted: "It forces you to change." Miss Arroyo had repeated ninth grade twice because of truancy. "I suddenly thought to myself, 'I'll be 20 years old and still in high school,'" she recalled. After taking 13 courses each semester for a year—going to classes during the day and at night and attending summer school—she is now a senior and, she said with bemusement, "a role model."

Teachers, too, say they have benefited. "I've become much more tolerant, much fairer" both within the community and in other classes, said Allan Sternberg, a teacher of social studies with 28 years' experience and an admitted skeptic who said he was "subtly roped" into becoming the program's director.

The experiment's driving force is the public demand for some kind of moral education in schools. A 1987 nationwide survey by the Gallup Organization Inc. found that 43 percent of the 1,571 respondents questioned agreed that values and ethical behavior should be taught in public schools instead of being left to parents and churches; 36 percent wanted such values taught in churches or by parents. It was the first year the question had been asked.

The response among many school systems has been to institute programs based on any number of competing theories: the notion, for example, that "doing good things," involving children in activities

Democracy 101

Central to the life of a just community is a public discussion of issues that affect students. Through such discussion, students are supposed to listen to others and learn to appreciate their perspectives. Ann Higgins, one of the Harvard University researchers supervising the just community program, says these are both prerequisites for moral development. The resolution of a particular issue by voting may not satisfy all parties involved, as seen in the following exchange within the R.C.S. community at Theodore Roosevelt High School in the Bronx. But that is often the case in the democratic process—which is part of the lesson the just community teaches.

Cheryl Ives, a teacher, had lowered Rubel Hastu's grade in the just community because he had been disrupting the social studies class that followed. Rubel, a 17-year-old with a flair for the dramatic, argued that he should not be penalized in one class for what had happened in another. He told the community that he was particularly angry with Ms. Ives for telephoning his grandmother about the incident. As he talked about his grandmother, he struggled visibly with his temper and finally stalked from the room, shouting as he left, "With all due respect, Ms. Ives, I'm mad at you."

Allan Sternberg, who heads the community project, suggested moving on to the next item on the agenda, since this "personal grievance" had not been listed for discussion. However, he was overruled by the students. Within a few minutes, Rubel returned, looked directly at Ms. Ives and said firmly, "You have no right to lower my sixth-period grade on the basis of what happens in seventh period." Many of his classmates applauded.

Natalie Codner was one of the exceptions. Taking the floor, she explained, "I like you and everything, Rubel, but if you're going to practice something, you have to practice it all the time. You can't say, practice it in sixth period, but not continue to practice it in seventh. That's like saying, I go to church on Sunday, so I can be a bad person the rest of the week."

No applause, but a murmur.

Ms. Ives then spoke, the only time she did so during the 40-minute discussion. "When Rubel stands up here in the community and talks about respect and caring and sharing and doesn't practice it after he leaves the room, his participation in this community is a lie," she said. "He can't say one thing and then act any way he chooses the rest of the time. That's why I lowered his grade."

A teacher moved that the issue be sent to the fairness committee; the motion was voted on and passed overwhelmingly. The committee debated the issue over several sessions. Finally, a committee member recalled that according to state law, only a teacher may change a student's grade.

Given that constraint, the committee concluded that the community could not infringe on Ms. Ives's rights. It wasn't the result that Rubel Hastu wanted, but having had his case debated in a public forum, he indicated that he was satisfied.

helpful to the school and community, promotes a sense of moral responsiblity. Edward Wynne, an education professor at the University of Illinois at Chicago, is directing such a program in about 50 of Chicago's elementary and secondary schools. Then there is the more classical approach taken by Kevin Ryan, an education professor at Boston University and director of its Character Education Program, who uses ideas in literature and history to point out moral issues.

At the heart of the Roosevelt experiment are the theories of Lawrence Kohlberg, a psychologist and educator who was director of Harvard University's Center for Moral Education for 20 years. Mr. Kohlberg, who died in 1987, believed that moral development hinges on the notion of justice. Children, he said, will not accept the idea of justice unless their schools are democratic, a state reached by having students discuss and decide on issues that affect them. In contrast to having youngsters obey authority, Mr. Kohlberg took as his model Socrates, who asked questions and elicited, rather than dic-

tated, answers. The result, he said, would be conditions requisite for moral development: students listen, consider other viewpoints and take the perspective of others.

Applying this theory to schools sounds simple. In practice, it has proved demanding for students and draining for teachers, who must eschew the role of authority figure and adopt that of adviser promoting debate and encouraging ever more complex levels of moral reasoning. It was first tried in 1974 with small programs at the Cluster School in Cambridge, a public high school, and Brookline High School, both near Boston; in 1979 the Alternative School at Scarsdale High School in New York adopted it.

Ann Higgins, a professor of education at Harvard and the chief evaluator of just-community programs around the nation, described Roosevelt as one of the "most interesting" places in which Kohlberg's model has been established—and "one of the least likely" places for it to work. Most other schools that try it, as one Roosevelt student put it, "have smart and mostly

6-Stage Gauge

In his studies, Lawrence Kohlberg, a psychologist and director of the Center for Moral Education at Harvard University, found evidence for the existence of six stages of moral reasoning. As Mr. Kohlberg sketched them, they begin with the stage at which people must have rules of morality imposed; they end at a stage in which people are society-minded, having internalized a system of morality, and can contemplate the larger philosophical questions confronting their community.

Stage one is based on obedience and punishment. Rules of conduct derive their force from the power of those who back them. Individuals who are at this stage have no sense that rules play a necessary role in a social system.

Stage two is the relativist, or pragmatic "You scratch my back and I'll scratch yours" level. Individuals still have no sense of a larger social system.

Stage three finds individuals conforming to the expectations of others, to please them.

Stage four is based on law and order. Those at this stage have as their main goal the establishment of rules and maintenance of social order, rather than satisfying personal desires.

Stage five shifts the focus to the notion of a social contract. Individuals who are at this level of moral development have a sense that right actions are those that have been agreed upon by society, but are aware that values and opinions are relative and can be changed. They place particular value on procedures for change such as elections, constitutional conventions and the like.

Stage six emphasizes universal moral principles, like justice.

Mr. Kohlberg's studies, which cut across several cultures, led him to conclude that these stages are universal and that each represents a structured, distinct way of thinking about the self and society. Mr. Kohlberg theorized that most people settle at one of these stages. The most common stage, he said, is four—law and order; the rarest is six, and reflects the thinking of such moral leaders as Mohandas K. Gandhi and the Rev. Dr. Martin Luther King Jr.

---

well-off kids," while Roosevelt has "the good, the bad and the ugly."

Still, with $379,000 in research funding provided by the W.T. Grant Foundation, which supports mental-health research on children, a three-year pilot program requested by New York State began in 1985 at Roosevelt and the Bronx High School of Science—two schools selected to represent opposite ends of the academic scale.

Roosevelt currently supports two just communities, each consisting of 5 teachers and about 100 students, grades 9 through 12, who have volunteered for the program. One community represents a cross-section of the student population; the other includes chronic truants.

Each community meets for two consecutive 40-minute class periods one day a week, during which a leader is chosen for that session only. Once the meeting is called to order, the community deals with the agenda, which typically contains items that range in significance from class trips to truancy and drugs. Agendas are established by standing committees and "core groups" of about 25 students and one teacher that have met beforehand. The community's three standing committees—fairness, agenda and activities—also bring issues to the larger forum. All matters are decided by an open vote; students and teachers have one vote each.

The fairness committee, which includes two teachers and eight students, mediates disputes and decides on punishment for rule infractions within the community. A fight between students, for example, required apologies all around and a letter to the assistant principal on why fighting doesn't solve disagreements. A student who defaced school property with graffiti was ordered to perform community service in the school equivalent to the cost of clean-up, and to write a letter of apology to the principal and custodial staff.

Though governed by Robert's Rules of Order, community discussions can be dramatic and chaotic. The community of truants (called R.C.R. for Roosevelt Community Renaissance) established rules for last spring's outing to a state park that specified "no weapons, no fighting, no radios, no sex"—but only with a disgruntled minority arguing until the very end in favor of weapons and sex.

Discussions can just as easily bog down, as they did last year over a four-week period when the R.C.S. community (for Roosevelt Community School) debated whether to expel a member for continually disrupting meetings and for his arrogance shown toward decisions of the fairness committee. He was finally given one more chance when a teacher pointed out that it was "hardly arrogant to sit and take criticism for four weeks without complaint."

Some educators have criticized the Kohlberg approach as fuzzy "60's-think," born of a time when educators were reluctant to impose their own values on students. Professor Ryan of Boston University says that rather than spending time "studying the Holocaust, the Constitution and learning to analyze social policy," students using the Kohlberg method participate in "huge amounts of debate over the simplest of things." This focus, he said, "ignores the role of content in moral education."

Professor Wynne of the University of Illinois agreed that more imposition of moral values on students was needed, arguing that the responsibility of adults is to "articulate their values and, when necessary, defend them and use discipline to enforce them."

As Professor Higgins of Harvard, who evaluates just communities, sees it: "The critics have basically said, 'We don't care how students think; we care about how they act.' And we say if that act doesn't derive from a thoughtful position, when the circumstances are different the student won't know how to act."

QUESTIONS ABOUT THE READING

1. The report notes that, according to Kohlberg, "moral development hinges on the notion of justice." How do the "just communities" at Theodore Roosevelt High School attempt to help participants develop the notion of justice?

2. The material headed "Six-Stage Gauge," is a brief summary of Kohlberg's stages of moral reasoning. Is it similar to the description of the six stages in Chapters 12 and 15 of your text? Which of Kohlberg's stages does Rubel Hastu (the student described under the heading "Democracy 101") appear to be at? Natalie Codner?

3. According to the article, Kohlberg believed that listening to and considering the viewpoints of others are prerequisites to moral development. How does this apply to Hastu?

4. According to the final section of the report, people begin with imposed rules, then internalize their society's rules, and finally reach a point where they "can contemplate the larger philosophical issues confronting their community." Which of these levels of moral reasoning does the "just community" appear to be aimed at achieving?

5. Kohlberg's highest stage of moral reasoning involves independent thinking about abstract moral principles. Does a program in which moral decisions are made by majority rule seem likely to help students move toward that goal?

6. The participants in the program at Theodore Roosevelt High School seem generally positive in their responses to it. But the article reports some criticisms by other educators. What are they, and how would you evaluate them? Are they similar to or different from the criticisms of Kohlberg's theory presented in Chapters 12 and 15 of your text?

ANSWER KEY FOR CHAPTER 15

Note: Numbers in parentheses refer to pages in the textbook where answers can be found.

CHAPTER 15 REVIEW

Important Terms for Section I

1. abstractly (page 537)
2. imaginary audience (540)
3. fable (541)

Learning Objectives for Section I

1. (pages 537-539)
2. (539)
3. (539-540)
4. (540-542)
5. (542-543)
6. (543-544)

Learning Objectives for Section II

1. (page 545)
2. (546)
3. (545-549)
4. (549)
5. (549-551)

Learning Objectives for Section III

1. (pages 551-552)
2. (552-555)
3. (553)

CHAPTER 15 QUIZ

Matching—Numbers

1. 53 (page 539)
2. 77 (545)
3. 15 (549)
4. 12 (538)
5. 80 (551)
6. 23 (549)
7. 20 (545)
8. 27 (550)
9. 44 (553)
10. 5 (549)

Multiple-Choice

1. d (page 537)
2. d (538)
3. a (540)
4. b (541)
5. b (542)
6. c (542)
7. a (545)
8. a (548)
9. d (548)
10. c (549)
11. b (549)
12. d (551)
13. c (552)
14. d (553)
15. b (554)

True or False?

1. T (pages 536, 540)
2. F—According to the Piagetian perspective, adolescents' idealism is a sign of attainment of the highest level of cognitive development, the capacity for abstract thought. (537)
3. F—Up to one-half of American adults never reach cognitive maturity, as measured by formal operations tasks. (539)
4. F—Factors other than cognition affect moral reasoning; advanced cognitive development is necessary for advanced moral development but does not guarantee it. (542)
5. T (542)
6. F—According to Kohlberg, moral thinking is universal—it transcends cultural boundaries. (543)
7. F—Average high school graduates in previous generations, when fewer people finished school, were better educated than the average graduate today. (545)
8. T (546)
9. T (547)
10. F—Difficulties in parents' marital relationships do not seem to affect teenagers' grades. (548)
11. T (548)
12. F—Boys are more likely to drop out than girls. (549)
13. T (550)
14. T (550)
15. T (550)
16. F—Many high school seniors (about half in one study) do not plan on getting the appropriate amount of education to meet their career goals. (552)
17. T (553)
18. F—A father's occupation seems to have no influence on his daughter's career choice. (553)
19. T (554)
20. T (555)

PERSONALITY AND SOCIAL DEVELOPMENT IN ADOLESCENCE

OVERVIEW

Chapter 16 focuses on the profound and sometimes disquieting personality developments that accompany the physical and cognitive changes of adolescence. In this chapter, the authors:

■ Present five historical and contemporary theoretical perspectives on adolescents' personality development

■ Describe ways in which boys and girls seek identity

■ Discuss teenagers' relationships with parents and peers

■ Examine prevailing sexual attitudes and practices among American adolescents

■ Explore causes, consequences, and prevention of teenage pregnancy and delinquency

■ Identify adolescents' special personality strengths

CHAPTER 16 REVIEW

Section I   Theoretical Perspectives on Adolescents' Personality Development

FRAMEWORK FOR SECTION I

A. G. Stanley Hall: "Storm and Stress"
B. Margaret Mead: The Cultural Factor
C. Sigmund Freud: The Genital Stage
D. Anna Freud: Ego Defenses of Adolescence
E. Erik Erikson: Crisis 5—Identity versus Identity Confusion

IMPORTANT TERMS FOR SECTION I

Completion: Fill in the blanks to complete the definitions of key terms for this section of Chapter 16.

1. **storm and stress:** In Hall's terminology, the idea that adolescence is necessarily a time of strong and variable _____ ; from the German *Sturm und Drang.*

2. _____ **stage:** In Freud's terminology, the psychosexual stage of mature sexuality; it occurs during adolescence.

3. _____: In Freud's terminology, the basic energy that fuels the sexual drive.

4. **reaction formation:** Defense mechanism characterized by replacement of an anxiety-producing feeling with the expression of its _____.

5. **intellectualization:** In the terminology of Anna Freud, a defense mechanism characterized by participating in abstract intellectual discussions to avoid unpleasant, _____-producing feelings.

6. **asceticism:** In Anna Freud's terminology, a defense mechanism characterized by _____ in response to the fear of loss of control over one's impulses.

7. **identity versus identity _____:** In Erikson's theory, the fifth crisis of psychosocial development, in which an adolescent must determine his or her own sense of self (identity), including the role he or she will play in society.

LEARNING OBJECTIVES FOR SECTION I

After reading and reviewing this section of Chapter 16, you should be able to do the following.

1. Explain how Hall's concept of "storm and stress" contributed to developmentalists' thinking about adolescence.

2. Contrast Margaret Mead's interpretation of her findings about stress in adolescence with Hall's view.

3. Explain how adolescents achieve mature sexuality according to Sigmund Freud, and cite aspects of his theory that have been challenged by research.

4. Describe two ego defenses of adolescence proposed by Anna Freud.

5. Discuss how identity formation occurs, according to Erik Erikson.

Section II The Search for Identity

FRAMEWORK FOR SECTION II

A. Research on Identity
1. Identity Statuses: Crisis and Commitment
2. Gender Differences in Identity Formation
B. Personal Relationships in Adolescence
1. Relationships with Parents
a. Conflict with Parents
(1) The Roots of Conflict
(2) The Nature of Conflict
b. What Adolescents Need from Their Parents
c. When Adolescents Care for Themselves
d. Adolescents with Single Parents
2. Relationships with Peers
a. How Adolescents Spend Their Time—and with Whom
b. Parents "versus" Peers
c. Friendships in Adolescence
C. Achieving Sexual Identity
1. Studying Adolescents' Sexuality
2. Sexual Attitudes and Behavior
a. Masturbation
b. Sexual Preference: Heterosexuality and Homosexuality
(1) Homosexuality
(2) Heterosexuality
(a) Attitudes versus Behavior
(b) Early Sexual Activity
3. Communicating with Parents about Sex

IMPORTANT TERMS FOR SECTION II

Completion: Fill in the blanks to complete the definitions of key terms for this section of Chapter 16.

1. **crisis:** Period of conscious decision making related to _____ formation.

2. **commitment:** Personal investment in an occupation or a system of _____.

3. **adolescent rebellion:** Break with parental and societal _____ undergone by some but not all adolescents.

4. _____: Sexual self-stimulation.

5. **sexual** _____: Whether a person is heterosexual or homosexual.

6. **heterosexual:** Sexually interested in members of the _____ sex.

7. **homosexual:** Sexually interested in members of the _____ sex.

LEARNING OBJECTIVES FOR SECTION II

After reading and reviewing this section of Chapter 16, you should be able to do the following.

1. Name the two elements that determine identity status, according to Erikson and James Marcia; describe four categories of identity status; and describe gender differences in identity formation.

2. Identify the source and nature of most adolescent conflict with parents, and explain why discord is generally greatest during early adolescence.

3. Describe how parent-child relationships may both influence and reflect the timing of puberty.

4. Identify the kind of parenting that seems to meet adolescents' needs best, and list at least five suggestions to promote understanding between adolescents and parents.

5. Assess the risk of antisocial behavior in "self-care" adolescents and those who do not live with their fathers.

6. Summarize how and with whom teenagers typically spend their time, and discuss the relative influence of parents and peers.

7. Describe the nature of friendship in adolescence.

8. Explain some of the difficulties of studying adolescents' sexuality.

9. Describe sexual attitudes and behavior among adolescents today and the extent to which teenagers and parents communicate about sex.

Section III Problems of Adolescence

FRAMEWORK FOR SECTION III

A. Pregnancy
　1. Trends in Teenage Pregnancy
　2. Consequences of Teenage Pregnancy
　3. Understanding Teenage Pregnancy
　　a. Why Do Teenagers Become Pregnant?
　　b. Who Is Likely to Become Pregnant?
　4. Preventing Teenage Pregnancy
　5. Helping Pregnant Teenagers
B. Juvenile Delinquency
　1. Statistics
　2. Who Are Juvenile Delinquents?
　　a. Personal Characteristics of Delinquents
　　b. The Delinquent's Family
　3. Dealing with Delinquency

IMPORTANT TERM FOR SECTION III

Completion: Fill in the blank to complete the definition of the key term for this section of Chapter 16.

1. **status offender:** Juvenile charged with committing an act that is considered criminal only because the offender is a(n) _____ (for example, truancy, running away from home, or engaging in sexual intercourse).

LEARNING OBJECTIVES FOR SECTION III

After reading and reviewing this section of Chapter 16, you should be able to do the following.

1. Summarize current statistical trends in teenage pregnancy, and cite consequences of teenage pregnancy for mothers, fathers, and babies.

2. Give reasons why teenagers become pregnant, and identify characteristics shared by teenagers who are likely to become pregnant.

3. List guidelines for preventing teenage pregnancy, and identify ways of helping expectant teenagers.

4. Differentiate between the two types of juvenile delinquency, and cite statistical trends in juvenile offenses by boys and girls.

5. Identify characteristics typical of juvenile delinquents and their families, and discuss the difficulty of predicting how delinquents will turn out.

Section IV Personality Strengths of Adolescents

LEARNING OBJECTIVES FOR SECTION IV

After reading and reviewing this section of Chapter 16, you should be able to do the following.

1. Identify several personality strengths adolescents see in themselves.

2. List at least five distinctive personality strengths of adolescents identified by researchers.

CHAPTER 16 QUIZ

Matching—Who's Who: Match each name in the left-hand column with the appropriate description in the right-hand column.

1. G. Stanley Hall _____
2. Margaret Mead _____
3. D. Freeman _____
4. Sigmund Freud _____
5. Anna Freud _____
6. Erik Erikson _____
7. James Marcia _____
8. Carol Gilligan _____
9. Laurence Steinberg _____

a. criticized Mead's research
b. categorized identity statuses
c. proposed adolescent defense mechanisms
d. studied timing of puberty and parent-child relationships
e. held that adolescent conflict paves the way for mature sexuality
f. formulated the first psychological theory of adolescence
g. held that the chief task of adolescence is to resolve the identity crisis
h. studied adolescence in Samoa and New Guinea
i. studied women's identity achievement

Multiple-Choice: Circle the choice that best completes or answers each item.

1. The theorist who described adolescence as a time of "storm and stress" was
   a. G. Stanley Hall
   b. Sigmund Freud
   c. Anna Freud
   d. Erik Erikson

2. Margaret Mead's research on stress in adolescence highlights the importance of
   a. heredity
   b. culture
   c. sexuality
   d. maturation

3. According to Sigmund Freud, conflict in adolescence originates in
   a. physiological changes
   b. psychological changes
   c. societal pressures
   d. repression of sexual energy

4. According to Sigmund Freud, through reaction formation adolescents replace sexual longing for a parent with
   a. sexual attraction to young persons of the other sex
   b. masturbation
   c. independence
   d. hostility

5. Anna Freud
   a. broke away from her father's psychosexual theory
   b. emphasized personality formation in adolescence
   c. rejected her father's concept of ego defenses
   d. expanded her father's concept of reaction formation

6. According to Erik Erikson, a major aspect of the adolescent's search for identity is the
   a. first sexual relationship
   b. changing relationship with parents
   c. career decision
   d. choice of a peer group

7. The virtue that arises from Erikson's fifth crisis is
   a. fidelity
   b. industry
   c. self-esteem
   d. independence

8. Erin has never experienced an identity crisis. She and her father have always been close. When he advised her to get an MBA and go into business, she took his advice. After getting her degree, she accepted a position with a large bank and made a down payment on a house. When she sees her friends agonizing over their career choices, Erin smiles with a trace of superiority. James Marcia would place Erin in the category of
   a. identity achievement
   b. foreclosure
   c. identity confusion
   d. moratorium

9. According to Gilligan, women achieve identity primarily through
   a. cooperation
   b. competition
   c. crisis
   d. careers

10. Studies have found that the percent of families in which serious conflict between adolescents and parents occurs is approximately
    a. 10
    b. 20
    c. 35
    d. 50

11. Which of the following is usually *not* an issue in arguments between adolescents and their parents?
    a. values
    b. schoolwork
    c. chores
    d. friends

12. Discord between adolescents and parents generally
    a. increases steadily during the teenage years
    b. increases during early adolescence, then decreases steadily during middle and late adolescence
    c. increases during early adolescence, then stabilizes during middle adolescence and decreases in late adolescence
    d. does not follow any particular pattern

13. According to self-reports, teenagers are *least* happy when they are
    a. alone
    b. with their classmates
    c. with their parents
    d. with other adults

14. Teenagers tend to rely more on the influence of parents than of peers in situations involving
    a. dress
    b. dating
    c. school problems
    d. job choices

15. Adolescents tend to choose friends who are
    a. physically attractive
    b. outgoing
    c. athletic
    d. like themselves

16. Research on adolescents' sexual practices may not be accurate because
    a. volunteers tend to be less sexually active than the population as a whole
    b. sexual mores are constantly changing
    c. subjects may not be truthful, and self-reports cannot be corroborated
    d. all of the above

17. Today, homosexuality is most widely attributed to
    a. mental illness
    b. genetic factors
    c. family constellation
    d. a combination of hormonal factors and environmental events

18. The main reason teenagers give for early sexual activity is
    a. sexual desire
    b. curiosity
    c. social pressure
    d. media influence

19. What percent of adolescent nonvirgins reportedly did not seek information about prevention of pregnancy and infection before their first sexual experience?
    a. 25
    b. 45
    c. 65
    d. 85

20. The pregnancy rate in the United States for girls aged 15 to 19 is
    a. 5 percent or less
    b. nearly 10 percent
    c. about 25 percent
    d. approaching 40 percent

21. Which of the following is *not* a likely consequence of teenage pregnancy today?
    a. complications of pregnancy
    b. birth of babies with neurological defects
    c. marriage
    d. end of schooling

22. Which of the following is apparently *not* a major factor in a girl's likelihood of becoming pregnant?
    a. age
    b. sexual knowledge
    c. sexual practices
    d. amount of sexual experience

23. According to one study, the single most important consideration cited by young teenagers in choosing a birth control clinic is
    a. location
    b. cost
    c. service
    d. confidentiality

24. Which of the following is a relatively poor predictor of delinquency?
    a. record of imprisonment among family members
    b. lack of parental supervision and discipline
    c. low socioeconomic status
    d. poor educational achievement

25. Special personality strengths of adolescents identified by researchers do *not* include
    a. idealism
    b. energy and vitality
    c. awareness and perceptivity
    d. organization and planning

True or False? In the blank following each item, write T (for *true*) or F (for *false*). In the space below each item, if the statement is false, rewrite it to make it true.

1. According to Sigmund Freud, masturbation declines with age and sexual activity. _____

2. According to Anna Freud, adolescents' intellectual discussions of world problems stem from their search for identity and their capacity for abstract thought. _____

3. According to Erikson, women cannot achieve intimacy until they have achieved identity. _____

4. According to Marcia, it may be just as healthy for women to achieve identity with or without going through a crisis. _____

5. Adolescents are more likely to have conflicts with their fathers than with their mothers. _____

6. Research shows that girls who argue more with their mothers mature physically more rapidly than other girls. _____

7. Permissive parenting is the most effective style with adolescents because it gives them freedom consistent with their cognitive growth. _____

8. Self-care makes adolescents vulnerable to peer pressure for antisocial behavior. _____

9. Adolescents who do not live with their biological fathers tend to be susceptible to peer pressure to get into trouble. _____

10. According to self-reports, adolescents spend about 5 percent of their time with their parents. _____

11. Adolescent friendships tend to be closer than childhood or adult friendships. _____

12. The proportion of teenagers who say that they masturbate has increased since the 1960s. _____

13. Homosexual behavior has increased during the past 30 years. _____

14. Today's teenagers are more sexually active than those of the previous generation. _____

15. Teenagers who have talked with their parents about sex are more likely to use birth control than teenagers who have not. _____

16. Girls who feel guilty about premarital sex are more likely than other girls to use effective contraception. _____

17. A 15-year-old who robs a liquor store is considered a status offender. _____ .

18. Boys are more likely than girls to be arrested. _____

19. Juvenile delinquents, on the average, have lower IQs than law-abiding youths. _____

20. Adolescents tend to overrate their own personality strengths. _____

TOPICS FOR THOUGHT AND DISCUSSION

---

1. According to Sigmund Freud, an important difference between infantile and mature sexuality is the capacity to reproduce. But birth control permits adults who are capable of reproduction to engage in sexual intercourse for pleasure alone. Do you think Freud would consider such activity immature? Why or why not?

2. Freud's theory agrees with Hall's view that storm and stress are inevitable in adolescence. But research shows that severe turmoil seems to occur only in a minority of adolescents. How might Freud explain this finding?

3. Your text mentions two other challenges to Freud's theory: older adolescents masturbate more than younger ones; and clitoral orgasm is characteristic of many normal, mature women. How seriously do these findings weaken the theory?

4. Are essential elements of Freud's theory supported by observations of adolescent

behavior? For example, might the theory help explain teenagers' reticence with their parents regarding sex?

5. Both Freud and Erikson saw differences in the ways men and women achieve identity. Aside from taking the male pattern as the norm, to what extent is each of their theories consistent or inconsistent with the findings of Marcia and Gilligan concerning gender differences in identity achievement?

6. What similarities and differences do you see between Marcia's four categories of identity achievement and the three stages of career development described in Chapter 15? What factors are stressed by each?

7. Research suggests bidirectional (two-way) influences between the timing of puberty and parent-child relationships. What other bidirectional effects, previously discussed in your text, can you recall?

8. Why does your text call the change in sexual behavior and attitudes since the 1920s a sexual "evolution" rather than a sexual "revolution"? What is the difference in the connotation of the two terms? Which do you consider more appropriate?

9. The Harris pollsters found it more effective to ask teenagers why *other* teenagers do not use birth control rather than why the respondents themselves do not use it. What other areas of research might benefit from this technique? Does it have an inherent flaw?

10. Researchers have credited adolescents with distinctive personality strengths of which they are often unaware. Are these characteristics related or contrary to the egocentric behaviors Elkind attributes to adolescents, as described in Chapter 15?

CHAPTER 16 READING

INTRODUCTION

Maya Angelou, born Marguerite Johnson, surmounted racial prejudice, the trauma of a rape at the age of 8, a teenage pregnancy, and a descent into prostitution to become a noted writer, dancer, and activist.

Marguerite, whose parents separated when she was 3 years old, was brought up by her strict, pious grandmother in a small, segregated town in Arkansas during the depression. For a brief period, she lived with her mother in the black ghetto of St. Louis, until she was raped by her mother's boyfriend.

Most of her sometimes unsettled teenage years were spent with her mother in San Francisco. The girl, who had always loved reading, got high grades in high school and took dance and drama classes at night on a scholarship.

This selection is from Maya Angelou's highly acclaimed autobiography, *I Know Why the Caged Bird Sings*, published in 1969. It is startlingly frank, remarkably objective, and impressively clear-sighted—qualities to be found in all of Angelou's work.

An Excerpt from "I Know Why the Caged Bird Sings"

by Maya Angelou

A classmate of mine, whose mother had rooms for herself and her daughter in a ladies' residence, had stayed out beyond closing time. She telephoned me to ask if she could sleep at my house. Mother gave her permission, providing my friend telephoned her mother from our house.

When she arrived, I got out of bed and we went to the upstairs kitchen to make hot chocolate. In my room we shared mean gossip about our friends, giggled over boys, and whined about school and the tedium of life. The unusualness of having someone sleep in my bed (I'd never slept with anyone except my grandmothers) and the frivolous laughter in the middle of the night made me forget simple courtesies. My friend had to remind me that she had nothing to sleep in. I gave her one of my gowns, and without curiosity or interest I watched her pull off her clothes. At none of the early stages of undressing was I in the least conscious of her body. And then suddenly, for the briefest eye span, I saw her breasts. I was stunned.

They were shaped like light-brown falsies in the five-and-ten-cent store, but they were real. They made all the nude paintings I had seen in museums come to life. In a word, they were beautiful. A universe divided what she had from what I had. She was a woman.

My gown was too snug for her and much too long, and when she wanted to laugh at her ridiculous image I found that humor had left me without a promise to return.

Had I been older I might have thought that I was moved by both an esthetic sense of beauty and the pure emotion of envy. But those possibilities did not occur to me when I needed them. All I knew was that I had been moved by looking at a woman's breasts. So all the calm and casual words of Mother's explanation a few weeks earlier and the clinical terms of Noah Webster did not alter the fact that in a fundamental way there was something queer about me.

I somersaulted deeper into my snuggery of misery. After a thorough self-examination, in the light of all I had read and heard about dykes and bulldaggers, I reasoned that I had none of the obvious traits—I didn't wear trousers, or have big shoulders or go in for sports, or walk like a man or even want to touch a woman. I wanted to be a woman, but that seemed to me to be a world to which I was to be eternally refused entrance.

What I needed was a boyfriend. A boyfriend would clarify my position to the world and, even more important, to myself. A boyfriend's acceptance of me would guide me into that strange and exotic land of frills and femininity.

Among my associates, there were no takers. Understandably the boys of my age and social group were captivated by the yellow- or light-brown-skinned girls, with hairy legs and smooth little lips, whose hair "hung down like horses' manes." And even those sought-after girls were asked to "give it up or tell where it is." They were reminded in a popular song of the times, "If you can't smile and say yes, please don't cry and say no." If the pretties were expected to make the supreme sacrifice in order to "belong," what could the unattractive female do? She who had been skimming along on life's turning but never-changing periphery had to be ready to be a "buddy" by day and maybe by night. She was called upon to be generous only if the pretty girls were unavailable.

I believe most plain girls are virtuous because of the scarcity of opportunity to be otherwise. They shield themselves with an aura of unavailableness

(for which after a time they begin to take credit) largely as a defense tactic.

In my particular case, I could not hide behind the curtain of voluntary goodness. I was being crushed by two unrelenting forces: the uneasy suspicion that I might not be a normal female and my newly awakening sexual appetite.

I decided to take matters into my own hands. (An unfortunate but apt phrase.)

Up the hill from our house, and on the same side of the street, lived two handsome brothers. They were easily the most eligible young men in the neighborhood. If I was going to venture into sex, I saw no reason why I shouldn't make my experiment with the best of the lot. I didn't really expect to capture either brother on a permanent basis, but I thought if I could hook one temporarily I might be able to work the relationship into something more lasting.

I planned a chart for seduction with surprise as my opening ploy. One evening as I walked up the hill suffering from youth's vague malaise (there was simply nothing to do), the brother I had chosen came walking directly into my trap.

"Hello, Marguerite." He nearly passed me.

I put the plan into action. "Hey," I plunged. "Would you like to have a sexual intercourse with me?" Things were going according to the chart. His mouth hung open like a garden gate. I had the advantage and so I pressed it.

"Take me somewhere."

His response lacked dignity, but in fairness to him I admit that I had left him little chance to be suave.

He asked, "You mean, you're going to give me some trim?"

I assured him that that was exactly what I was about to give him. Even as the scene was being enacted, I realized the imbalance in his values. He thought I was giving him something, and the fact of the matter was that it was my intention to take something from him. His good looks and popularity had made him so inordinately conceited that they blinded him to that possibility.

We went to a furnished room occupied by one of his friends, who understood the situation immediately and got his coat and left us alone. The seductee quickly turned off the lights. I would have preferred them left on, but didn't want to appear more aggressive than I had been already—if that was possible.

I was excited rather than nervous, and hopeful instead of frightened. I had not considered how physical an act of seduction would be. I had anticipated long soulful tongued kisses and gentle caresses. But there was no romance in the knee which forced my legs, nor in the rub of hairy skin on my chest.

Unredeemed by shared tenderness, the time was spent in laborious gropings, pullings, yankings and jerkings.

Not one word was spoken.

My partner showed that our experience had reached its climax by getting up abruptly, and my main concern was how to get home quickly. He may have sensed that he had been used, or his lack of interest may have been an indication that I was less than gratifying. Neither possibility bothered me.

Outside on the street we left each other with little more than "Okay, see you around."

Thanks to Mr. Freeman nine years before, I had had no pain of entry to endure, and because of the absence of romantic involvement neither of us felt much had happened.

At home I reviewed the failure and tried to evaluate my new position. I had had a man. I had been had. Not only didn't I enjoy it, but my normality was still a question.

What happened to the moonlight-on-the-prairie feeling? Was there something so wrong with me that I couldn't share a sensation that made poets gush out rhyme after rhyme, that made Richard Arlen brave the Arctic wastes and Veronica Lake betray the entire free world?

There seemed to be no explanation for my private infirmity, but being a product (is "victim" a better word?) of the southern Negro upbringing, I decided that I "would understand it all better by and by." I went to sleep.

Three weeks later, having thought very little of the strange and strangely empty night, I found myself pregnant.

QUESTIONS ABOUT THE READING

1. What motivated Marguerite's sexual encounter? How does her motivation compare with those found by the Harris poll cited in the discussion of early sexual activity in Chapter 16 of your text?

2. "Why do teenagers become pregnant?" is a question raised in your text. Does Marguerite's experience illustrate one or more of the causes noted in the text, or does it suggest a different reason or reasons?

3. In what ways did Marguerite fit the pattern, described in Chapter 16, of adolescent girls who are likely to become pregnant? In what ways did she not fit the pattern?

4. Marguerite appears to have given no thought to the possibility that she might become pregnant. Does her behavior demonstrate any of the adolescent thought processes discussed in Chapter 15?

5. This passage was written years after the incident it recounts. What indications can you find that this is the case? If Marguerite had been writing in a diary at the time of the event, what might have been different about the narrative? What (if anything) might be much the same?

ANSWER KEY FOR CHAPTER 16

Note: Numbers in parentheses refer to pages in the textbook where answers can be found.

CHAPTER 16 REVIEW

Important Terms for Section I

1. emotions (page 561)
2. genital (562)
3. libido (562)
4. opposite (562)
5. anxiety (563)
6. self-denial (563)
7. confusion (564)

Learning Objectives for Section I

1. (page 561)
2. (562)
3. (562-563)
4. (563)
5. (564-565)

Important Terms for Section II

1. identity (page 566)
2. beliefs (566)
3. values (569)
4. masturbation (580)
5. orientation (580)
6. other (580)
7. same (580)

Learning Objectives for Section II

1. (pages 566-568)
2. (569-572)
3. (571)
4. (572-573)
5. (573-574)
6. (574-577)
7. (578-579)
8. (579-580)
9. (580-584)

Important Term for Section III

1. minor (page 590)

Learning Objectives for Section III

1. (pages 584-586)
2. (585, 586-587)
3. (588-590)
4. (590-591)
5. (590-592)

Learning Objectives for Section IV

1. (pages 592-594)
2. (594-595)

CHAPTER 16 QUIZ

Matching—Who's Who

1. f (page 561)
2. h (562)
3. a (562)
4. e (562)
5. c (563)
6. g (564-565)
7. b (566-567)
8. i (568)
9. d (571)

Multiple-Choice

1. a (page 561)
2. b (562)
3. a (562)
4. d (562-563)
5. b (563)
6. c (564)
7. a (565)
8. b (567)
9. a (568)
10. b (569)
11. a (570, 572)
12. c (570)
13. b (576)
14. d (577)
15. d (579)
16. c (579-580)
17. d (581)
18. c (582-583)
19. d (583)
20. b (584)
21. c (585, 586)
22. c (587)
23. d (589)
24. c (591-592)
25. d (593-595)

True or False?

1. T (page 563)
2. F—According to Anna Freud, adolescents' intellectual discussions are a way of avoiding the anxiety created by their awakening sexual urges. (563)

3. F—According to Erikson, men cannot achieve intimacy until they have achieved identity, but women achieve both intimacy and identity at the same time. (565)
4. T (568)
5. F—Adolescents are more likely to have conflicts with their mothers than with their fathers. (569)
6. T (571)
7. F—Authoritative parenting is the most effective style with adolescents because it takes their cognitive growth into account by explaining reasons behind the stands parents take. (573)
8. F—Self-care does not, in itself, create vulnerability; parenting style and closeness of potential contact with parents are important factors. (573)
9. T (574)
10. T (576)
11. T (578)
12. T (580)
13. F—Although homosexuality is far more visible today, homosexual behavior has declined or been stable during the past 30 years. (581)
14. T (581)
15. T (584)
16. F—Girls who feel guilty about premarital sex are less likely than other girls to use effective contraception. (587)
17. F—Robbing a liquor store is an adult crime; status offenses involve violations of laws regulating minors only. (590)
18. T (591)
19. T (591)
20. F—Researchers found that adolescents tend to underrate their own personality strengths. (594)